Ham Radio Technician Class License Study Guide

From Beginner to Licensed! Master the Fundamentals of Amateur Radio, Ace the FCC Exam and Get on the Air with Confidence

Morse Code Publishing

Contents

Introduction   1

Section 1: The Technician Class Exam

  The Technician Class Exam   #

  1. Design of this Book   #

  2. The Exam   #

  3. How to Study: Techniques That Work   #

Section 2: The Science of Radio

  The Science of Radio   #

  4. The Metric System   #

  5. Electrical Principles   #

  6. The Control of Electrical Principles   #

  7. Radio Waves   #

  8. Frequency Bands   #

  9. Propagation: How Your Signal Travels   #

  10. The Atmosphere   #

  11. The Electromagnetic Spectrum and the Radio Bands   #

  12. Modulation and Bandwidth   #

Section 3: The Physical Radio Station

  The Physical Radio Station   #

  13. Electronic And Electrical Components   #

  14. Essential Tools and Techniques for Electronics   #

  15. The Ham Radio Station   #

  16. Antenna Basics   #

  17. Feedline Basics   #

18. Power Sources and Electrical Safety   #

19. Antennas, Feedlines and Safety   #

Section 4: Operating Your Radio

Operating Your Radio   #

20. Decoding Ham Radio Jargon   #

21. Making Your First Contact   #

22. Repeaters   #

23. Space (Satellites and Stations)   #

24. Exploring Other Modes   #

25. Troubleshooting   #

26. Privacy and Ethics   #

Section 5: Rules & Regulations

Rules & Regulations   #

27. Understanding the FCC's Role   #

28. What's Legal for a Technician?   #

29. Public Service in Ham Radio   #

30. The Amateur Station and Control   #

Section 6: Expanding Your Ham Experience

Expanding Your Ham Experience   #

31. Hams Having Fun   #

32. Upgrading Your License: From Technician to General   #

Keeping the Hobby Alive   249

Conclusion   250

Exam Question Index   251

Glossary   254

References   262

Introduction

AMATEUR RADIO! HAM RADIO! Welcome to a hobby or a lifestyle, as some would say, that will transform your simple curiosity into a lifetime of enjoyment, challenges, duty, and connection. Welcome to the fascinating world of ham radio.

As someone who embarked on the thrilling adventure of becoming a ham radio operator from a complete beginner, I understand the highs and lows of this journey. My passion for ham radio was sparked by a simple desire to explore a new hobby that combined my love of electronics, the thrill of a challenge, and the joy of connecting with others. This journey led me to create a resource that would make ham radio accessible to everyone, especially beginners like you and me when I first started.

This book was really created for me to help me pass my Technician Class License. It was never meant to be shared with others. It wasn't until my friend wanted to get his license and saw how well I did in preparing that I shared my notes with him. I put this together through his encouragement and am now sharing it with you. Thank you, Brian, for your encouragement and confidence in me!

This book is designed to demystify the process and equip you with everything you need to succeed. It includes a deep dive into all possible questions from the exam pool so that you feel 100% confident and ready to take your license exam.

You don't need prior experience or knowledge in ham radio to start. That's right! This guide is tailored for absolute beginners (like I was), aiming to transform daunting technical challenges into manageable, understandable concepts. I remember initially how overwhelming the technical jargon and concepts seemed, and this guide intends to break down those barriers. It combines accurate, detailed explanations with real-world applications, ensuring you grasp the theory and its application in practical scenarios.

The book includes all the questions you could see on the exam and a comprehensive breakdown of all sections of the Technician Class exam. Each chapter is structured to build your understanding progressively, turning complex regulations and technical details into explicit, actionable knowledge.

I assure you that this book will guide you from confusion to clarity. You will transition from feeling daunted by the complexity of ham radio to confidently passing the FCC exam. Through this guide, you'll prepare for the exam and be ready to join the vibrant global community of licensed amateur radio enthusiasts with a sense of accomplishment and confidence.

As we progress, remember that every expert was once a beginner—don't be fooled into thinking otherwise! So, take this first step with an open mind and an excited spirit, ready to explore the airwaves and connect with people worldwide. Your enthusiasm and open-mindedness will be your greatest assets on this journey.

To conclude with a personal touch, here's a favorite quote that has inspired me throughout my ham radio journey: "The biggest barrier to learning something new is the belief that you can't do it." Let this book be the tool that helps you break down that barrier, inviting you into a world where curiosity leads to discovery and learning becomes an exciting adventure.

Ready to start this rewarding journey? Let's dive in!

Jared Johnson, KF0RTU @ Morse Code Publishing

The Technician Class Exam

Your Gateway to Ham Radio

WELCOME TO HAM RADIO! Before you can start exploring the airwaves, you'll need to pass the Technician Exam—the first step to becoming a licensed amateur radio operator. This exam covers the basics of radio theory, regulations, and operating practices, and it's your gateway to a lifetime of learning and communication. In this section, we'll break down everything you need to know to prepare so you can approach the exam with confidence and excitement.

Chapter 1

Design of this Book

THE GOAL OF THIS book is to help you accomplish three key things:

1. Master the fundamental principles of amateur radio.

2. Prepare you to ace the FCC exam and earn your Technician license.

3. Give you the confidence to get on the air!

The exam part of this book is divided into four main sections: Rules & Regulations, Science of Radio, The Physical Radio Station, and Operating the Radio. We then end with a final section about growing your skills and knowledge in ham radio.

Each section of this book represents a quadrant in our teaching strategy. Each is interconnected and will reinforce your learning and deepen your understanding of ham radio.

Rules & Regulations	Science of Radio
The Radio Station	Operating the Radio

Science of Radio

This section delves into the technical and scientific principles behind radio communications. You'll explore concepts such as wave propagation, modulation, and frequency. We'll also discuss the different types of signals and how they travel through the atmosphere. This knowledge is the backbone of understanding radio waves and how to make the most of your communications.

The Physical Radio Station

Here, we'll focus on the hardware and setup of your radio station. From antennas and feedlines to transceivers and power supplies, this section will guide you through the essential components of a functioning amateur radio station. You'll learn the design of a station and how to troubleshoot your equipment, ensuring you're always ready to communicate.

Operating the Radio

This section is all about putting your knowledge into practice. You'll learn the procedures for making contacts, using repeaters, and operating in CW, SSB, and digital modes. We'll cover best practices for clear communication, handling interference, and staying safe. By the end of this section, you'll feel confident in your ability to operate your station effectively and responsibly.

Rules & Regulations

In this section, you'll learn about the legal aspects of amateur radio. We'll cover the Federal Communications Commission (FCC) rules, band plans, licensing requirements, and the responsibilities of being a licensed amateur radio operator. Understanding these regulations is paramount because they ensure that all operators use the radio spectrum responsibly and avoid causing interference.

Teaching Framework

Our teaching framework integrates learning across four main sections: Rules & Regulations, Science of Radio, The Physical Radio Station, and Operating the Radio. Each section interconnects, enriching your understanding as you progress. For instance, grasping radio wave propagation enhances your station setup and operation skills, while regulatory knowledge aids proper procedures.

This holistic approach ensures a well-rounded grasp of amateur radio, preparing you for the Technician exam and active participation in the radio community. At the book's end, you'll find a glossary of radio terms and a "Technician's Cheat Sheet" to reinforce key concepts and provide quick references. Let's embark on this exciting journey together!

A final word of encouragement: learning amateur radio can feel overwhelming, but it's all about simplifying and focusing on core principles. You don't need to memorize everything; instead, identify the key concepts that govern the field. Many details are simply variations or combinations of these fundamentals.

This book is designed to be concise and direct, providing the essential knowledge to succeed without getting bogged down in extraneous details. By focusing on the core principles and understanding how they interconnect, you'll find that what initially seems complex is manageable and intuitive.

Accuracy and Updates

Every effort has been made to ensure that the information in this book is accurate, up-to-date, and aligned with current standards and regulations. However, human errors can occur, and the world of amateur radio is constantly evolving. If you find any discrepancies, outdated information, or errors, please don't hesitate to reach out and let us know. Your feedback is invaluable in maintaining the quality and reliability of this resource. You can contact me at Jared@MorseCodePublishing. com, and I will do my best to address any concerns or updates in future editions. Thank you for your understanding and for contributing to this book's continued improvement.

Chapter 2

The Exam

HAVE YOU EVER STOOD at the base of a mountain, looking up at the peak, wondering how you will ever reach the top? The path might seem daunting initially, but with the correct map and tools, what seemed impossible becomes a series of manageable steps. Similarly, preparing for the Technician Class Exam might initially appear overwhelming (over 400 possible questions to know!). This chapter is your guide, mapping out the structure and nuances of the exam and equipping you with strategies to navigate this challenge effectively. From understanding the exam format to grasping the scoring system, you'll be prepared and ready to excel.

Exam Overview

The Technician Class License exam, often your first formal encounter in the ham radio community, is designed to test your understanding of basic regulations, operating practices, and electronics theory. The exam consists of 35 multiple-choice questions. Usually, the test takes about an hour. However, you will likely be given all the time you need to take the test. These questions are randomly selected from a pool of 412, covering various topics to ensure a comprehensive assessment of your beginner-level knowledge of amateur radio operations.

The Question Pool

Imagine the question pool as a well-organized library, where books are sorted into specific topics and subtopics, making it easier to find exactly what you need. Similarly, the question pool for the exam is meticulously organized into categories and subcategories, each focusing on a distinct aspect of amateur radio knowledge. Within each category, subcategories break down the material further, providing a detailed roadmap for your study. This structured setup helps you systematically approach your preparation, allowing you to tackle one area at a time and cumulatively build your knowledge.

How to Read the Exam Question Format

When preparing for the exam, you will see questions "numbered" in the following format: T5B01.

In the Technician exam, each question is labeled with a unique identifier like 'T5B01.' This identifier helps you understand the question's context:

- 'T' stands for the Technician license class. The questions are changed periodically. The current pool of questions is good through June 30, 2026.

- The first number, '5,' indicates the main topic or sub-element. In our example, 5 refers to the sub-element "Electrical Principles."

- The letter 'B' specifies a subtopic within the main topic.

- The final number '01' represents the question's specific number within that subtopic.

This structure helps you quickly locate and understand the question's context.

Sub-Element Weights

Understanding how the exam content is weighted helps prioritize your study efforts. The exam sub-elements are not weighted equally, which means that some sub-elements will have more questions on the exam than others. This insight directs your focus to areas needing a more robust review.

For instance, you will see three times as many questions about FCC rules (6 questions) as you will for antennas and feed lines (2). While having well-rounded knowledge is essential, emphasizing these heavier-weighted areas can increase your chances of a successful outcome. See below for each sub-element and the number of questions for each sub-element on the exam.

Sub-elements on the technician's exam:

1. Commission's Rules: six questions from this sub-element will be on the exam (6)

2. Operating Procedures: three questions from this sub-element will be on the exam (3)

3. Radio Wave Propagation (3)

4. Amateur Radio Practices (2)

5. Electrical Principles (4)

6. Electronic And Electrical Components (4)

7. Practical Circuits (4)

8. Signals And Emissions (4)

9. Antennas And Feed Lines (2)

10. Safety (often just written as zero) (3)

For a total of 35 exam questions.

Question Types

The questions in the Technician Class exam are structured to assess your memory and understanding. Each question offers four choices, one correct answer, and three distractors. These distractors are not random but carefully crafted to challenge common misunderstandings or computational errors. It's crucial to approach each question critically to understand why an answer is correct. This approach helps tackle distractors, which might seem correct at a surface level.

For example, a question might ask about acceptable frequency ranges for technician operators. The distractors might include frequency ranges close to correct but outside the allocated bands.

Scoring System

The scoring system of the Technician Class exam is straightforward: each correct answer earns one point. There is no benefit to leaving a question blank, which strategically implies that guessing if you're unsure is better than leaving an answer blank. This aspect of the scoring system should influence how you handle questions you find challenging. It's good practice to tackle questions you are confident about and then return to the more challenging ones, making educated guesses if needed.

By dissecting the exam structure this way, you are better prepared to allocate your study time effectively, understand what to study, and approach the exam strategically. This foundation is essential as we progress through further details and strategies in the following sections, each designed to build upon this initial groundwork, ensuring you confidently approach the exam with a clear plan.

You must score at least 74% to pass, which means getting 26 out of 35 questions correct. While this might sound straightforward, the breadth of topics requires a solid preparation strategy to ensure you cover all necessary material.

It's Time to Schedule Your Exam

Let's get you ready for the Ham Radio Technician Class exam! There are a few key steps to ensure you're fully prepared and have everything in place to take the test—think of it as your final homework before the big day. Here's what you need to do:

Step 1: FCC Registration Number (FRN)

Preparing for your amateur radio exam requires some essential items to ensure a smooth process.

First, you need an FCC Registration Number (FRN), which you can obtain by registering your Social Security Number on the FCC's website. This number is necessary for all licensing transactions.

This must be done before taking your exam. This is your homework!

Start with this website: https://www.fcc.gov/new-users-guide-getting-started-universal-licensing-system-uls

- You can also type 'New Users Guide To Getting Started With Universal Licensing System' into Google; it will be the first site to appear.

Follow the steps for a new user to register with the FCC's Commission Registration System (CORES).

- Click on 'Register.' Then follow the prompts to 'Create New Account.'
- Once you complete the steps, you will receive an email asking you to verify your account creation. Click the link in the email to confirm.
- Then click the button that says, "Go to CORES."

Next, you click on the link to 'Register New FRN."

- Follow the step-by-step instructions and register for an 'Individual FRN.'
- You will know you have completed this step when you see your new FCC Registration Number (FRN).
- Print this page and save your FRN!

Step 2: Find and Register for an Exam Session

Search for Exam Session: Visit the ARRL website and navigate to the search for exam session page.

- https://www.arrl.org/find-an-amateur-radio-license-exam-session
- Or type into Google, "Find an Amateur Radio License Exam in Your Area," and click on the ARRL site.

On the ARRL website, you can search for in-person or an online exam session. Select the type of exam you prefer. I'd recommend the in-person where possible. Especially if you are new to ham radio, it's an excellent opportunity to meet people and start networking with other hams.

Assuming you want to be in person:

- **Enter Zip Code:** Enter your zip code to get the best results and find nearby exam sessions.

- **Results:** The ARRL will provide a list of exams, including details such as the sponsoring club, location, time, and whether walk-ins are allowed.

- **Registration:** Walk-ins are usually not permitted, so you must register beforehand. For more details and contact information, click on the specific exam session to schedule your appointment.

It's that easy! You know you have been successful when you have an exam date set.

Step 3: Take the Exam

The dawn of your exam day is not just another sunrise; it marks the culmination of your diligent preparation and heralds a significant step forward in your journey as an amateur radio operator. Today, all the knowledge you've absorbed, the concepts you've untangled, and the practice tests you've navigated converge to a pivotal point.

You must also bring a legal photo ID, such as a driver's license or passport. If you don't have a photo ID, two other forms of identification, such as a birth certificate and a social security card, are required. Students and minors can present a school ID; if they are under 18, they might also need a guardian's ID. That's right! There is no age requirement to obtain your Ham radio license. Any person of any age who can pass the exam can acquire a license. But you do have to pass the exam without help.

Bring any previous Amateur Radio license or Certificates of Successful Completion of Examination (CSCE). Also, **carry two pencils, a pen, and a calculator with cleared memory**. Cell phones and other electronic devices with calculator capabilities are not allowed. Lastly, ensure you have a check, money order, or cash to cover the exam fee.

Arrive at the test location with ample time to spare. When you check-in, you'll be directed to a specific area where the exam will take place. The environment is typically set up to minimize distractions. Desks are spaced appropriately, and there may be dividers. Understanding that this setup is designed to give everyone an equal opportunity to concentrate can help ease any nerves about the testing environment.

When taking the exam, use the strategies you've practiced from our next chapter. Approach each question methodically: read the entire question and all answer choices before marking your sheet. If a question is challenging, mark it and move on, returning to it later. This helps you manage your time and avoid getting stuck on challenging problems. Keep a steady pace to ensure you cover all the questions within the allotted time, and periodically review your answers, especially those you were unsure of on your first pass.

Stay calm and focused during the exam. If you feel anxious, practice deep breathing:

- Inhale slowly through your nose. Hold for a few seconds. Exhale slowly through your mouth.

This can reduce tension and refocus your mind. Positive affirmations, like "I am prepared" or "I can do this," can help maintain your confidence.

As you sit down to take your Technician Class License exam, acknowledge the hard work you've put in and trust in your preparation. You are ready to take this important step toward joining the global community of amateur radio enthusiasts.

Now that we have an overview of the exam and how to study, let's begin our study!

Chapter 3

How to Study: Techniques That Work

WHEN MASTERING THE MATERIAL for the Technician Class exam, the effectiveness of your study techniques can make all the difference between just passing and genuinely understanding. Engaging actively with the content prepares you for the exam. It sets a solid foundation for your future as a ham radio operator. Let's explore some active learning strategies that have proven successful for many who are now licensed operators.

Active learning is a process that involves more than just reading; it requires you to engage with the material dynamically. For instance, **in this book, as you progress through it, you will want to read the questions and answers just as if they are part of the normal text—because they are! They are set up to be read as part of the teaching in the order you find them.**

You will see the exam question and the four possible answers. The correct answer will be **BOLDED** in the question. The key information you need to answer the exam question will be underlined in the text. So anywhere you see underlined text, pay attention, as that is key information you will need to know.

For example, here is an actual question from the exam. In this book, we will give you the question along with each possible answer. The **bolded** text is the correct answer—in this example, the letter 'A' is the correct answer.

> **T5B02: Which is equal to 1,500,000 hertz?**
>
> **A. 1500 kHz**
> B. 1500 MHz
> C. 15 GHz
> D. 150 kHz

An additional active learning strategy is using flashcards. Picture this: each card holds a question on one side and the answer on the other. As you shuffle through the deck, you're testing your knowledge, reinforcing the information, and identifying areas that need more attention.

Another powerful tool is summarization. After reading a section, explain it in your own words, as if you were teaching it to someone else. This method ensures you have truly grasped the concepts rather than memorizing words.

Creating a customized study plan is helpful, as it respects the uniqueness of your schedule, learning pace, and prior knowledge. Start by assessing how many days or weeks you have until the exam, then break down the topics into manageable chunks. Allocate more time to sections with more weight or topics entirely new for you. Remember, consistency is vital in a study plan; even if it's just 20 minutes a day, it's better than cramming all the material into a few lengthy sessions.

Visual aids and mnemonics make learning more enjoyable and enhance your ability to recall the information later. Diagrams, for instance, can be invaluable for visualizing complex concepts such as signal paths or antenna designs. Mnemonics, on the other hand, are tools designed to help remember lists or sets of information. For example, to remember the order of operations in adjusting your radio settings, use a phrase where the first letter of each word stands for a step in the process. These visual and mnemonic aids transform abstract information into tangible, memorable content.

Lastly, remember the importance of feedback loops. This involves regular testing of your knowledge through practice exams, which are core in preparing for the format and time constraints of the actual test. This process helps identify weak areas and builds confidence as your scores improve.

Memorization Techniques vs. Understanding Concepts

Proper comprehension is about grasping the underlying concepts that make the facts work, enabling a more profound and enduring mastery of the subject matter. This approach prepares you for the exam and equips you with practical knowledge that enhances your participation in the amateur radio community. Let's explore how you can elevate your study methods beyond rote memorization to understand better and retain the material.

The essence of learning in any field, especially one as technical and diverse as amateur radio, lies in understanding concepts over memorizing facts. While memorization might help you recall specific answers, understanding the concepts ensures that you can apply this knowledge in various contexts, solve problems, and adapt to new situations. This is particularly relevant in amateur radio, where operating conditions and technologies constantly evolve.

For instance, understanding the concept of radio wave propagation involves more than memorizing that specific frequencies travel farther at night. It requires an appreciation of why this happens—the interaction between radio waves and the ionosphere changes characteristics based on time of day and solar activity. This deeper understanding allows you to select optimal frequencies for communication at different times, enhancing your effectiveness as a radio operator.

Integrating concepts with practical examples is another powerful tool in your study arsenal. This method involves linking theoretical knowledge to real-world applications, cementing your understanding, and making the information more relatable and easier to recall. For example, when studying the types of antennas, instead of just memorizing their names and features, consider how each type would perform under specific operating conditions. Imagine setting up a dipole antenna in your backyard and consider how its orientation and height above the ground affect your ability to communicate with other local or distant stations. Visualizing these scenarios transforms abstract information into concrete understanding that sticks with you far beyond the exam.

Analogies are particularly useful in breaking down complex technical concepts into digestible pieces. They compare a new, unfamiliar concept and something you already understand. For instance, if you're struggling to grasp the idea of electrical impedance in antennas, you might think of it as similar to water pressure in a hose. Just as water flow in a hose can be optimal at a certain pressure, radio signals transmit most effectively when the antenna impedance matches the transmitter. Such analogies not only make challenging concepts more accessible but also make the learning process more engaging and enjoyable.

Finally, practicing with purpose is about engaging with practice questions to reinforce your understanding, not just your ability to recall facts. This active practice approach prepares you for the diversity of questions you might face during the exam. It deepens your understanding, ensuring that you retain the knowledge long after you have passed the test.

By focusing on understanding concepts, integrating practical examples, utilizing analogies, and practicing with purpose, you transform your exam preparation from a task of memorization to an enriching process of learning.

Recognizing Patterns and Tricky Questions

When preparing for the Technician Class License exam, understanding the intricacies of the question pool goes beyond knowing the correct answers. It involves recognizing patterns in how questions are structured and developing strategies to handle tricky questions effectively.

Pattern Recognition

In the vast array of questions that make up the exam, specific patterns emerge that can guide you to the correct answers. Recognizing these patterns involves paying close attention to the phrasing of questions and the structure of the answers provided. For instance, examiners often use a particular phrasing style for questions that require a regulatory answer, such as those about FCC rules. These questions might include specific keywords like "regulation," "legal," or "permissible," which signal that the answer will likely involve a rule or a standard procedure.

Another typical pattern involves the use of qualifiers such as "always," "never," or "must." Questions using these terms typically test absolutes and are designed to see if you understand amateur radio operations' fundamental, non-negotiable aspects. On the other hand, options that contain qualifiers like "usually," "sometimes," or "typically" may hint at more general knowledge and understanding, which requires you to think about the most common or likely scenarios rather than absolute rules.

As you practice, reflect on why specific answers are correct and how they align with the question's phrasing. This practice will prepare you for similar questions you might face and help you feel more at ease with the exam format.

Analyzing Tricky Questions

Tricky questions are a staple of any standardized test, designed to assess your depth of understanding and ability to apply knowledge in less straightforward contexts. These questions often include extra information to distract from the core issue or subtly mislead with closely related but incorrect answers. To navigate these challenges, start by carefully reading the question to identify precisely what is being asked. Strip away any details that do not directly relate to answering the question.

Once you've isolated the main query, consider each answer choice methodically. Ask yourself why each option could be correct or incorrect based on the facts and concepts you have studied. This analytical approach helps prevent the common pitfall of rushing to select an answer that seems right at a glance but falls apart under scrutiny. Suppose an answer seems too obvious or straightforward, especially if the question is complex. In that case, it's worth taking a second look to ensure a straightforward surface-level interpretation.

Common Pitfalls and How to Overcome Them

As you prepare for the Technician Class exam, knowing and learning to navigate potential pitfalls is necessary for a smooth study experience and success. Let's explore some common challenges and how to overcome them effectively.

Overconfidence can be a subtle obstacle, often stemming from initial successes. It can lead to a false sense of readiness. The solution? Regular practice exams. They provide reality checks, highlighting areas needing more attention, like complex FCC regulations. This helps ensure you're genuinely prepared, not just feeling ready, and familiarizes you with the exam format, reducing anxiety and boosting efficiency.

Procrastination often results from the daunting nature of the material or unclear study goals. Combat this by setting small, achievable goals. Break down large topics, like "FCC regulations," into manageable chunks, such as "Frequency Allocations." This focused approach makes sessions more productive and rewarding. Additionally, create a structured study schedule with specific times dedicated to studying, making it a regular part of your day rather than an optional task.

Information overload is a significant challenge with the detailed content of the Technician Class exam. Avoid this by breaking study sessions into topic-specific chunks and allocating specific days or times to subjects. This prevents information from blurring together and helps build a solid knowledge base. Summarizing topics in your own words or creating simple mind maps can aid in consolidating information and ease recall during the exam.

Burnout is a real risk with intense studying. It can lead to decreased motivation and resentment towards the subject. Maintain a healthy study-life balance by taking regular breaks—short ones every hour—to retain information and stay focused. Engage in activities you enjoy, like hobbies or exercise, to alleviate stress and refresh your mind. Recognize signs of burnout, such as chronic fatigue or irritation, and give yourself time to rest. Remember, this journey is a marathon, not a sprint.

Adopting these strategies allows you to navigate the common pitfalls in preparing for the Technician Class exam. These approaches aid in efficient learning and make the experience enjoyable, helping you become a licensed operator with confidence and ease!

Time Management for Aspiring Hams

Balancing work, family, and other commitments while studying for your Technician Class License can feel like finding a quiet moment in a busy city—challenging but possible. Prioritizing study time means integrating it into your daily routine rather than seeing it as an interruption. Think of your time as a garden; careful planning and attention help everything flourish, including your personal, professional, and educational goals.

To prioritize study time effectively, assess your typical day or week to identify less busy periods, such as early mornings, lunch breaks, or quiet moments after dinner. Consistency is key; even 20-30 minutes daily can add up significantly over time. Communicate your goals and schedule with family or housemates to minimize interruptions and enhance productivity during these study periods.

Efficiency during study sessions is crucial. Start each session with a clear objective, such as covering a specific topic or focusing on certain question types. Use active recall techniques by reciting or writing down what you remember after reading a section, reinforcing memory, and highlighting areas needing further review. Focus on weaker areas to improve your skills. Use tools like timers to keep sessions focused and short, as prolonged periods can lead to diminishing returns.

Establishing a study routine reduces the mental effort needed to start each session. Like brushing your teeth daily, a routine eliminates the decision-making about studying. Find a distraction-free location, such as a particular desk at home, a library, or a quiet coffee shop. Consistently studying in the same spot can help trigger 'study mode.' Keep all your study materials—books, notes, flashcards—readily accessible to reduce setup time.

Setting goals is key for motivation. Begin with a broad goal, like passing the Technician Class exam by a specific date, and break it into smaller, measurable objectives, such as mastering a chapter or completing practice questions. These goals should be SMART: Specific, Measurable, Achievable, Relevant, and Time-bound. They provide clear targets and regular opportunities to celebrate your achievements, keeping motivation high.

By integrating these time management strategies into your study practices, preparing for the Technician exam becomes less about finding time and more about maximizing it. This efficient, structured approach not only prepares you for the exam but also enhances your ability to manage responsibilities across all areas of life. The goal is to seamlessly and sustainably integrate learning into your life, turning time management challenges into personal growth and success opportunities.

Practice Exams

The use of practice exams in your study routine is akin to a dress rehearsal before a major performance; it provides a vital snapshot of your current knowledge and readiness, allowing you to adjust your preparations effectively before the event. Integrating practice exams into your study schedule is essential for evaluating your memory of the material and getting comfortable with the exam format and time constraints.

We have 14 practice exams for you — yes, 14 exams! Why 14 exams? To be fully prepared for the test, you must answer each question at least once in exam format. Because section T5D has fourteen possible questions, and only one will be on the exam, we need fourteen practice tests.

Scheduling Practice Exams

As your exam date approaches, increase the frequency of the practice exams. In the last few weeks before your test, try to simulate the exam environment as closely as possible. Find a quiet, uninterrupted space and time yourself as if you were in the exam room. This not only helps with retention but also eases any anxiety you might feel about the process and timing of the actual exam. Moreover, it allows you to practice managing your time efficiently across different exam sections, ensuring you can comfortably complete all questions within the allotted time.

Access the 14 practice exams here:

14 Practice Exams!

www.MorseCodePublishing.com/TechExam

Frequency of Practice

Finding the right balance for practice exams is key to steady improvement without burnout. Start with taking exams every other week, increasing to weekly as the exam date nears. Allow time between tests to absorb the material and focus on the weaknesses identified. Avoid cramming too many practice exams before the actual test, which can lead to fatigue and diminish returns. Instead, use the final days before the exam to review material gently, concentrate on weak areas, and ensure you're well-rested and relaxed on exam day.

Analyzing Results

Analyzing practice exam results is crucial. Review incorrect answers and identify patterns in the questions you miss, whether by topic or format. This helps you adjust your study focus. Revisit your study materials for each wrong answer, ensuring you understand the concept fully. For challenging topics, seek additional resources like tutorials, extra reading, or help from a study group. Integrating practice exams into your study routine helps prepare for the exam format and pressure while deepening your material understanding, making your study time more effective. Each exam should build your knowledge and confidence, leading to success on the Technician Class License exam.

The Science of Radio

Introduction to the Science Behind Radio

UNDERSTANDING THE PRINCIPLES OF radio science is essential for mastering amateur radio operations. Radio technology is based on physics, especially electromagnetism, and encompasses electromagnetic wave generation, transmission, and reception.

By delving into the science that powers radio communication, we uncover the intricate processes that enable signals to travel vast distances through the air, allowing us to communicate across town or worldwide.

This section will explore the core concepts of electricity, radio wave propagation, frequency, modulation, and the role of antennas, providing a solid foundation of technical knowledge to ace your exam. Through this exploration, you'll better appreciate the technological marvels that make ham radio a unique and fascinating hobby.

Chapter 4

The Metric System

THE METRIC SYSTEM IS essential for mastering the technical aspects of the hobby. The metric system is a simple, standardized system of measurement based on units of ten, making it easy to learn and use.

This system's beauty lies in its simplicity and consistency. All you need to know are the base units and a few prefixes, and you can easily understand and convert between different measurements. This simplicity makes the metric system a common language in science and engineering, allowing for clear communication and accurate calculations.

So, let's dive into the metric system.

Prefixes, Values, and Symbols

Prefixes	Value	Standard form	Symbol
Tera	1 000 000 000 000	10^{12}	T
Giga	1 000 000 000	10^{9}	G
Mega	1 000 000	10^{6}	M
Kilo	1 000	10^{3}	k
Deci	0.1	10^{-1}	d
Centi	0.01	10^{-2}	c
Milli	0.001	10^{-3}	m
Micro	0.000 001	10^{-6}	μ
Nano	0.000 000 001	10^{-9}	n
Pico	0.000 000 000 001	10^{-12}	p

Here is a table highlighting the labeling of metric values. Review and memorize the prefixes, their symbols, and their values. The base value will be '1', and then you will multiply or divide by tens to get to the correct prefix.

The key to all this is memorizing the metric chart above. Now, let's help you memorize the metric units that are important for Ham Radio – from giga to pico, you can use the following mnemonic:

Giant Monsters Kick Big Mountains, Making New Paths

Giant = (Giga - G)
Monsters = (Mega - M)
Kick = (Kilo - k)
Big = (base unit)
Mountains = (Milli - m)
Making = (Micro - µ)
New = (Nano - n)
Paths = (Pico - p)

Do you want a cheat code to help you remember when the unit symbol is capitalized or not? Be a Millionaire! All unit symbols are lowercase until you get to be a Millionaire (Mega = M = Millions). At Mega (million) and up, symbols are capitalized.

No more delays. Are you ready to jump into some exam questions? Let's go!

Frequency is measured in hertz (more on this later). But the base unit of frequency is 1 hertz (Hz). Notice that in hertz, the 'H' is also capitalized. That info will help with this exam question:

> ### T5C07: What is the abbreviation for megahertz?
>
> A. MH
> B. mh
> C. Mhz
> **D. MHz**

The chart shows that Mega means one million and is represented by the symbol 'M' (a capital M). That means the abbreviation for megahertz is MHz.

Using the metric chart again...

> ### T5C13: What is the abbreviation for kilohertz?
>
> A. KHZ
> B. khz
> C. khZ
> **D. kHz**

Again, our base unit is hertz (Hz). Kilo means 1,000 and is represented by the 'k' (lowercase k) symbol. The abbreviation for kilohertz is kHz.

The Metric Scale

Several questions in your technician's exam are designed to ensure you understand how the metric system works. Although the questions and units of measure will change, the principle of 10s still applies.

Start with the base unit and move left (get bigger) or right (get smaller). Each unit you move is a factor of 10 (or think of it as moving one decimal place). In ham radio, we focus on the bigger prefixes. This means we move by larger units of 1,000 or 10^3 - (10^3 is just a fancy way of writing 10 x 10 x 10, which equals 1,000). In most cases, we will move our decimal place three spaces left or right based on our direction in the scale.

For example, 1,000,0000 Hz equals 1 MHz (M is for mega, meaning millions), or 1,000 Hz is equal to 1 kHz (k is for kilo, meaning thousand). We moved our units, or decimals, in groupings or multiples of 1,000s.

Metric Scale for Ham Radio

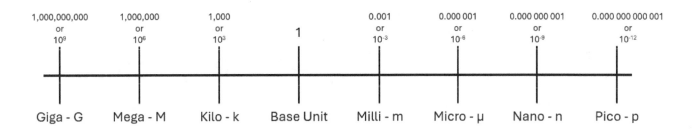

Let's practice one and then throw some exam questions at you.

T5B01: How many milliamperes is 1.5 amperes?

A. 15 milliamperes
B. 150 milliamperes
C. 1500 milliamperes
D. 15,000 milliamperes

To solve this problem, start with the base unit of amperes.

Starting at amperes, we move to the right on our number chart one space to Milli (10^3 or 1,000). <u>Moving right means the number gets bigger.</u>

On our Ham Scale, we move to the <u>right</u> one jump, which means we multiply by 1,000 (10^3 means 10 x 10 x 10 or 1,000) or think about moving the decimal three spaces.

1.5 amperes x 1,000 = 1500

But it's no longer amperes. It has now become milliamperes. So, the correct answer is 1,500 milliamperes.

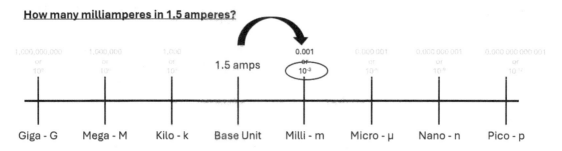

Let's try another one, this time moving to the left.

T5B02: Which is equal to 1,500,000 hertz?

A. 1500 kHz
B. 1500 MHz
C. 15 GHz
D. 150 kHz

To solve, start with the base unit of hertz.

Starting at hertz (the base unit), we move to the left on our number chart one space to kilo. <u>Moving left means the number gets smaller.</u>

We move one "Ham Unit" to the <u>left</u> – which is equal to 10^3 or 1,000 units or 3 decimal places. They all mean the same thing!

1,500,000 hertz divided by 1,000 = 1500 (we basically dropped off three zeros)

But it's no longer hertz. It has now become kilohertz or simply kHz. So, the correct answer is 1500 kHz. If you do this for the other possible answers, none of them make sense and are incorrect.

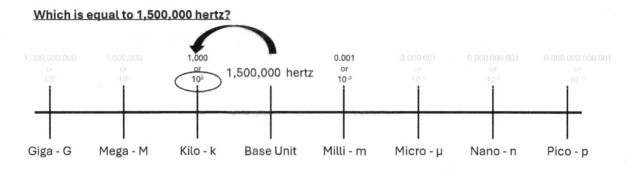

Let's try some more.

T5B03: Which is equal to one kilovolt?

A. One one-thousandth of a volt
B. One hundred volts
C. One thousand volts
D. One million volts

Refer to the numbers table again. A kilo is a thousand, so one kilovolt is a thousand volts.

Now, a tricky one.

T5B04: Which is equal to one microvolt?

A. One one-millionth of a volt
B. One million volts
C. One thousand kilovolts
D. One one-thousandth of a volt

On the table, a micro is written as 0.000 001. Micro means millionths, which in basic terms means millions to the right of the zero. Confusing, I know!

Here is how I like to think about it. Look at the chart again. Micro is written as 0.000 001. There are, in fact, six zeros, just like a million has six zeros (a different but easy way to think about it). So, a micro is a million, but it is written in the funny metric system as a million**th.** This gives us the answer that 'one microvolt' is 'one-million**th** of a volt.'

Remember, when looking at things to the right of the decimal, we will add '**th**'.

Let's try some more.

T5B05: Which is equal to 500 milliwatts?

A. 0.02 watts
B. 0.5 watts
C. 5 watts
D. 50 watts

We start at milliwatts and move "one Ham Unit" to the left. Again, our "Ham Unit" on this metric scale is 10^3 or 1,000 or three decimal points. Moving left means the number gets smaller. We divide by 1,000. Moving the decimal three places to the right.

500.0 milliwatts divided by 1,000 = 0.5. We must update the prefix from milliwatts to watts, so 500 milliwatts equals 0.5 watts.

For reference, you will see on our metric scale 10^{-3}. That negative sign is the fancy technical way of indicating that we divide or make our big number smaller. As you become familiar with the metric system, it will become second nature. But for now, don't let it confuse you. Just remember which way to move the decimal point.

Exam Questions

The following questions are all part of the exam pool. Work your way through each one using the concepts above. The units will change, but moving right or left on the numbers line (or up and down on the table – whichever is easier for you) will remain valid.

Exam Tip: When taking the exam, draw out the metric line and use it. The visualization will help. Just remember, "Giant Monsters Kick Big Mountains Making New Paths." Draw it out and use it for the following questions.

T5B06: Which is equal to 3000 milliamperes?

A. 0.003 amperes
B. 0.3 amperes
C. 3,000,000 amperes
D. 3 amperes

Moving from milliamperes to amps (our base unit), the "number" out front gets smaller. It goes from 3,000 to 3 (as there are 1,000 or 10^3 places between milli and base unit). So, our answer is 3 amps.

T5B07: Which is equal to 3.525 MHz?

A. 0.003525 kHz
B. 35.25 kHz
C. 3525 kHz
D. 3,525,000 kHz

Refer to the scale again. Moving from megahertz to kilohertz (all answers are in kilohertz) will increase our number. There are 1,000 or 10^3 places between mega and kilo. So, we move from 3.525 to 3,525 (our decimal moved three places). We update our units from MHz to kHz and get 3,525 kHz.

T5B08: Which is equal to 1,000,000 picofarads?

A. 0.001 microfarads
B. 1 microfarad
C. 1000 microfarads
D. 1,000,000,000 microfarads

Moving from picofarads to microfarads (all answers are in microfarads) will decrease our number. There are 1,000,000 or 10^6 places between pico and micro. So, we chop off six zeros and move from 1,000,000 to 1 (our decimal moved over six zeros). We update our units from picofarads to microfarad.

T5B12: Which is equal to 28400 kHz?

A. 28.400 kHz
B. 2.800 MHz
C. 284.00 MHz
D. 28.400 MHz

Moving from kHz to MHz (all answers are in MHz, except answer 'A,' which doesn't make sense because it's the same units) will decrease our number. There are 1,000 or 10^3 places between kilo and mega. So, we move 3 decimal places and go from 28,400 to 28.400 (our decimal moved over three spaces left). We update our units from kHz to MHz.

T5B13: Which is equal to 2425 MHz?

A. 0.002425 GHz
B. 24.25 GHz
C. 2.425 GHz
D. 2425 GHz

Look back to the base scale. Moving from MHz to GHz (all answers are in GHz) will decrease our big number out front. There are 1,000 or 10^3 places between mega and giga. Again, we moved three decimal places and went from 2,425 to 2.425 (our decimal moved over three spaces left). We update our units from MHz to GHz.

Our method emphasizing the "big numbers out front" will aid you in memorization and is a technique that works with the metric system. Although somewhat unconventional, it is effective.

In conclusion, always remember, "**G**iant **M**onsters **K**ick **B**ig **M**ountains **M**aking **N**ew **P**aths!"

Chapter 5

Electrical Principles

Introduction to Electrical Principles

ELECTRICITY AND ELECTRICAL PRINCIPLES form the backbone of amateur radio. Understanding these principles helps you pass the Technician Class license exam. It equips you with the skills to troubleshoot, repair, and optimize your radio equipment. This chapter will introduce you to the fundamentals of electricity, including voltage, current, resistance, and power, Ohm's Law, and the basics of electrical circuits. By grasping these concepts, you'll be better prepared to handle the technical aspects of ham radio, ensuring your station operates efficiently and effectively. Whether building a simple antenna or setting up a sophisticated communication system, a solid foundation in electrical principles is pivotal for your success in the amateur radio world.

Current

Current is a fundamental concept in electricity. It refers to the flow of electrons in an electric circuit, like the current or flow of the ocean, but with electrons, through a conductor, such as a wire. Measured in amperes (amps - A), current represents the rate at which electrons move past a specific point in a circuit.

You will see many examples of current compared to a watering hose. Let's get creative and use the analogy of a person running through a maze. Think of current as how fast our person is running through the maze (it's a dumb analogy, but that will help it stick!).

T5A03: What is the name for the flow of electrons in an electric circuit?

A. Voltage
B. Resistance
C. Capacitance
D. Current

T5A01: Electrical current is measured in which of the following units?

A. Volts
B. Watts
C. Ohms
D. Amperes

Electrical current is driven by <u>voltage, which provides the necessary force</u> to push the electrons. In our fanciful analogy, voltage is the force (the electrical zap!) making our runner run through the maze. The higher the 'zap,' or voltage, the faster our runner runs.

T5A05: What is the electrical term for the force that causes electron flow?

A. Voltage
B. Ampere-hours
C. Capacitance
D. Inductance

Different Types of Current

The primary current types are direct (DC) and alternating (AC).

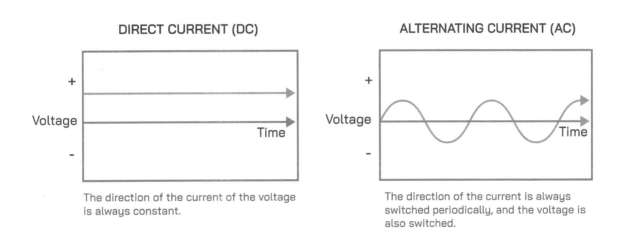

DIRECT CURRENT (DC)

The direction of the current of the voltage is always constant.

ALTERNATING CURRENT (AC)

The direction of the current is always switched periodically, and the voltage is also switched.

Direct Current (DC)

Direct current (DC) is characterized by the unidirectional flow of electric charge. In a DC circuit, electrons move in a single, consistent direction from the negative terminal to the positive terminal. This current type is typically produced by batteries, solar cells, and DC power supplies. DC is commonly used in low-voltage applications and electronic devices, including many components of amateur radio equipment. The steady voltage and current are ideal for powering transceivers, amplifiers, and other sensitive electronic circuits.

Alternating Current (AC)

Alternating current (AC) differs from DC in that the flow of electric charge periodically reverses direction. In an AC circuit, <u>the voltage alternates between positive and negative values</u>, causing the current to oscillate back and forth. This current type is generated by AC power sources such as power plants. It is delivered to homes and businesses through the electrical grid. AC is used for high-voltage applications, powering household appliances, and larger electronic devices. In amateur radio, AC is typically used to power base stations and other equipment that require a connection to the mains electricity supply.

T5A09: Which of the following describes alternating current?

A. current that alternates between a positive direction and zero
B. current that alternates between a negative direction and zero
C. Current that alternates between positive and negative directions
D. All these answers are correct

Electrical Resistance

Electrical resistance is the property of a material that opposes the flow of electric current, measured in ohms (Ω). It is a crucial concept in electrical circuits, determining how much current flows for a given voltage. In our unique analogy about a runner in a maze, resistance can be thought of as material inside the maze—perhaps mud, snow, or wind. The material's resistance, the space inside our maze, slows our runner down.

Resistance can be influenced by various factors, including the material's composition, length, and cross-sectional area. Understanding resistance is essential for designing efficient circuits and selecting appropriate components in ham radio. High resistance can limit current flow, potentially leading to voltage drops and reduced performance. In contrast, low resistance ensures more efficient power transfer.

T5A04: What are the units of electrical resistance?

A. Siemens
B. Mhos
C. Ohms
D. Coulombs

Need help in remembering Ohms? I think about Ohms as a police officer saying, "Ohmmm, going to have to ask you to slow down." Which is resistance slowing our runner down.

Power

I need more power!

Power in electrical circuits is the rate at which electrical energy is used or transferred, measured in watts (W). This concept is fundamental in ham radio, as it directly relates to the efficiency and performance of your equipment. How well can we get our runner through the maze?

Knowing your transmitter's power output in radio communications is necessary for effective signal propagation and compliance with regulatory limits.

T5A02: Electrical power is measured in which of the following units?

A. Volts
B. Watts
C. Watt-hours
D. Amperes

T5A10: Which term describes the rate at which electrical energy is used?

A. Resistance
B. Current
C. Power
D. Voltage

Decibels and the Power Ratio

Decibels (dB) are a logarithmic unit that measures the relative strength of signals, power levels, and gains in ham radio. They are invaluable for quantifying the performance of antennas, amplifiers, and other radio equipment. Using decibels, ham radio operators can easily compare signal strengths, assess the effectiveness of their setups, and make informed adjustments to improve communication quality.

Wait, what? What is logarithmic? A logarithmic scale is a way of showing numbers that grow very quickly by multiplying instead of adding. For example, on a regular scale, you count 1, 2, 3, and 4. But on a logarithmic scale, you jump by tens. If you started at 1, you would count 1, 10, 100, and 1000. This scale makes comparing very large or small numbers easier.

One common application of decibels in ham radio is measuring antenna gain. Antenna gain measures how well an antenna can focus energy in a particular direction. This measurement helps operators choose the suitable antenna for their needs and optimize its placement for better signal reception and transmission.

The Math Behind Decibels

I'm not going to lie; this is one of the most complex math parts for me. But let's work our way through it slowly.

The decibel is a logarithmic unit that expresses the ratio of two values, typically power levels. Because it is based on a logarithmic scale, a small change in decibels represents a significant change in the actual value. Memorize this formula.

1. **Power Ratio**:

$$\text{dB} = 10 \log_{10}\left(\frac{P_2}{P_1}\right)$$

In the decibel formula for power, P_1 (the initial power) is always in the denominator, and P_2 (the final power) is in the numerator. This is because decibels measure the ratio of the final power to the initial power, indicating how much the power has increased or decreased or how many times one power level is greater or smaller.

T5B09: Which decibel value most closely represents a power increase from 5 watts to 10 watts?

A. 2 dB
B. 3 dB
C. 5 dB
D. 10 dB

Solving the Decibel Increase from 5 Watts to 10 Watts

To determine the decibel (dB) increase when power goes from 5 watts to 10 watts, we use the power formula. Let's break it down step by step:

1. Identify the power values:

- Initial power (P₁): 5 watts

- Final power (P₂): 10 watts

2. Calculate the power ratio:

$$\frac{P_2}{P_1} = \frac{10}{5} = 2$$

3. Find the logarithm of the ratio:

$$\log_{10}(2) \approx 0.3$$

On your calculator, find the 'Log' key and press it. Then enter '2', and press the 'equal' key to get 0.301029957 or simply 0.3.

4. Multiply by 10 to find the decibel increase:

$$dB = 10 \times 0.3 = 3 \text{ dB}$$

So, a power increase from 5 to 10 watts is most closely represented by the rise of **3 dB**.

Quick Tip: Easy Way to Remember

A simple way to remember this is that doubling the power increases approximately 3 dB. So, when you see the power going from 5 watts to 10 watts (which is double), you can quickly recall that the increase is about 3 dB. The same is true if it's 20 watts to 40 or 25 watts to 50 watts; they are all 3 dB.

T5B10: Which decibel value most closely represents a power decrease from 12 watts to 3 watts?

A. -1 dB
B. -3 dB
C. -6 dB
D. -9 dB

Work through the steps above.

1. Identify values:

   - Initial = 12 watts (the bottom number)

   - Final = 3 watts (the top number)

2. Divide the two numbers: Final power divided by initial power or (3 watts divided by 12 watts)

- ◦ Equals 0.25

3. Find the Log ratio: Press the Log key and then 0.25; press enter.

- ◦ Equals -0.602059913 or call it -0.6.

4. Multiply by 10

- ◦ -0.6 times 10 = **-6 dB**

One more time:

T5B11: Which decibel value represents a power increase from 20 watts to 200 watts?

A. 10 dB
B. 12 dB
C. 18 dB
D. 28 dB

Work through steps 1-4 again. The ending power is on top, and the starting power is on bottom. Do you get 10 dB?

Understanding and using decibels allows ham radio operators to measure and optimize their equipment and signal quality effectively. The logarithmic nature of decibels simplifies calculations and comparisons, making it an essential tool in the technical aspects of amateur radio.

You will want to memorize this formula for the exam.

Frequency

Frequency, measured in hertz (Hz), refers to the number of complete cycles an alternating current completes per second. Each cycle has one complete wave, including a positive and negative half-cycle. The frequency of an AC signal determines how many times the current changes direction in one second. The unit of frequency is hertz (Hz), with one hertz equaling one cycle per second. Standard frequencies for household AC power are 60 Hz.

Our memorization technique: our runner in the maze has to change direction, back and forth, running this way and then that way. How frequently he changes direction is measured in hertz... because it hurts to have to change direction so frequently (see how nicely both hertz and frequency get memorized together)! And remember, this is a simple and silly memorization technique, that's it. Don't take it too seriously. But silly helps things stick in memory.

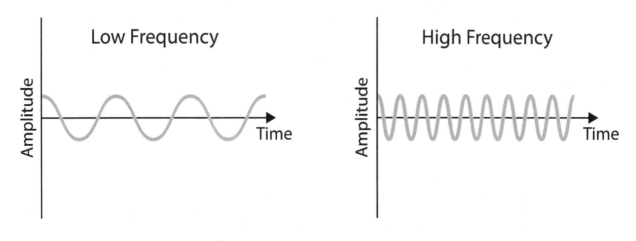

T5A12: What describes the number of times per second that an alternating current makes a complete cycle?

A. Pulse rate
B. Speed
C. Wavelength
D. Frequency

T5A06: What is the unit of frequency?

A. Hertz
B. Henry
C. Farad
D. Tesla

Importance of Frequency in Ham Radio

Understanding AC frequency is fundamental in ham radio for several reasons. First, radio signals are high-frequency AC signals transmitted through the air. The frequency of these signals determines their wavelength (more on this later) and propagation characteristics. Second, many radio transceivers and other equipment use AC power from the electrical grid. Hence, knowledge of the local frequency standard is essential for proper operation and compatibility.

Understanding the terminology is one of the most essential things about ham radio. So, let's start with an easy one: RF = Radio Frequency. Easy enough!

T5C06: What does the abbreviation "RF" mean?

A. Radio frequency signals of all types
B. The resonant frequency of a tuned circuit
C. The real frequency transmitted as opposed to the apparent frequency
D. Reflective force in antenna transmission lines

Furthermore, radio communications often involve modulating a carrier AC signal to encode information. Understanding how frequency affects modulation techniques (such as AM, FM, and SSB) is essential for effective communication (again more later).

Conductors and Insulators

Through what do electrons flow?

Conductors

Conductors are materials that allow the easy flow of electric current due to their low electrical resistance. They are characterized by having free electrons that can move easily from one atom to another when an electric potential is applied. This property makes conductors ideal for use in electrical circuits and wiring.

Common examples of conductors include metals such as copper, aluminum, silver, and gold, with copper being widely used in electrical wiring due to its high conductivity and relative affordability. Graphite and saltwater are also conductors, although metals are more efficient.

T5A07: Why are metals generally good conductors of electricity?

A. They have relatively high density
B. They have many free electrons
C. They have many free protons
D. All these choices are correct

Insulators

Insulators, on the other hand, are materials that resist the flow of electric current due to their high electrical resistance. Their electrons are tightly bound to their atoms, preventing free movement. Insulators are fundamental in preventing unintended current flow and protecting against electric shocks.

Remember our previous section about the police officer saying, "Ohmmmm, going to slow you down?" Resistance opposes the flow of all current types (DC, AC, and RF).

T5A11: What type of current flow is opposed by resistance?

A. Direct current
B. Alternating current
C. RF current
D. All these choices are correct

Common examples of insulators include plastics, rubber, glass, and ceramics. Plastics are commonly used to insulate electrical wires and components. In contrast, rubber is often used in protective gear and insulating covers for electrical tools and wires. Glass and ceramics are used in high-voltage applications and as insulators in radio equipment.

In ham radio, insulators isolate different circuit parts, preventing short circuits and protecting sensitive components from high voltages. They are also used in antenna systems to separate the conductive elements from supporting structures, ensuring efficient signal transmission without losses due to unintended grounding.

T5A08: Which of the following is a good electrical insulator?

A. Copper
B. Glass
C. Aluminum
D. Mercury

Proper selection and use of these materials ensures the reliability and safety of radio equipment. Conductors create efficient pathways for electrical signals, while insulators prevent unwanted current flow and protect the operator and the equipment.

Circuit Types: Parallel vs. Series

Circuits are the pathways through which electric current flows. Understanding the different types of circuits—particularly parallel and series circuits—is a fundamental electrical concept. Each type of circuit has its unique characteristics and applications.

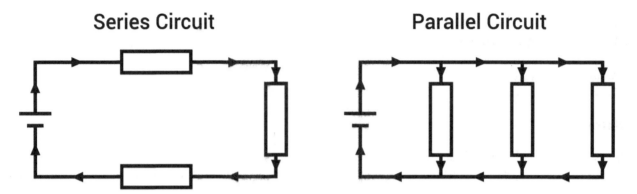

Series Circuits

In a series circuit, components are connected end-to-end in a single path for the current to flow. This means that the same current passes through each component one after another. Here are some points about series circuits:

1. Current: The current (I) is the same through all components in series. Because there is only one path to take.

2. Voltage: The total voltage (V) is the sum of the voltages across each component. If you have three resistors in series, the total voltage is the sum of the voltage drops across each resistor.

3. Resistance: The total resistance (R) is the sum of the individual resistances. Adding more resistors in series increases the total resistance.

T5D13: In which type of circuit is DC current the same through all components?

A. Series
B. Parallel
C. Resonant
D. Branch

Don't let the word 'DC current' in the question throw you off. It's an example of a "filler word" that we talked about back in chapter 3.

Parallel Circuits

In a parallel circuit, components are connected across the same two points, creating multiple paths for the current to flow. Here are some points about parallel circuits:

1. Current: The total current (I) is the sum of the currents through each parallel branch. Different branches can have different currents depending on their resistance.

2. Voltage: The voltage (V) across each component is the same and equal to the source's total voltage. Everywhere gets "zapped" the same amount.

3. Resistance: The total resistance (R) of a parallel circuit is <u>less than the resistance of the smallest</u> individual resistor.

T5D14: In which type of circuit is voltage the same across all components?

A. Series
B. Parallel
C. Resonant
D. Branch

Practical Applications

Series Circuits: Series circuits are often used in applications where the same current must pass through all components, such as string lights or certain types of sensors.

Parallel Circuits: Parallel circuits are used in applications where components must operate independently, such as in-home electrical wiring, where each appliance gets the same voltage but can draw different currents.

Understanding the differences between series and parallel circuits is key to designing effective and efficient electronic systems. Mastering these concepts will better equip you to build, troubleshoot, and optimize your ham radio equipment.

Ohm's Law

Ohm's Law is one of the fundamental principles of electronics and ham radio, and it forms the foundation for understanding how electrical circuits work. This Law describes the relationship between voltage (V), current (I), and resistance (R) in a simple and intuitive way. Think of it as the "rule of three" for electricity. You can easily calculate the third if you know two of these quantities.

The Formula

Ohm's Law is expressed by the formula:

$$E = I \times R$$

Where:

- **E** (voltage) is the electrical potential difference measured in volts (V).

  - 'E' what? It goes back to when and where things were named. Skipping the history lesson, remember that E = voltage.

- **I** (current) is the flow of electric charge measured in amperes (A).

  - 'I'? Again, it is a fascinating historical story, but it is unnecessary for the exam. Just remember that I = current.

- **R** (resistance) opposes the current flow measured in ohms (Ω).

  - Finally, an easy one to remember!

Breaking It Down

To understand this better, let's use the ever-present water analogy. Imagine a garden hose:

- **Voltage (E)** is like the water pressure in the hose. Higher pressure pushes more water through.

- **Current (I)** is the amount of water flowing through the hose. More water flow means a higher current.

- **Resistance (R)** is like the width of the hose. A narrow hose (higher resistance) makes water flow harder, while a wide hose (lower resistance) allows more water to pass through easily.

The Ohm's Law Triangle is a simple tool for visualizing how the three interact and is useful for memorization on the exam. Start with the "E" on top and then go alphabetically counterclockwise- "I", then "R".

Using the Triangle: If you want to find voltage (E), cover up the "E" in the triangle. You're left with "I" next to "R," which means Voltage = Current × Resistance ($E = I \times R$).

- To find current (I), cover up the "I". You'll see "E" over "R," which means Current = Voltage ÷ Resistance ($I = E \div R$).

- To find resistance (R), cover up the "R". You'll see "E" over "I", which means Resistance = Voltage ÷ Current ($R = E \div I$).

This simple triangle allows you to quickly solve problems involving voltage, current, and resistance without having to memorize each formula separately.

Write out the triangle on a piece of paper. This will help with memorization. Then, answer the three exam questions, which involve rewriting the formula to solve for each measurement.

T5D01: What formula is used to calculate current in a circuit?

A. $I = E * R$
B. $I = E / R$
C. $I = E + R$
D. $I = E - R$

Draw the triangle. To find current (I), cover up the "I". You'll see "E" over "R", which means Current = Voltage ÷ Resistance ($I = E \div R$).

T5D02: What formula is used to calculate voltage in a circuit?

A. $E = I \times R$
B. $E = I / R$
C. $E = I + R$
D. $E = I - R$

If you want to find voltage (E), cover up the "E" in the triangle. You're left with "I" next to "R", which means Voltage = Current × Resistance ($E = I \times R$).

T5D03: What formula is used to calculate resistance in a circuit?

A. R = E x I
B. R = E / I
C. R = E + I
D. R = E - I

To find resistance (R), cover up the "R". You'll see "E" over "I", which means Resistance = Voltage ÷ Current (R = E ÷ I).

Now, let's try using some numbers.

T5D04: What is the resistance of a circuit in which a current of 3 amperes flows when connected to 90 volts?

A. 3 ohms
B. 30 ohms
C. 93 ohms
D. 270 ohms

The Easy 4-Step Approach

Step 1: look at the values we have been given. 90 volts and 3 amps.

Step 2: fill in the triangle.

- E = 90 volts

- I = 3 amps

Step 3: do the math.

- 90 divided by 3 = 30

- Since we are solving for resistance (R), we have 30 ohms!

The following problems are part of the exam pool. Use the triangle and solve for the missing measurement.

Remember, what are they asking for? What measurement: resistance (R), current (I), or voltage (E)?

Create your triangle on a piece of paper and then fill in the numbers from the question. With your triangle, you should easily complete the following exam questions.

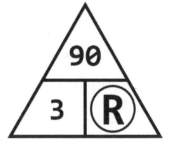

Voltage	Current	Resistance
E = I.R	I = E/R	R = E /I

T5D05: What is the resistance of a circuit for which the applied voltage is 12 volts, and the current flow is 1.5 amperes?

A. 18 ohms
B. 0.125 ohms
C. 8 ohms
D. 13.5 ohms

Resistance = Voltage ÷ Current (R = E ÷ I) = 12 volts divided by 1.5 amps = 8 ohms of resistance

T5D06: What is the resistance of a circuit that draws 4 amperes from a 12-volt source?

A. 3 ohms
B. 16 ohms
C. 48 ohms
D. 8 ohms

Resistance = Voltage ÷ Current (R = E ÷ I) = 12 volts divided by 4 amps = 3 ohms

T5D07: What is the current in a circuit with an applied voltage of 120 volts and a resistance of 80 ohms?

A. 9600 amperes
B. 200 amperes
C. 0.667 amperes
D. 1.5 amperes

Current = Voltage ÷ Resistance (I = E ÷ R) = 120 volts divided by 80 ohms = 1.5 amps of current

T5D08: What is the current through a 100-ohm resistor connected across 200 volts?

A. 20,000 amperes
B. 0.5 amperes
C. 2 amperes
D. 100 amperes

Current = Voltage ÷ Resistance (I = E ÷ R) = 200 volts divided by 100 ohms = 2 amps

T5D09: What is the current through a 24-ohm resistor connected across 240 volts?

A. 24,000 amperes
B. 0.1 amperes
C. 10 amperes
D. 216 amperes

Current = Voltage ÷ Resistance (I = E ÷ R) = 240 volts divided by 24 ohms = 10 amps

T5D10: What is the voltage across a 2-ohm resistor if a current of 0.5 amperes flows through it?

A. 1 volt
B. 0.25 volts
C. 2.5 volts
D. 1.5 volts

Voltage = Current × Resistance (E = I × R) = 0.5 amps multiplied by 2 ohms = 1 volt

T5D11: What is the voltage across a 10-ohm resistor if a current of 1 ampere flows through it?

A. 1 volt
B. 10 volts
C. 11 volts
D. 9 volts

Voltage = Current × Resistance (E = I × R) = 1 amp multiplied by 10 ohms = 10 volts

T5D12: What is the voltage across a 10-ohm resistor if a current of 2 amperes flows through it?

A. 8 volts
B. 0.2 volts
C. 12 volts
D. 20 volts

Voltage = Current × Resistance (E = I × R) = 2 amps multiplied by 10 ohms = 20 volts

That's a lot of math! Just remember the Ohm Triangle, and you will be able to move between Voltage (E), Current (I), and Resistance (R).

The Power Pyramid

Just when you thought it was safe to move on, we have one more triangle for you. The triangle of power!

In addition to Ohm's Law, the power formula is another essential formula. This formula helps you calculate the electrical power in a circuit, which is key to understanding how much energy your devices use or generate. The power formula relates power (P) to current (I) and voltage (E).

The Formula

The power formula is expressed as:

$$P = I \times E$$

Where:

- **P** (power) is the amount of electrical energy transferred or consumed per unit of time, measured in watts (W). And yes! P for power is easy!

- **I** (current) is the flow of electric charge, measured in amperes (A).

- **E** (voltage) is the electrical potential difference, measured in volts (V).

Remember, there is Power in PIE!

Why It Matters in Ham Radio

Understanding the power formula is essential for ham radio operators because it helps manage your equipment's energy consumption and output. Knowing how much power your transmitter uses or how much power your antenna can handle ensures that your setup operates efficiently and safely. It also helps you make informed decisions when choosing power supplies and other components.

To remember the order of the pyramid, spell P-I-E counterclockwise—the power of pie.

T5C08: What is the formula used to calculate electrical power (P) in a DC circuit?

A. P = E * I
B. P = E / I
C. P = E - I
D. P = E + I

The Power Triangle works the same way. Simply know which values you have and the ones for which you are solving. Plug them into the pyramid and solve. Let us practice!

Power	Current	Voltage
P = E × I	I = P / E	E = P / I

T5C09: How much power is delivered by a voltage of 13.8 volts DC and a current of 10 amperes?

A. 138 watts
B. 0.7 watts
C. 23.8 watts
D. 3.8 watts

Power = Voltage × Current (P = V × I) = 13.8 volts multiplied by 10 amps = 138 watts of power. Here is another example of DC just being filler for this question.

T5C10: How much power is delivered by a voltage of 12 volts DC and a current of 2.5 amperes?

A. 4.8 watts
B. 30 watts
C. 14.5 watts
D. 0.208 watts

Power = Voltage × Current (P = V × I) = 12 volts multiplied by 2.5 amps = 30 watts of power

T5C11: How much current is required to deliver 120 watts at a voltage of 12 volts DC?

A. 0.1 amperes
B. 10 amperes
C. 12 amperes
D. 132 amperes

Current = Power ÷ Voltage (I = P ÷ V) = 120 watts of power divided by 12 volts = 10 amps

Having any trouble getting the correct answer? Go back to the Easy 4-Step Approach and follow each one. The only difference between the Ohm and Power pyramids is the units of measurement. The formula and math work the same.

Chapter 6

The Control of Electrical Principles

Capacitance

CAPACITANCE IS A FUNDAMENTAL electrical property that describes <u>a component or circuit's ability to store and release electrical energy. It is measured in farads (F).</u> Capacitance is typically found in capacitors, essential components in many electronic circuits, including ham radios. Think about, "I have the capacity to store energy in an ELECTRIC field!" That electric piece is important.

A capacitor consists of two conductive plates separated by an insulating material called a dielectric (more on this in the physical radio station section). When a voltage is applied across the plates, an electric field is created, allowing the capacitor to store energy as an electrostatic charge.

This stored energy can be released when the circuit requires it, helping to smooth out fluctuations in voltage and maintain stable operation. In ham radio, capacitors are used for various purposes, such as filtering signals, tuning antennas, and coupling or decoupling different circuit stages.

T5C01: What describes the ability to store energy in an electric field?

A. Inductance
B. Resistance
C. Tolerance
D. Capacitance

I don't have a good way to remember this one, so just memorize it!

T5C02: What is the unit of capacitance?

A. The farad
B. The ohm
C. The volt
D. The henry

Inductance

Inductance is the electrical property that describes the <u>ability of a component or circuit to store energy in a magnetic field</u> when an electric current flows through it. That seems like capacitance! So, the key here is that inductance refers to the MAGNETIC field.

Inductance is measured in Henry's (H). It is primarily associated with inductors, which are components made by winding a coil of wire around a core. When current flows through the coil, it creates a magnetic field, storing energy within the inductor. This stored energy can then be released when the current changes, providing a means to regulate current flow and filter signals.

In ham radio, inductors play an important role in various applications, such as tuning circuits, filtering out unwanted frequencies, and forming part of oscillators and transformers. Understanding inductance is essential for designing and troubleshooting radio equipment, as it helps ensure that circuits operate efficiently and effectively. By mastering the principles of inductance, amateur radio operators can enhance their ability to create and maintain stable, high-performing communication systems.

T5C03: What describes the ability to store energy in a magnetic field?

A. Admittance
B. Capacitance
C. Resistance
D. Inductance

T5C04: What is the unit of inductance?

A. The coulomb
B. The farad
C. The henry
D. The ohm

So, who is still confused? One more look at the difference between capacitance and inductance.

Capacitance and inductance are fundamental electrical properties but operate based on different principles and serve distinct circuit functions.

Capacitance is storing and releasing electrical energy in an electrostatic field. Capacitance, measured in farads (F), helps smooth out voltage fluctuations, filter signals, and couple or decouple circuit stages.

Inductance is the ability to store and release energy in a magnetic field. Measured in henrys (H), it regulates current flow, filters unwanted frequencies, and creates oscillators and transformers.

In essence, capacitors oppose changes in voltage by storing and releasing energy quickly. In contrast, inductors oppose changes in current by generating a counteracting voltage. Understanding these differences is crucial for designing and optimizing circuits, giving us control over electricity in our radios.

Memorization technique.

We have four ideas here: 1) **C**apacitance, 2) **I**nductance, 3) **E**lectric Field, and 4) **M**agnetic Field. Lucky for us, if we put the words in alphabetical order, partners line up. **C – E – I – M**

- **C**apacitance = **E**lectric Field

- **I**nductance = **M**agnetic Field

Impedance

Impedance is <u>a circuit's total opposition to the flow of alternating current</u> (AC).

It includes resistance (which opposes the flow of direct current) and reactance (which comes from capacitors and inductors in the circuit).

What was that?

Impedance affects how much current flows for a given AC voltage. <u>Like resistance, it's measured in ohms (Ω).</u> Any time our cop slows us down, it's an ohm.

Matching impedance between components, like a transmitter and antenna, is crucial in ham radio. Proper impedance matching ensures efficient power transfer and reduces signal loss, improving radio equipment performance. Understanding impedance helps design, tune, and troubleshoot your ham radio setup.

T5C12: What is impedance?

A. The opposition to AC current flow
B. The inverse of resistance
C. The Q or Quality Factor of a component
D. The power handling capability of a component

T5C05: What is the unit of impedance?

A. The volt
B. The ampere
C. The coulomb
D. The ohm

Understanding the electrical principles of current, resistance, power, capacitance, inductance, and impedance is fundamental for any aspiring ham radio operator. These concepts form the backbone of radio equipment operating and interacting with the surrounding environment.

By grasping these principles, you can effectively design, build, and troubleshoot circuits, ensuring your equipment performs at its best. Whether you're smoothing out voltage fluctuations with capacitors, managing current flow with inductors, or ensuring optimal power transfer through impedance matching, a solid foundation in these electrical principles will enhance your skills and confidence as a ham radio operator.

Mastery of these topics further prepares you for the Technician Class license exam.

Chapter 7

Radio Waves

IMAGINE STANDING ON A cliff overlooking the ocean, where the waves travel tirelessly from the horizon to the shore. This relentless movement of water is much like how radio waves traverse through space, an invisible force carrying voices and data across vast distances. In this chapter, we'll decode the mystique of radio waves and their propagation, transforming the seemingly complex into something understandable. By grasping these fundamentals, you'll be equipped to pass your exam and engage effectively in amateur radio, making connections that were once beyond reach.

Physics of Radio Waves

Radio waves are electromagnetic radiation, akin to the light you see with your eyes but with much longer wavelengths and lower frequencies. They are part of the electromagnetic spectrum, which includes other types of waves such as microwaves, infrared radiation, ultraviolet light, X-rays, and gamma rays.

These waves are generated by moving electric charges, typically in a piece of metal called an antenna. When an electric current flows through an antenna, it creates an electromagnetic field that radiates outwards as radio waves. Depending on their frequency, the length of these waves can range from about one millimeter to over 100 kilometers.

The frequency of radio waves, measured in hertz (Hz), is the number of times the wave oscillates per second. Radio frequencies used in ham radio range from 30 kHz (kilohertz) to 300 GHz (gigahertz), covering a broad spectrum of wavelengths.

When you speak into a ham radio's microphone, your voice is converted into electrical signals. These signals are then used to alter (modulate) a radio wave generated by the transmitter. The modulated wave travels through the air (and even the vacuum of space) at the <u>speed of light – 300,000 kilometers per second</u>, carrying your message.

T3B04: What is the velocity of a radio wave traveling through free space?

A. speed of light
B. speed of sound
C. Speed inversely proportional to its wavelength
D. Speed that increases as the frequency increases

For comparison, the Earth's circumference at the equator is 40,075 kilometers. Radio waves travel at the speed of light, which is why communication is instantaneous anywhere in the world.

T3B11: What is the approximate velocity of a radio wave in free space?

A. 150,000 meters per second
B. 300,000,000 meters per second
C. 300,000,000 miles per hour
D. 150,000 miles per hour

For this question, remember that we are in the metric system, which rules out a few answers. Also, we saw the speed of light written in kilometers above. Now, we have to convert kilometers to meters. Remembering our chapter on the metric system, we move to the right (the big number out front gets bigger) by 1,000 or three decimal places.

The speed of light changes from 300,000 kilometers per second to 300,000,000 meters per second.

Components of Radio Waves:

- **Electric Field (E-field):** This component oscillates <u>perpendicular (at a right angle)</u> to the wave's direction of travel. <u>The electric field's strength and orientation determine the radio wave's polarization.</u>

- **Magnetic Field (H-field):** This component oscillates <u>perpendicular (at a right angle)</u> to both the direction of travel and the electric field. The magnetic field is always in phase with the electric field.

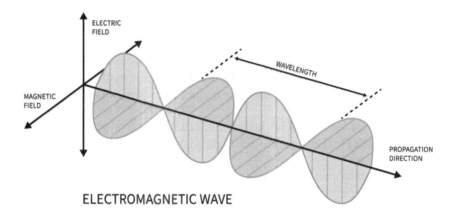

T3B03: What are the two components of a radio wave?

A. impedance and reactance
B. voltage and current
C. Electric and magnetic fields
D. Ionizing and non-ionizing radiation

T3B01: What is the relationship between the electric and magnetic fields of an electromagnetic wave?

A. They travel at different speeds
B. They are in parallel
C. They revolve in opposite directions
D. They are at right angles

The property of a radio wave that defines its polarization is the <u>orientation of its electric field (E-field).</u> Polarization refers to the direction in which the electric field oscillates as the radio wave travels through space.

T3B02: What property of a radio wave defines its polarization?

A. The orientation of the electric field
B. The orientation of the magnetic field
C. The ratio of the energy in the magnetic field to the energy in the electric field
D. The ratio of the velocity to the wavelength

Polarization

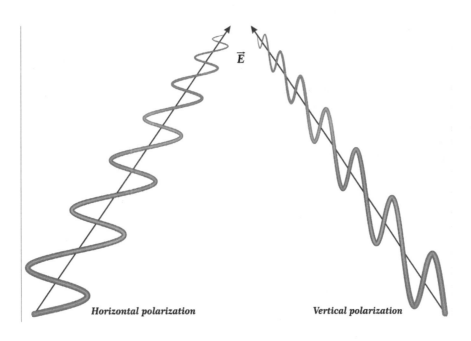

Horizontal polarization   *Vertical polarization*

- **Vertical Polarization**:

  - In vertically polarized waves, the electric field oscillates in a vertical direction.

  - These waves are commonly used in mobile and handheld radio communications because vertically oriented antennas are easy to mount and use.

- **Horizontal Polarization**:

    ○ In horizontally polarized waves, the electric field oscillates in a horizontal direction.

    ○ This type of polarization is often used in television broadcasting and some forms of long-distance communication, where horizontal antennas can be more practical.

- **Circular Polarization**:

    ○ Circularly polarized waves have an electric field that rotates in a circular motion as they propagate. This can be either right-hand circular polarization (RHCP) or left-hand circular polarization (LHCP).

    ○ Circular polarization is used in satellite and space communications because it can reduce the effects of signal fading due to rotation or orientation changes of the transmitting and receiving antennas.

- **Elliptical Polarization**:

    ○ Elliptically polarized waves have an electric field that traces an ellipse as it propagates. This more general form of polarization includes linear and circular polarization.

Matching the polarization of the transmitting and receiving antennas is crucial for efficient communication. If the polarizations are mismatched, signal strength can be significantly reduced, leading to poor reception and communication quality. For example, a vertically polarized antenna will not effectively receive a horizontally polarized signal.

The orientation of a radio wave's electric field defines its polarization. Understanding and matching the polarization of antennas in radio communication systems is essential for maximizing signal strength and communication efficiency.

Memorization technique.

Think about holding a "walkie-talkie." I know, I know, but don't hurt me. It's just for memorization. You hold a walkie-talkie straight up and down... or vertically. The antenna is vertical. Meaning it is vertically polarized. Suppose you turned the walkie-talkie sideways. The antenna is now parallel to the ground and so horizontally polarized.

Remember that, and you have this polarization stuff down!

Chapter 8

Frequency Bands

IN REAL-WORLD APPLICATIONS, THE choice of frequency band can dramatically affect the success and scope of communication.

Each band, with its unique propagation characteristics, opens up different aspects of the hobby to explore, from local emergency preparedness networks to worldwide digital communication networks, each offering its own set of challenges and rewards.

Look at some of those characteristics and relate them to real-world usage.

Short-Hand Name	VLF	LF	MF	HF	VHF	UHF	SHF	EHF
Name	Very Low Frequency	Low Frequency	Medium Frequency	High Frequency	Very High Frequency	Ultra High Frequency	Super High Frequency	Extremely High Frequency
Frequency	3 – 30 kHz	30 – 300 kHz	300 – 3,000 kHz	3 MHz – 30 MHz	30 – 300 MHz	300 – 3,000 MHz	3 GHz – 30 GHz	30 – 300 GHz
Wavelength	100 – 10 km	10 – 1 km	1,000 m – 100 m	100 – 10 m	10 – 1 m	1 – 0.1 m	10 cm – 1 cm	1 – 0.1 cm

Frequency Band Table

Characteristics of Radio Bands

VLF (Very Low Frequency)

- Propagation: Ground waves capable of long-distance communication.

- Uses: Submarine communication, navigation beacons.

- Penetration: Good penetration through water and Earth.

- Antenna Size: Huge antennas are needed due to long wavelengths.

LF (Low Frequency)

- Propagation: Ground waves are reliable over long distances.

- Uses: Long-range navigation, time signals, AM broadcasting.

- Antenna Size: Large antennas are required.

- Penetration: Good ground penetration, useful for geophysical surveys.

MF (Medium Frequency)

- Propagation: Ground waves during the day, skywaves at night.

- Uses: AM radio broadcasting, maritime communication.

- Antenna Size: Medium-sized antennas.

- Night-time Reach: Better long-distance propagation at night due to skywave reflections.

HF (High Frequency)

- Propagation: Skywave (ionospheric) propagation is capable of global communication.

- Uses: Shortwave radio, amateur radio, international broadcasting, military communication.

- Antenna Size: Practical antenna sizes for home and portable use.

- Day/Night Variability: Propagation conditions vary with time of day and solar activity.

VHF (Very High Frequency)

- Propagation: Line-of-sight, limited by the horizon.

- Uses: FM radio, television broadcasting, air traffic control, amateur radio.

- Antenna Size: Relatively small antennas.

- Penetration: Good penetration through buildings, suitable for mobile communication.

UHF (Ultra High Frequency)

- Propagation: Line-of-sight, affected by obstacles.

- Uses: Television broadcasting, mobile phones, Wi-Fi, Bluetooth, amateur radio.

- Antenna Size: Very small antennas.

- Penetration: Limited building penetration, but suitable for urban environments with many repeaters.

SHF (Super High Frequency)

- Propagation: Line-of-sight, very sensitive to obstacles and atmospheric conditions.

- Uses: Radar, satellite communication, microwave links, Wi-Fi.

- Antenna Size: Tiny, often parabolic dishes.

- Atmospheric Effects: Affected by rain, fog, and other atmospheric conditions.

EHF (Extremely High Frequency)

- Propagation: Line-of-sight, very short range.

- Uses: Advanced radar, experimental communication systems, scientific research.

- Antenna Size: Tiny antennas.

- Atmospheric Effects: Highly affected by atmospheric absorption, limited practical use in open air.

Technician Band Access

As a Technician class licensee, you will have full access to the UHF (Ultra High Frequency) and VHF (Very High Frequency) bands allocated for amateur radio use in the United States. These bands are ideal for local and regional communication.

In this section, we will explore the characteristics of VHF and UHF bands, including their propagation properties, typical uses, and practical tips to help you make the most of your operating privileges. Understanding these aspects will enhance your ability to communicate effectively, enjoy the full benefits of your technician license, and pass your exam.

Insights into VHF and UHF for Technician Licensees

VHF (Very High Frequency)

- **Frequency Range**: 30 to 300 MHz

- **Wavelength**: 10 meters to 1 meter

- **Characteristics**:

    o **Propagation**: VHF signals primarily travel by line-of-sight, which means they usually do not bend around obstacles or follow the curvature of the Earth. However, they can reflect off buildings, hills, and other large objects, extending their range slightly beyond the horizon.

    o **Penetration**: VHF signals can penetrate through foliage and buildings better than UHF signals, making them suitable for mobile and portable communication.

    o **Typical Uses**: FM radio, television broadcasting (channels 2-13), public service communications (police and fire departments), marine communications, and amateur radio.

- **Advantages**:

    o **Range**: This is effective for medium-range communication, typically up to 30 miles, depending on the terrain and antenna height.

    o **Less Interference**: VHF is less affected by man-made electrical noise than lower frequency bands.

    o **Antenna Size**: VHF antennas are generally manageable, making them suitable for home use and mobile installations.

- **Disadvantages**:

    o **Obstructions**: Large buildings, hills, and other obstructions can significantly reduce signal strength.

- o **Bandwidth:** Less bandwidth compared to UHF, which can limit the number of available channels.

UHF (Ultra High Frequency)

- **Frequency Range:** 300 MHz to 3 GHz

- **Wavelength:** 1 meter to 0.1 meter

- **Characteristics:**

  - o **Propagation:** UHF signals also travel by line-of-sight but are more affected by physical obstructions than VHF signals. They tend to have a shorter range but can penetrate through buildings better than VHF signals.

  - o **Penetration:** UHF signals can pass through walls and buildings more effectively than VHF, making them ideal for indoor communication and urban environments.

  - o **Typical Uses:** Television broadcasting (channels 14-83), mobile phones, Wi-Fi, Bluetooth, GPS, and amateur radio.

- **Advantages:**

  - o **Bandwidth:** UHF offers more bandwidth, allowing for more channels and higher data transmission rates.

  - o **Antenna Size:** UHF antennas are smaller and more compact, making them easy to install in confined spaces.

  - o **Urban Use:** More effective for use in densely populated urban areas with many buildings and obstacles.

- **Disadvantages:**

  - o **Range:** UHF typically has a shorter range than VHF due to its higher frequencies and greater susceptibility to obstacles.

  - o **Interference:** More prone to interference from other electronic devices and appliances.

Practical Applications for Technicians

VHF in Ham Radio:

- **2-Meter Band:** This is the most popular VHF band for amateur radio, ranging from 144 to 148 MHz. It is widely used for local communication, repeater operation, and emergency services.

- **Simplex and Repeater Operation:** Technician licensees can use VHF frequencies for simplex (direct radio-to-radio) communication and through repeaters, which extend the communication range.

UHF in Ham Radio:

- **70-centimeter Band:** This band ranges from 420 to 450 MHz and is another popular amateur radio band. It is ideal for local communication, especially in urban areas where building penetration is essential.

- **Linked Repeaters:** UHF repeaters are often linked to other repeaters via the internet or other means, allowing for long-distance communication through a network of repeaters.

Tips for Using VHF and UHF:

- **Antennas**: Use high-gain antennas to improve signal strength and range. Vertical antennas are common for VHF for mobile and base stations. In contrast, smaller and more directional antennas are effective for UHF.

- **Line-of-Sight**: Ensure that antennas are placed as high as possible and in a clear line of sight to minimize obstructions and maximize range.

- **Repeaters**: Utilize local repeaters to extend your communication range. Familiarize yourself with the location and frequencies of repeaters in your area.

Understanding the characteristics and best practices for using VHF and UHF bands will help Technician licensees maximize their privileges and enhance their communication capabilities in the amateur radio community.

Let's tackle some exam questions.

T3A02: What is the effect of vegetation on UHF and microwave signals?

A. Knife-edge diffraction
B. Absorption
C. Amplification
D. Polarization rotation

When dealing with UHF (Ultra-High Frequency) and microwave signals, one key factor to consider is how vegetation, like trees and shrubs, can impact these signals. The main effect here is absorption. Unlike lower-frequency signals, UHF and microwave signals have shorter wavelengths, making them more susceptible to being absorbed by water-containing materials, like the leaves and branches of plants.

Think of it like this: when UHF and microwave signals pass through vegetation, the plants absorb part of the signal's energy, weakening it. This is why you might experience reduced signal strength or even signal loss when operating in areas with dense foliage.

T3A12: What is the effect of fog and rain on signals in the 10-meter and 6-meter bands?

A. Absorption
B. There is little effect
C. Deflection
D. Range increase

Unlike higher frequency signals, which can be heavily impacted by moisture in the air, the signals in the 10-meter and 6-meter bands are largely unaffected by fog and rain.

This minimal impact occurs because the wavelengths of these bands are relatively long compared to the size of raindrops and fog droplets. These water particles are simply too small to significantly scatter or absorb the radio waves in these bands. So, while you might notice some interference in other situations, you can generally expect clear communication on these frequencies, regardless of the weather.

But:

T3A07: What weather condition might decrease range at microwave frequencies?

A. High winds
B. Low barometric pressure
C. Precipitation
D. Colder temperatures

When working with microwave frequencies, one important factor to keep in mind is how weather can affect your signal's range. Precipitation, such as rain, snow, or sleet, can significantly reduce the range of microwave signals. Because of their high frequency and short wavelength, microwave signals are particularly sensitive to weather conditions. When it rains or snows, the tiny water droplets or ice particles in the air interact with these signals in two main ways: absorption and scattering.

Summary

In summary, for ham radio operators with a Technician license, several bands are particularly popular due to their accessibility and the range of activities they support. The 2-meter and 70-centimeter bands are the most popular for everyday use, while the 6-meter and 10-meter bands offer opportunities for more specialized and long-distance communications.

10-Meter Band (HF)

- **Wavelength**: Approximately 10 meters

- **Frequency Range**: 28.0–28.5 MHz (Technician operators have limited privileges in the 28.0–28.5 MHz range. See Privileges Cheat Sheet for exact details.)

- **Usage**: This band can support long-distance (DX) communications, especially during periods of high solar activity. It offers a great introduction to HF operating and is a favorite among Technicians interested in experimenting with digital modes or single-sideband (SSB) phone operations.

6-Meter Band (VHF)

- **Wavelength**: Approximately 6 meters

- **Frequency Range**: 50–54 MHz

- **Usage**: Known as "The Magic Band," the 6-meter band can provide both local and long-distance communications, depending on atmospheric conditions. It can exhibit characteristics of both HF and VHF bands, making it a versatile choice for Technician operators.

2-Meter Band (VHF)

- **Wavelength**: Approximately 2 meters

- **Frequency Range**: 144–148 MHz

- **Usage**: This is the most popular VHF band for Technician operators. It is widely used for local communications, especially through repeaters. It is also popular for simplex (direct, station-to-station) communications and emergency services.

70-Centimeter Band (UHF)

- **Wavelength**: Approximately 70 centimeters

- **Frequency Range**: 420–450 MHz

- **Usage**: This band is popular for local communications, often using repeaters. The shorter wavelength allows for better performance in urban environments, where signals can penetrate buildings and other obstacles more effectively than VHF signals.

Memorization technique: repetition. We saw a lot of repetition in this chapter. These radio bands are a core fundamental part of radio. Through repetition, you will begin to remember and know these bands until one day, this knowledge is just second nature.

Chapter 9

Propagation: How Your Signal Travels

PROPAGATION REFERS TO RADIO waves traveling through the atmosphere from a transmitter to a receiver. This is a critical concept in ham radio, as understanding how different propagation mechanisms work can help operators optimize their communication range and reliability.

The environment through which radio waves travel can influence their behavior. Like sound waves, which can echo off walls or be muffled by cushions, radio waves interact with objects and atmospheric conditions in various ways. Understanding these interactions is imperative for effective transmission and reception.

Propagation Modes

Different environments require different propagation modes to transmit signals effectively. As a Technician licensee, you will primarily encounter three modes:

1. **Ground Wave Propagation**: This occurs when radio waves travel along the surface of the Earth. Ground waves are predominantly used for local communications within about 50 to 100 miles, ideal for chatting with fellow hams in your region. These waves tend to follow the Earth's curvature and can be reliable during the day and night.

2. **Skywave Propagation**: At higher frequencies, radio waves can be reflected to Earth by the ionosphere, an ionized layer of the atmosphere. This mode allows for international communication, as the waves can 'bounce' between the ionosphere and the Earth, covering vast distances. However, this type of propagation is highly dependent on solar and atmospheric conditions, and thus, it can be pretty variable.

3. **Line-of-Sight Propagation**: As the name suggests, this mode requires no physical obstruction between the transmitting and receiving antennas. Line-of-sight propagation is perfect for applications like FM radio and television broadcasts, where clarity and consistency are essential. The range can be extended beyond the visual line of sight by the slight bending of waves in the atmosphere, known as tropospheric ducting.

Factors Affecting Propagation

Several environmental factors can influence how well your radio signals travel. Solar activity, such as sunspots and solar flares, can dramatically affect the ionization levels of the ionosphere, altering its ability to reflect radio waves. Higher solar activity generally enhances skywave propagation conditions but can also lead to increased levels of disruptive solar noise.

The Earth's atmosphere, with its varying layers of temperature and ionization, plays a significant role in radio wave propagation. Weather conditions, particularly storms and heavy cloud cover, can absorb or scatter radio waves, reducing signal strength and clarity. Understanding these factors can help you choose the best times and frequencies for your radio activities.

Knife-edge diffraction

<u>Knife-edge diffraction is a phenomenon that allows radio signals to bend around sharp edges, such as the tops of mountains or buildings, enabling them to travel beyond obstacles that would typically block direct line-of-sight communication.</u> When a radio wave encounters a sharp edge (like hitting the edge of a building in the image below), part of the wave is bent, or diffracted, around the obstacle, continuing on the other side. This effect helps signals reach areas that would otherwise be in a shadow zone due to the obstruction.

Remembering knife-edge diffraction is easy if you think of a knife slicing through the air, creating a path for the radio wave to follow. This effect is particularly useful in urban environments or mountainous regions where obstacles frequently interfere with line-of-sight communication.

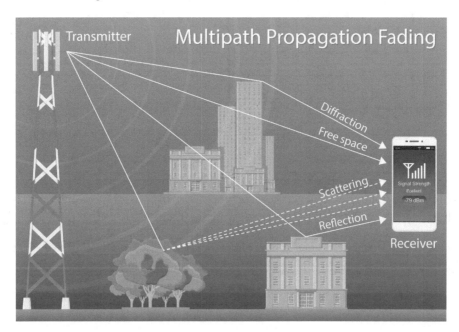

T3C05: Which of the following effects may allow radio signals to travel beyond obstructions between the transmitting and receiving stations?

A. Knife-edge diffraction
B. Faraday rotation
C. Quantum tunneling
D. Doppler shift

Multipath Propagation

Multipath propagation is a phenomenon where radio signals travel from a transmitter to a receiver along multiple paths. These paths include direct line-of-sight, reflections off buildings, mountains, or other obstacles, and even refraction through the atmosphere.

As a result, <u>the signal arriving at the receiver combines these multiple paths, which can cause constructive or destructive interference.</u> This can lead to signal strength and quality variations, sometimes resulting in fading or distortion.

Look back at the image above on propagation. A radio wave can take many paths from its transmitter to its intended receiver.

When these multiple signal paths converge at the receiving antenna, they can cancel or reinforce each other depending on their phase relationships.

In Phase and Out of Phase

Phase relationships describe the relative positions of waves in time, specifically how the peaks and troughs of one wave align with those of another. When discussing radio signals, phase relationships become crucial, especially in multipath propagation.

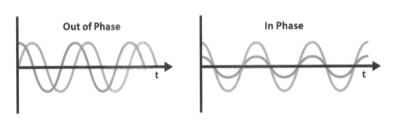

In Phase

When two waves are in phase, their peaks (highest points) and troughs (lowest points) align perfectly. This means that the waves reach their maximum and minimum values at the same time. When in-phase waves combine, they reinforce each other, producing a more robust overall signal. This is known as constructive interference.

For example, suppose two VHF signals arrive at an antenna in phase. In that case, their combined effect will be stronger than either of the individual signals alone. This can improve the clarity and strength of the received signal.

Out of Phase

When two waves are out of phase, their peaks and troughs do not align. Instead, the peak of one wave aligns with the trough of another. If two waves are entirely out of phase (180 degrees out of phase), one wave's peak aligns perfectly with the other wave's trough. When out-of-phase waves combine, they can cancel each other out, resulting in a weaker or even null signal. This is known as destructive interference.

For instance, if two VHF signals arrive at an antenna out of phase, their combined effect may be a much weaker signal or, in some cases, no signal. This can lead to signal fading or dead spots.

Importance in Radio Communication

Understanding phase relationships is key for optimizing radio communication. In multipath propagation, signals often arrive at the receiver through different paths, each with a phase relationship. <u>Small changes in the position of the receiving antenna can cause significant changes in the phase relationships of these signals, leading to variations in signal strength.</u>

Understanding that VHF signals are especially prone to these effects—due to their relatively short wavelengths (1 to 10 meters), VHF signals can easily reflect off buildings, terrain, and other obstacles —helps clarify why signal strength can vary so dramatically with minor changes in antenna position.

T3A01: Why do VHF signal strengths sometimes vary greatly when the antenna is moved only a few feet?

A. The signal path encounters different concentrations of water vapor
B. VHF ionospheric propagation is very sensitive to path length
C. Multipath propagation cancels or reinforces signals
D. All these choices are correct

By understanding how in-phase and out-of-phase signals interact, radio operators can better position their antennas to maximize constructive interference and minimize destructive interference, ensuring clearer and more reliable communication.

Picket Fencing

"Picket fencing" refers to the rapid fluttering or fading of mobile radio signals caused by multipath propagation. When a vehicle with a mobile radio moves through an area, the transmitted signal can reflect off various objects such as buildings, trees, and other structures. These reflections create multiple paths for the signal to reach the receiver. As the vehicle moves, the relative phases of these numerous signals constantly change, causing the received signal to rapidly fluctuate in strength.

This rapid variation in signal strength resembles the visual effect of looking through the gaps in a picket fence while moving past it, hence the name "picket fencing."

T3A06: What is the meaning of the term "picket fencing"?

A. Alternating transmissions during a net operation
B. Rapid flutter on mobile signals due to multipath propagation
C. A type of ground system used with vertical antennas
D. Local vs long-distance communications

The irregular fading of signals is often caused by the random combination of signals that arrive via different paths. Transmitted radio signals can travel to the receiver through multiple routes, such as direct paths, reflections off the ionosphere, or even numerous reflections. Each path may vary in length and the conditions it encounters, causing the signals to arrive at slightly different times and with different phases.

T3A08: What is a likely cause of irregular fading of signals propagated by the ionosphere?

A. Frequency shift due to Faraday rotation
B. Interference from thunderstorms
C. Intermodulation distortion
D. Random combining of signals arriving via different paths

So, what effect does all this multipath propagation have? What's the real problem with it?

T3A10: What effect does multipath propagation have on data transmissions?

A. Transmission rates must be increased by a factor equal to the number of separate paths observed
B. Transmission rates must be decreased by a factor equal to the number of separate paths observed
C. No significant changes will occur if the signals are transmitted using FM
D. Error rates are likely to increase

And that is the ultimate problem. Error rates are likely to increase, making our transmissions less reliable.

Chapter 10

The Atmosphere

THE ATMOSPHERE PLAYS AN interesting role in radio wave propagation and significantly impacts radio communications. Understanding these layers helps operators predict and optimize their transmission ranges and reception quality, making the atmosphere important enough for an overview and then a deep dive into it.

Understanding how radio waves travel through the atmosphere is essential for optimizing ham radio communication. The atmosphere, with its various layers and properties, significantly influences the behavior and propagation of radio waves. This section will explore the complex interactions between radio waves and the atmosphere, including the roles of the troposphere, stratosphere, mesosphere, and thermosphere.

By delving into these atmospheric relationships, you will gain valuable insights into how different frequencies are affected by atmospheric conditions, how to predict and utilize favorable propagation paths, and how to overcome environmental challenges. This knowledge will enhance your ability to make reliable long-distance contacts and improve communication effectiveness.

> **T3C06: What type of propagation is responsible for allowing over-the-horizon VHF and UHF communications to ranges of approximately 300 miles on a regular basis?**
>
> **A. Tropospheric ducting**
> B. D region refraction
> C. F2 region refraction
> D. Faraday rotation

The troposphere is the part we live in. VHF and UHF work within the troposphere. Answers 'B' and 'C' relate to the ionosphere. Faraday rotation is the phenomenon where the polarization plane of an electromagnetic wave, such as a radio wave, rotates as it passes through a magnetic field in a medium like the ionosphere (key word here: ionosphere).

So, the only answer that makes sense is 'A' tropospheric ducting.

Tropospheric ducting is a phenomenon that allows radio waves to travel much greater distances than usual by being trapped in a layer of the atmosphere called the troposphere. This occurs mainly during temperature inversions, where a layer of warmer air lies above a layer of cooler air, reversing the normal temperature gradient – colder air tends to be on top because things get really cold as you move closer to space.

The inversion creates a refractive index gradient, bending radio waves downward and trapping them between the layers. As the waves reach the lower boundary, they are refracted back upwards, effectively guiding them along the curvature of the Earth.

This guided path enables radio waves, especially VHF and UHF signals, to propagate hundreds of miles beyond their typical line-of-sight range. Tropospheric ducting often provides stable signal paths, which can be advantageous for long-distance communication.

Ham radio operators can leverage this phenomenon to make contacts far beyond their usual range, particularly during specific weather conditions that favor temperature inversions, such as clear, calm nights or over large bodies of water. This extended range capability enhances the effectiveness and reliability of VHF and UHF communications.

T3C08: What causes tropospheric ducting?

A. Discharges of lightning during electrical storms
B. Sunspots and solar flares
C. Updrafts from hurricanes and tornadoes
D. Temperature inversions in the atmosphere

T3C11: Why is the radio horizon for VHF and UHF signals more distant than the visual horizon?

A. Radio signals move somewhat faster than the speed of light
B. Radio waves are not blocked by dust particles
C. The atmosphere refracts radio waves slightly
D. Radio waves are blocked by dust particles

Radio waves can travel over the visual horizon with help from the atmosphere. However, the atmosphere doesn't really impact light waves, so radio waves get the boost and travel a little further.

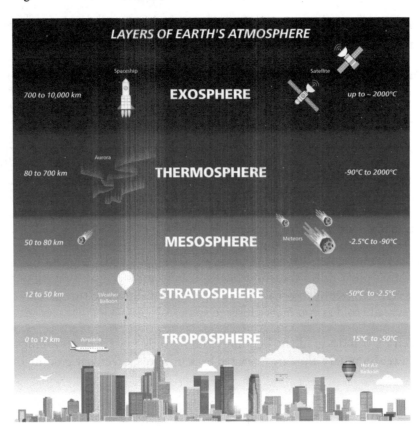

Layers of the Atmosphere

1. **Troposphere:**

   - **Location**: Extends from the Earth's surface to about 12 kilometers (~8 miles).

   - **Characteristics**: Contains most of the atmosphere's water vapor and weather phenomena. We live here!

   - **Impact on Radio Waves**: Primarily affects VHF and UHF signals through tropospheric refraction, which can extend their range. Weather conditions like temperature inversions can also enhance or hinder propagation.

2. **Stratosphere:**

   - **Location**: Ranges from about 12 to 50 kilometers (31 miles) above the Earth's surface.

   - **Characteristics**: It contains the ozone layer, which absorbs and scatters ultraviolet solar radiation.

   - **Impact on Radio Waves**: Generally, it has minimal direct effect on radio wave propagation.

3. **Mesosphere:**

   - **Location**: Extends about 50 to 80 kilometers (~50 miles) above the Earth's surface.

   - **Characteristics**: The middle layer of the atmosphere where temperatures decrease with altitude.

   - **Impact on Radio Waves**: This layer plays a minor role in radio wave propagation, but meteors burn up, occasionally affecting radio signals.

4. **Thermosphere:**

   - **Location**: Ranges from about 80 to 700 kilometers (435 miles) above the Earth's surface.

   - **Characteristics**: Temperatures rise significantly with altitude as high-energy solar radiation heats the sparse gas molecules present, increasing their energy and raising the temperature with height. Contains the ionosphere.

   - **Impact on Radio Waves**: The ionosphere within the thermosphere is central for HF radio wave propagation.

The Ionosphere

The ionosphere reflects or refracts radio waves primarily due to its unique composition and the presence of ionized particles—a quick detour about the difference between reflecting and refracting.

- **Reflection** occurs when a wave, like light or a radio signal, hits a surface and bounces back at the same angle it arrived. This resembles seeing your reflection in a mirror, where the light waves bounce back to your eyes.

- **Refraction** happens when a wave passes from one medium to another and changes direction due to a change in speed. For example, a straw appears bent in water because light waves slow down and bend when they move from air to water.

In short, reflection is the bouncing back of waves from a surface, while refraction is the bending of waves as they pass through different materials.

This region of the Earth's upper atmosphere, extending from about 60 kilometers (37 miles) to 1,000 kilometers (620 miles) above the Earth's surface, contains a high concentration of ions and free electrons. These ions and electrons are created by ionizing atmospheric gases due to solar radiation, particularly ultraviolet (UV) light and X-rays from the Sun.

When solar radiation hits the molecules and atoms in the upper atmosphere, it strips away electrons, creating ions and free electrons. An ion is an atom or molecule that has gained or lost one or more electrons, giving it a net electrical charge. Atoms typically have an equal number of protons (positively charged) and electrons (negatively charged), making them neutral. However, when an atom gains extra electrons, it becomes negatively charged and is called an anion. Conversely, it becomes positively charged when it loses electrons and is called a cation.

Ions are core in many chemical reactions and processes, such as in batteries, where the flow of ions generates an electric current.

This ionization process creates layers within the ionosphere that can reflect or refract radio waves. Radio waves, being electromagnetic waves, interact with these charged particles in the ionosphere. This interaction affects the speed and direction of the radio waves. At specific frequencies, the density of ions in the ionosphere is high enough to reflect radio waves back toward the Earth, acting like a mirror. This reflection is <u>more effective at lower frequencies within the HF band (3 to 30 MHz).</u>

The ability of the ionosphere to reflect or refract radio waves is influenced by several factors, including frequency, solar activity, time of day, and seasonal changes. <u>While lower-frequency radio waves are more likely to be reflected</u> (HF), in contrast, <u>higher-frequency waves (UHF) usually pass through</u> or are refracted. Increased solar activity enhances ionization, improving reflective and refractive properties, while low solar activity reduces ionization. The ionosphere's properties also change between day and night, with higher solar radiation during the day increasing ionization. Seasonal variations further impact ionization levels, with higher levels typically occurring in the summer due to increased solar exposure.

Layers of the Ionosphere

1. **D Layer**:

   - **Location**: Approximately 60 to 90 kilometers (37 to 56 miles) above the Earth's surface.

   - **Characteristics**: Exists only during the daytime and absorbs lower-frequency HF signals, causing attenuation. Attenuation refers to the gradual weakening of a signal as it travels.

   - **Impact on Radio Waves**: <u>Absorbs and weakens HF signals</u> during the day, especially at frequencies below 10 MHz.

2. **E Layer**:

   - **Location**: Approximately 90 to 120 kilometers (56 to 75 miles) above the Earth's surface.

   - **Characteristics**: Can reflect HF waves and is more pronounced during the daytime.

   - **Impact on Radio Waves**: Provides helpful reflection for HF signals in the daytime, aiding short to medium-range communication (up to 2,000 kilometers or 1,200 miles).

3. **F Layers (F1 and F2)**:

   - **Location**: The F1 layer is about 150 to 220 kilometers (93 to 137 miles) above the Earth's surface during the daytime and merges into the F2 layer at night. The F2 layer extends from about 220 to 800 kilometers (137 to 500 miles).

   - **Characteristics**: The most important layers for long-distance HF propagation. The <u>F1 layer disappears at night</u>, while the F2 layer remains, providing reliable reflection for HF waves.

   - **Impact on Radio Waves**: The F2 layer supports long-distance HF communication (up to 3,000 kilometers or 1,900 miles per hop). This layer is highly variable and influenced by solar activity.

Practical Applications for Ham Radio Operators

Understanding the ionosphere and atmospheric layers allows ham radio operators to predict and optimize communication strategies. By selecting the appropriate frequencies and times for transmission, operators can take advantage of favorable ionospheric conditions to achieve longer and more reliable contacts.

T3A11: Which region of the atmosphere can refract or bend HF and VHF radio waves?

A. The stratosphere
B. The troposphere
C. The ionosphere
D. The mesosphere

T3C09: What is generally the best time for long-distance 10-meter band propagation via the F region?

A. From dawn to shortly after sunset during periods of high sunspot activity
B. From shortly after sunset to dawn during periods of high sunspot activity
C. From dawn to shortly after sunset during periods of low sunspot activity
D. From shortly after sunset to dawn during periods of low sunspot activity

---

As underlined in the 'F-Region,' this layer disappears at night, meaning we need to use it from dawn to dusk.

Sporadic E Propagation

Sporadic E propagation is a fascinating and somewhat unpredictable phenomenon. It allows occasional strong signals on the 10 (HF), 6, and 2-meter VHF bands beyond the typical radio horizon.

This type of propagation occurs when patches of highly ionized gas, known as Sporadic E layers, form in the lower part of the ionosphere (the E layer). These ionized patches can reflect VHF and upper HF signals, enabling communication over distances far greater than usual line-of-sight limits.

Sporadic E is most commonly associated with strong, intermittent signals on the 10, 6, and 2-meter bands, making it an exciting opportunity for ham radio operators to make long-distance contacts. These events typically occur during late spring and summer but can happen at any time of the year.

T3C04: Which of the following types of propagation is most commonly associated with occasional strong signals on the 10, 6, and 2-meter bands from beyond the radio horizon?

A. Backscatter
B. Sporadic E
C. D region absorption
D. Gray-line propagation

The key phrases to remember in this question are occasional, propagation, and beyond the horizon!

Auroral Backscatter

"Auroral" refers to phenomena related to the aurora, which are natural light displays in the Earth's sky typically seen in high-latitude regions around the Arctic and Antarctic. These displays, known as the Aurora Borealis in the Northern Hemisphere and the Aurora Australis in the Southern Hemisphere, are caused by the interaction of solar wind particles with the Earth's magnetic field and atmosphere.

Auroral backscatter occurs when VHF signals are reflected off the ionized particles in the aurora.

This type of propagation is fascinating but can also present some unique challenges. VHF signals received via auroral backscatter are typically distorted and exhibit considerable variations in signal strength. This happens because the reflecting auroral particles are in constant motion, creating a turbulent and fluctuating medium that affects the stability and clarity of the radio waves.

When you encounter auroral backscatter, you'll notice that the signal may sound "fluttery" or "hollow," which can rapidly change in strength. These characteristics make auroral backscatter a challenging and exciting mode of communication for operators.

T3C03: What is a characteristic of VHF signals received via auroral backscatter?

A. They are often received from 10,000 miles or more
B. They are distorted, and signal strength varies considerably
C. They occur only during winter nighttime hours
D. They are generally strongest when your antenna is aimed west

Sunspots

T3C10: Which of the following bands may provide long-distance communications via the ionosphere's F region during the peak of the sunspot cycle?

A. 6 and 10 meters
B. 23 centimeters
C. 70 centimeters and 1.25 meters
D. All these choices are correct

Recall the previous section. One key concept to remember for the exam is that whenever the exam talks about the atmosphere, it mainly refers to HF and VHF.

During the peak of the sunspot cycle, increased solar activity enhances the ionization of the ionosphere's F region, significantly improving its ability to reflect higher-frequency radio waves. This heightened ionization allows the 6-meter (50 to 54 MHz – VHF) and 10-meter (28 to 29.7 MHz – HF) bands to achieve long-distance communication.

The 6-meter band, typically used for line-of-sight communication, can exhibit HF-like propagation characteristics during this period, enabling contacts over hundreds or thousands of miles.

Similarly, the 10-meter band, already known for its long-distance capabilities, becomes even more effective, allowing global communication with relatively low power and simple antennas.

The F region's enhanced ionization during the sunspot peak allows these bands to refract signals back to Earth, facilitating long-distance propagation. This phenomenon enables amateur radio operators to take advantage of optimal conditions for communication, making the 6-meter and 10-meter bands particularly valuable for achieving extended-range contacts during periods of high solar activity.

Meteor Scatter

Meteor scatter communication (yes, there is such a thing as communicating by bouncing signals off parts of meteors!!!) takes advantage of the ionized trails left by meteors as they enter the Earth's atmosphere. When a meteor burns up, it leaves behind a trail of ionized particles that can reflect radio waves, allowing for brief periods of long-distance communication. The 6-meter VHF band (50 to 54 MHz) is best suited for this type of communication.

Again, we have a theme on which bands and frequencies to use with things in space.

The 6-meter band is ideal for meteor scatter because its frequency is high enough to take advantage of meteors' short, intense bursts of ionization. These ionized trails can reflect the 6-meter signals, allowing radio operators to make contacts over hundreds of miles for a few seconds to a few minutes. This makes the 6-meter band, often called the "magic band," remarkably effective for this unique mode of communication.

T3C07: What band is best suited for communicating via meteor scatter?

A. 33 centimeters
B. 6 meters
C. 2 meters
D. 70 centimeters

The Curvature of the Earth

Now that we have covered bands, frequencies, wavelengths, and the atmosphere, let's apply those concepts, starting with radio waves and the curvature of the Earth.

The ionosphere's ability to reflect and refract radio waves is critically vital for communication over long distances, especially due to the curvature of the Earth. Because the Earth is round, radio waves traveling in a straight line from a transmitter would quickly leave the surface and travel into space, making long-distance terrestrial communication impossible without some means of bending or reflecting the waves back toward the Earth's surface.

The ionosphere acts as a natural reflector or refractor for radio waves. When radio waves are transmitted upwards, they encounter the ionized layers of the ionosphere. Depending on the frequency and ionization density of the waves, they can be reflected back to the Earth or refracted at an angle, allowing them to follow the curvature of the Earth. This process enables signals to cover distances far beyond the line-of-sight horizon, effectively "bouncing" between the ionosphere and the Earth's surface in what is known as skywave propagation.

Long-distance radio communication would be severely limited without the ionosphere's ability to bend radio waves back toward the Earth. The curvature of the Earth would cause radio signals to dissipate into space, restricting effective communication to line-of-sight distances, which are typically at most 30-40 miles for ground-based transmissions. Thus, the ionosphere's role in radio wave propagation is crucial for overcoming the Earth's curvature and enabling global radio communication.

T3C02: What is a characteristic of HF communication compared with communications on VHF and higher frequencies?

A. HF antennas are generally smaller
B. HF accommodates wider bandwidth signals
C. Long-distance ionospheric propagation is far more common on HF
D. There is less atmospheric interference (static) on HF

This section is all about the ionosphere and its relationship with HF. That is one key concept separating HF from higher-frequency VHF or UHF bands.

T3C01: Why are simplex UHF signals rarely heard beyond their radio horizon?

A. They are too weak to go very far
B. FCC regulations prohibit them from going more than 50 miles
C. UHF signals are usually not propagated by the ionosphere
D. UHF signals are absorbed by the ionospheric D region

For this question, they used 'simplex,' a concept we haven't covered yet, to emphasize that this communication occurs directly between two radio stations without using intermediate relays such as repeaters or satellites. In simplex operation, both transmitting and receiving occur on the same frequency.

Because we are using UHF with no other resources (repeaters or satellites) and the question states that we are going 'beyond the horizon,' we understand that we would need to bounce signals off the ionosphere. However, UHF frequencies are generally too high to be reflected.

Chapter 11

The Electromagnetic Spectrum and the Radio Bands

YOU NEED TO CHOOSE the right frequency to maximize the reach and clarity of your transmissions. Depending on the time of day and atmospheric conditions, specific frequencies will be more effective than others.

Understanding the relationship between frequency and wavelength is akin to learning the notes on a piano; each note has a specific pitch and tone, essential for creating music. In radio communication, frequency refers to the number of times a wave oscillates per second, measured in hertz (Hz), and wavelength is the physical distance over which the wave's shape repeats.

These two concepts are inversely related: <u>the higher the frequency, the shorter the wavelength</u>. This fundamental relationship shapes all aspects of radio transmission and reception.

T3B05: What is the relationship between wavelength and frequency?

A. Wavelength gets longer as frequency increases
B. Wavelength gets shorter as frequency increases
C. Wavelength and frequency are unrelated
D. Wavelength and frequency increase as path length increases

---

ELECTROMAGNETIC RADIATION (FREQUENCY)

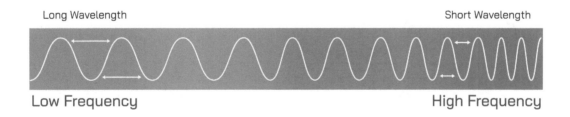

You will need to know a mathematical relationship between wavelength and frequency for the test. The relationship between frequency and wavelength is given by the formula:

Where:

- λ (pronounced lambda) is the wavelength in <u>meters</u>.

- *c* is the speed of light (approximately 300,000,000 <u>meters</u> per second).

- *f* is the frequency in hertz (Hz).

Now, on the test, the question is:

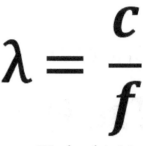

$$\lambda = \frac{c}{f}$$

Wavelength in Meters

T3B06: What is the formula for converting frequency to approximate wavelength in meters?

A. wavelength in meters equals frequency in hertz multiplied by 300
B. wavelength in meters equals frequency in hertz divided by 300
C. Wavelength in meters equals frequency in megahertz divided by 300
D. Wavelength in meters equals 300 divided by frequency in megahertz

---

Here, you can see they are being a little sneaky. Whereas our formula is in hertz, the question is looking at <u>megahertz</u>. So, let's adjust (plus, it makes the formula a little easier; that's why they do it, less about being sneaky and more about simplicity).

We must adjust the formula when using megahertz (MHz) for frequency. Since 1 MHz equals 1,000,000 Hz, the formula can be rewritten. Now:

- λ (pronounced lambda) is the wavelength in <u>meters</u>.

- *f* is the frequency in megahertz (MHz).

This new formula makes calculating the wavelength for any given frequency in megahertz easier.

$$\text{meters} = \frac{300}{\text{Frequency (MHz)}}$$

Memorize this formula, and remember that it has a frequency of megahertz (MHz).

Electromagnetic Spectrum

Radio makes up just one part of the overall electromagnetic spectrum. The electromagnetic spectrum also includes things like the light we see, the visible part of the spectrum, and x-rays (and gamma rays for any Hulk fans!).

THE ELECTROMAGNETIC SPECTRUM

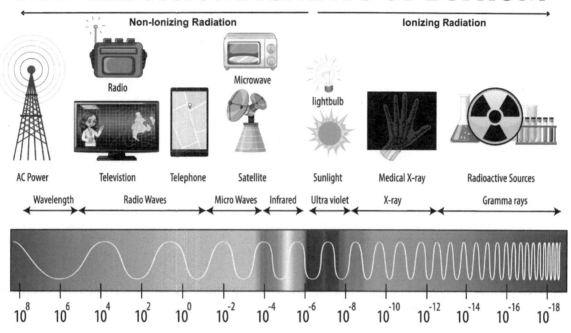

The radio spectrum encompasses all frequencies used for communication, which are meticulously organized into bands – think of them as sections or pieces of the electromagnetic spectrum.

Each band is allocated for specific use. And within particular bands, we amateur radio licensed operators have been given privileges to use parts of them for different types of communication and experimentation.

Radio Bands

Radio bands are broad categories that describe specific ranges of frequencies. Here, we name a few common ones. Yes! More repetition. Have you memorized them all yet?

- **VLF (Very Low Frequency)**

- **LF (Low Frequency)**

- **MF (Medium Frequency)**: includes AM radio

- **HF (High Frequency)**: includes shortwave radio and many ham bands

- **VHF (Very High Frequency)**: includes FM radio and TV channels

- **UHF (Ultra High Frequency)**: includes TV channels and mobile phones

- **SHF (Super High Frequency)**: used for radar and satellite communication

- **EHF (Extremely High Frequency)**

These names help quickly identify the general frequency range and the type of communication typically found there.

Short-Hand Name	VLF	LF	MF	HF	VHF	UHF	SHF	EHF
Name	Very Low Frequency	Low Frequency	Medium Frequency	High Frequency	Very High Frequency	Ultra High Frequency	Super High Frequency	Extremely High Frequency
Frequency	3 – 30 kHz	30 – 300 kHz	300 – 3,000 kHz	3 MHz – 30 MHz	30 – 300 MHz	300 – 3,000 MHz	3 GHz – 30 GHz	30 – 300 GHz
Wavelength	100 – 10 km	10 – 1 km	1,000 m – 100 m	100 – 10 m	10 – 1 m	1 – 0.1 m	10 cm – 1 cm	1 – 0.1 cm

Wavelength

Wavelength is the distance a radio wave travels in one cycle. Let's now add wavelengths to our names.

VLF (Very Low Frequency)

- **Wavelength**: 100 km to 10 km

  - For anyone new to the metric scale, 10 km is over 6 miles! This means in the time it takes for this wave to travel through its entire cycle, it travels over 6 miles.

  - Even though I'm adding in some miles, feet, and inches to help a beginner understand the metric system, ham radio uses the metric system.

LF (Low Frequency)

- **Wavelength**: 10 km to 1 km

  - 1 km is about 0.6 miles

MF (Medium Frequency)

- **Wavelength**: 1,000 meters (which is the same as 1 km) to 100 meters

  - 100 meters is about a football field (slightly longer but roughly)

HF (High Frequency)

- **Wavelength**: 100 meters to 10 meters

  - 10 meters is about 33 feet

VHF (Very High Frequency)

- **Wavelength**: 10 meters to 1 meter

  - 1 meter is about 3.28 feet

UHF (Ultra High Frequency)

- **Wavelength**: 1 meter to 0.1 meter (10 centimeters)

  - 10 cm is about 4 inches

SHF (Super High Frequency)

- **Wavelength**: 10 centimeters to 1 centimeter

  - 1 cm is a little under half an inch

EHF (Extremely High Frequency)

- **Wavelength**: 1 centimeter to 1 millimeter

At this point, it's helpful to start memorizing bands and wavelengths. Or, do what I do: print off a band chart. As Einstein said, use your mind to think, not memorize.

Printable band chart: **www.MorseCodePublishing.com/TechExam**

Band Chart

You will need to memorize part of this for the exam. Focus on the exam questions and memorize them. Otherwise, print off the included chart and hang it on your wall. Over time, as you become a wiser and older ham, it will sink into memory.

Frequency

Frequency describes how often a radio wave oscillates per second, measured in hertz (Hz). It indicates how many cycles occur in one second:

- **30 MHz**: The radio wave oscillates 30 million times per second. Remember, M = Mega, and Mega equals 1,000,000 (back from our metric system section).

- **144 MHz**: This means the wave oscillates 144 million times per second.

Higher frequencies correspond to shorter wavelengths, and lower frequencies correspond to longer wavelengths.

In the two examples above, 30 MHz has a lower frequency than 144 MHz, so a lower frequency means that 30 MHz has a longer wavelength than 144 MHz. A longer wavelength means it's easier to go farther, so if we wanted to consider a long-distance radio call, 30 MHz would be a better frequency than 144 MHz. There will be more on all this, but you can start to see how things are coming together!

Continuing to Connect the Concepts, Let's Add in Frequency

Remember, each term—whether a band name, wavelength size, or frequency —offers a different perspective on the same radio spectrum, making it easier to navigate and utilize. A few sections have been specifically called out as they are important to technicians.

VLF (Very Low Frequency)

- **Frequency**: 3 to 30 kHz (very low frequency)

- **Wavelength**: 100,000 meters to 10,000 meters (very long wavelengths)

LF (Low Frequency)

- **Frequency**: 30 to 300 kHz

- **Wavelength**: 10,000 meters to 1,000 meters

MF (Medium Frequency)

- **Frequency**: 300 kHz to 3 MHz (includes AM radio)

- **Wavelength**: 1,000 meters to 100 meters

Let's now highlight the ones important to use as Technicians.

HF (High Frequency)
- **Frequency**: 3 to 30 MHz (includes shortwave radio and many ham bands)

- **Wavelength**: 100 meters to 10 meters

VHF (Very High Frequency)
- **Frequency**: 30 to 300 MHz (includes FM radio and TV channels)

- **Wavelength**: 10 meters to 1 meter

UHF (Ultra High Frequency)
- **Frequency**: 300 MHz to 3 GHz (includes TV channels and mobile phones)

- **Wavelength**: 1 meter to 0.1 meter (10 centimeters)

SHF (Super High Frequency)

- **Frequency**: 3 to 30 GHz (used for radar and satellite communication)

- **Wavelength**: 10 centimeters to 1 centimeter

EHF (Extremely High Frequency)

- **Frequency**: 30 to 300 GHz (very, very fast frequency)

- **Wavelength**: 1 centimeter to 1 millimeter (very, very short wavelength)

Now, based on what we've learned, let's answer some questions. Refer specifically to the called-out bands above:

T3B07: In addition to frequency, which of the following is used to identify amateur radio bands?

A. The approximate wavelength in meters
B. Traditional letter/number designators
C. Channel numbers
D. All these choices are correct

Radio bands are often identified by wavelength in addition to frequency.

T3B08: What frequency range is referred to as VHF?

A. 30 kHz to 300 kHz
B. 30 MHz to 300 MHz
C. 300 kHz to 3000 kHz
D. 300 MHz to 3000 MHz

Stay tuned for the next section if you haven't memorized this yet.

T3B09: What frequency range is referred to as UHF?

A. 30 to 300 kHz
B. 30 to 300 MHz
C. 300 to 3000 kHz
D. 300 to 3000 MHz

T3B10: What frequency range is referred to as HF?

A. 300 to 3000 MHz
B. 30 to 300 MHz
C. 3 to 30 MHz
D. 300 to 3000 kHz

Do you need additional help with those last three questions or help remembering the frequencies? Here is my memory trick for this part. It's idiotic, but it works.

For Frequency:

1. I always start with High Frequency (HF) as my anchor. Then, High Frequency advances to '*Very*' High Frequency and then to '*Ultra*' High Frequency. Easy enough! Write it down. We now have the names in order.

2. Next, there are 3 ways to identify a band: the name, the wavelength, and the frequency—three different methods (3). Remember the #3.

3. Anchoring to High Frequency and the number 3, I now remember that the frequency for HF starts at 3 MHz. Nice and convenient!

4. HF begins at 3 MHz of frequency. A good start! Write it down.

5. Finally, the metric system is based on 10s. So, each band starts at a level and expands 10 times.

6. Putting this all together, HF starts at 3 MHz, and multiplied by 10, it ends at 30 MHz. Which is where VHF begins.

  ○ If VHF begins at 30 MHz, multiplying by 10, it must end around 300 MHz.

  ○ This is where UHF would start (300 MHz) and end around 3,000 MHz (or, using the metric system to simplify, it could be written as 3 GHz).

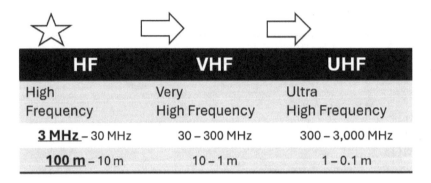

This exercise even works for wavelength.

For Wavelength:

1. Again, I will start with high-frequency (HF) as my anchor. Then, High Frequency advances to 'Very' High Frequency and then to 'Ultra' High Frequency. Easy enough! Write it down.

2. Next, we use the metric system, which is based on multiples of 10. So, we use 10s in the following steps.

3. Anchoring to High Frequency and using multiples of 10, I now remember that the wavelength for HF starts at 100 Meters. That's a nice, convenient round number!

4. HF begins at 100 meters of wavelength. Write it down.

5. Finally, the metric system is based on 10s. So, to move to the next band, we DIVIDE by 10.

6. Putting this all together, HF starts at 100 meters, and divided by 10, it ends at 10 meters. Which is where VHF begins.

  ○ If VHF begins at 10 meters, divided by 10, it must end at 1 meter.

  ○ This is where UHF would start at 1 meter and end at around 0.1 meter (10 cm).

Exam questions:

T1B03: Which frequency is in the 6-meter amateur band?

A. 49.00 MHz
B. 52.525 MHz
C. 28.50 MHz
D. 222.15 MHz

When we have either frequency or wavelength, and we want to know the other, we use our simplified formula.

$$\text{Frequency} = \frac{300}{\text{Wavelength in Meters}}$$

We want frequency. We have wavelength. We divide 300 by 6 meters to equal 50 MHz. But none of the answers equal 50!?!?

But we can at least eliminate 'C' and 'D,' which are far from 50. But we are still left with 'A' and 'B.' Remember the section about bands and the "magic 6-meter band." In that summary, we shared that the 6-meter band is from 50 to 54 MHz. Based on our math and memorization, we know the answer is 52.525 MHz, which is in the 6 m band.

> **T1B04: Which amateur band includes 146.52 MHz?**
>
> A. 6 meters
> B. 20 meters
> C. 70 centimeters
> **D. 2 meters**

Our math comes close to answering this question, and that counts! 300 divided by 146.52 equals 2.047 m, which is close enough to know that the answer is 'D.' The way to estimate this is that 146.52 MHz is very close to 150 MHz. Doing that math, 300 divided by 150 equals 2 meters.

$$\text{meters} = \frac{300}{\text{Frequency (MHz)}}$$

Radio Bands Summary

For a ham operator, knowing which bands are available and their specific characteristics is crucial for both regulatory compliance and effective communication. Not all frequencies are accessible for use, and frequency allocation is managed by national and international bodies to prevent interference. The Federal Communications Commission (FCC) oversees these regulations in the United States, assigning specific bands to different services, including amateur radio. Following these band plans is legally required and essential for ensuring clear and organized communication. These band plans provide a structured framework that supports efficient amateur radio operations.

Each band is further divided into segments dedicated to specific communication modes, such as Morse code (CW), digital modes, or voice communication, with recommended usage guidelines. More detailed rules and regulations will be covered in a later section.

It can be overwhelming to navigate terms like bands, wavelengths, frequencies, and the electromagnetic spectrum, along with UHF, VHF, and HF. Let's break it down: radio bands can be identified by different names, wavelength sizes (like 2 meters), or frequencies (like 30 MHz). These terms are interconnected and will become clearer as you delve deeper into amateur radio.

Chapter 12

Modulation and Bandwidth

Modulation

MODULATION IS AKIN TO understanding how different musical instruments can play the same note but sound distinct. Each instrument alters the sound wave in its unique way.

In amateur radio, modulation refers to how the basic form of a radio wave is changed to carry information, be it voice, data, or video. It involves combining speech with a radio frequency (RF) carrier signal.

T7A08: Which of the following describes combining speech with an RF carrier signal?

A. Impedance matching
B. Oscillation
C. Modulation
D. Low-pass filtering

There are several types of wave modulation, including Amplitude Modulation (AM), Frequency Modulation (FM), and Phase Modulation (PM). Each alters the carrier signal in different ways to encode the audio information.

AM (Amplitude Modulation)

AM (Amplitude Modulation) changes the height or strength of the radio wave to match the sound being sent. It was one of the first ways to send radio signals. It is still used today, especially in aviation and AM radio stations. AM is more susceptible to interference because changes in amplitude can be caused by various forms of electrical noise, such as thunderstorms and machinery.

Single Sideband (SSB) Modulation

Single Sideband (SSB) is a highly efficient type of amplitude modulation (AM) used extensively in ham radio. In traditional AM, a carrier signal is modulated with audio information, producing two identical sidebands (upper and lower) and a carrier, which consumes a lot of bandwidth and power. SSB improves on this by eliminating the carrier and one of the sidebands, leaving just one sideband (either upper or lower) to carry the information. This makes SSB much more efficient in terms of bandwidth and power usage.

Modulation

AM - Amplitude Modulation

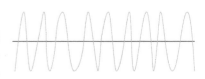

FM - Frequency Modulation

SSB is a streamlined version of AM. Instead of transmitting redundant information, SSB focuses all the power into a single sideband, making it more robust for long-distance communication. This efficiency is why SSB is so popular among amateur radio operators for voice communication on HF bands.

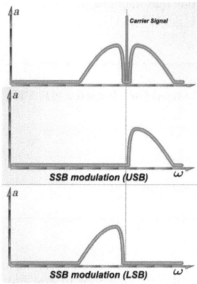

Visualization of Single Side Band

T8A01: Which of the following is a form of amplitude modulation?

A. Spread spectrum
B. Packet radio
C. Single sideband
D. Phase shift keying (PSK)

SSB for Long-Distance Contacts on VHF and UHF

Single-sideband (SSB) voice modulation is often used for long-distance, weak signal contacts on the VHF and UHF bands. SSB is the go-to mode for reaching long distances with low signal strength. Its efficiency in utilizing power and bandwidth allows for clearer communication even when the signal is faint.

SSB's efficiency is particularly suitable for long-distance communication, especially on the VHF and UHF bands, where conserving bandwidth and power is crucial.

T8A03: Which type of voice mode is often used for long-distance (weak signal) contacts on the VHF and UHF bands?

A. FM
B. DRM
C. SSB
D. PM

The upper sideband (USB) is typically used for SSB communications for these bands. This convention helps standardize operations and ensures compatibility between different stations. Operators can achieve better and more reliable communication over longer distances using the upper sideband, even when signals are weak.

Most modern ham radios have a mode selection button or dial. To use it, you will switch your radio to the appropriate SSB mode: USB (Upper Sideband) for 10-meter HF, VHF, and UHF bands or LSB (Lower Sideband) for other HF bands below 10 meters.

T8A06: Which sideband is normally used for 10-meter HF, VHF, and UHF single-sideband communications?

A. Upper sideband
B. Lower sideband
C. Suppressed sideband
D. Inverted sideband

FM (Frequency Modulation)

FM (Frequency Modulation) changes the speed of the radio wave to send information. FM is great for sending clear sound without much interference. It is perfect for radio stations playing music and public service broadcasts. FM is less susceptible to interference because it relies on changes in frequency rather than amplitude, making it better at rejecting noise and providing better sound quality.

Frequency Modulation (FM) or Phase Modulation (PM) is commonly used for VHF packet radio transmissions. Packet radio is a digital mode where data is transmitted in small packets, which requires a robust and reliable transmission method. FM is favored because it provides clear and consistent signal quality, which is central for accurately transmitting digital data. FM works by varying the carrier wave frequency to encode the data, making it less susceptible to noise and interference.

T8A02: What type of modulation is commonly used for VHF packet radio transmissions?

A. FM or PM
B. SSB
C. AM
D. PSK

VHF packet radio transmissions are a method of digital communication used by amateur radio operators to send data over Very High Frequency (VHF) bands. This method involves dividing data into small packets, transmitting them using Frequency Modulation (FM) or Phase Modulation (PM), and reassembling them at the receiving end. FM and PM are preferred due to their robust signal quality, which ensures accurate data transfer. VHF packet radio is commonly used for text messaging, weather data, and position reporting applications. It is especially valuable for emergency communications due to its reliability and efficiency in maintaining clear and accurate data transmission.

Similarly, Phase Modulation (PM) can also be used for packet radio. PM encodes data by varying the carrier wave phase, which, like FM, ensures that the digital signals are transmitted clearly and efficiently. Both FM and PM are well-suited for VHF packet radio because they maintain signal integrity over the distances typically covered by VHF frequencies.

Modulation for VHF and UHF Voice Repeaters

Frequency Modulation (FM) and Phase Modulation (PM) are also commonly used for VHF and UHF voice repeaters. These modulation types are preferred because they provide clear, reliable, high-quality voice communication, essential for effective repeater operation. FM works by varying the carrier wave frequency according to the voice signal, ensuring the transmitted audio is clear and less susceptible to noise and interference.

Similarly, Phase Modulation (PM) encodes the voice signal by varying the phase of the carrier wave. Both FM and PM are well-suited for the VHF (30-300 MHz) and UHF (300 MHz-3 GHz) bands because they can maintain signal integrity over longer distances and through various obstacles.

T8A04: Which type of modulation is commonly used for VHF and UHF voice repeaters?

A. AM
B. SSB
C. PSK
D. FM or PM

Digital Modulation

Digital modes, however, encode data into a series of digital signals, which are then used to modulate the carrier wave. These modes are increasingly popular in amateur radio because they provide efficient and reliable communication even under challenging conditions where traditional analog signals might fail.

More on digital later.

Bandwidth

Each modulation type inherently requires a certain amount of bandwidth, the range of frequencies the signal occupies on the radio spectrum. Bandwidth is pivotal in radio communications as it determines how much information can be transmitted and how susceptible the transmission might be to interference.

Said another way, bandwidth is the range of frequencies that a radio signal occupies. Imagine you're tuning a radio to a station. Each station has its own slice of frequencies. For example, an FM radio station might broadcast on 101.1 MHz. Still, it uses a small range of frequencies around that number to send its signal. This range is the station's bandwidth.

The wider the bandwidth, the more information the signal can carry. For instance, FM radio uses more bandwidth (about 200 kHz) than AM radio (10 kHz), so FM can deliver higher-quality sound. Each type of radio service (like AM, FM, or digital) uses a different amount of bandwidth to fit its needs.

Following this line of thinking and remembering what we learned about SSB (Single-Side Band), being part of AM, you should now be able to answer this question:

T8A07: What is a characteristic of single sideband (SSB) compared to FM?

A. SSB signals are easier to tune in correctly
B. SSB signals are less susceptible to interference
C. SSB signals have narrower bandwidth
D. All these choices are correct

SSB typically requires a bandwidth of about 2.5 to 3 kHz for effective transmission. This is much narrower than traditional amplitude modulation (AM), which requires twice the bandwidth due to transmitting both the upper and lower sidebands and the carrier.

T8A08: What is the approximate bandwidth of a typical single sideband (SSB) voice signal?

A. 1 kHz
B. 3 kHz
C. 6 kHz
D. 15 kHz

Typical Bandwidth by Mode

Mode	Bandwidth	Usage / Application
Digital Modes (e.g., PSK31)	31 Hz	Low bandwidth digital communication.
CW (Continuous Wave)	150-500 Hz	Morse code transmission.
SSB (Single Sideband)	2.5-3 kHz	Voice communication, HF ham radio.
AM (Amplitude Modulation)	10 kHz	Standard for AM broadcasting, voice communication.
NBFM (Narrowband FM)	10-15 kHz	Two-way radio, VHF repeaters, public safety.
WBFM (Wideband FM)	150-200 kHz	Commercial FM broadcasting (music and voice).
NTSC (Analog TV)	6 MHz	Analog television broadcasting.
ATSC (Digital TV)	6 MHz	Digital television broadcasting.

FM vs Single Sideband (SSB)

One of the main disadvantages of frequency modulation (FM) compared with single-sided band (SSB) is that FM can only receive one signal at a time at a given frequency. This limitation arises because FM signals occupy a wider bandwidth and are designed to be strong and clear, effectively blocking out other signals on the same frequency. In contrast, SSB signals use narrower bandwidth, allowing multiple signals to coexist on nearby frequencies and making it possible to tune in to and separate individual signals.

Remembering this fundamental difference can help you understand why SSB is often preferred for long-distance and crowded band conditions, where multiple stations may operate simultaneously. Knowing that FM allows only one signal per frequency will help you recall this concept for your exam, highlighting the trade-offs between signal clarity and bandwidth efficiency in different modulation modes.

T8A12: Which of the following is a disadvantage of FM compared with single sideband?

A. Voice quality is poorer
B. Only one signal can be received at a time
C. FM signals are harder to tune
D. All these choices are correct

Digital modes can also be designed to use very narrow bandwidths, which makes them less prone to interference and allows more simultaneous transmissions within a given part of the band.

Efficient spectrum use is fundamental to successful amateur radio operations. Managing bandwidth effectively ensures that multiple communications can co-occur without interfering with each other. This is not only a technical necessity but also a regulatory requirement, as the FCC allocates specific portions of the spectrum for different uses to prevent chaos on the airwaves.

Bandwidth of a VHF Repeater FM Voice Signal

Let's continue to learn more about ham radio by looking at actual questions on the exam.

The approximate bandwidth of a VHF repeater FM voice signal is between 10 and 15 kHz. This bandwidth range is necessary to accommodate the frequency variations required for transmitting clear and intelligible voice audio. Frequency Modulation (FM) works by varying the carrier wave frequency per the audio signal, and a bandwidth of 10 to 15 kHz ensures that the transmitted voice is clear and free from distortion.

This bandwidth is optimized to balance audio quality and spectrum efficiency, allowing multiple repeaters to operate within the VHF band without interfering with each other.

T8A09: What is the approximate bandwidth of a VHF repeater FM voice signal?

A. Less than 500 Hz
B. About 150 kHz
C. Between 10 and 15 kHz
D. Between 50 and 125 kHz

AM Fast-Scan TV Transmissions

Another question about bandwidths caused issues regarding where to place it within this book. We put it inside the bandwidth section because it was related to the exam question.

AM fast-scan TV, commonly called amateur television (ATV), transmits video and audio signals using amplitude modulation (AM) over radio frequencies. This form of television broadcasting is similar to commercial analog TV. Still, amateur radio operators use it for personal and experimental purposes.

In AM fast-scan TV, the video signal modulates the carrier wave's amplitude, meaning the carrier wave's strength varies per the brightness and detail of the picture. Audio is typically transmitted alongside the video by frequency modulation (FM) on a subcarrier or by using a separate carrier. The term "fast-scan" refers to the high frame rate, similar to standard broadcast television, providing smooth and continuous video, which contrasts with slow-scan television (SSTV), which transmits still images much slower.

AM fast-scan TV transmissions require substantial bandwidth, typically around 6 MHz, to carry the detailed video information and ensure high-quality image and sound. Amateur radio operators use AM fast-scan TV for various purposes, including personal communication, experimentation, and public service broadcasting. It allows them to share real-time video content, conduct remote surveillance, or provide visual information during emergency operations.

The relatively wide bandwidth (remember it was 6 MHz) is necessary to transmit the high-resolution video and accompanying audio signals that make up a television broadcast. Unlike voice transmissions, which require much narrower bandwidth, TV signals contain much more information and, therefore, need more space in the frequency spectrum.

The 6 MHz bandwidth allows for the detailed video data to be transmitted alongside the audio, ensuring that the received picture is clear and the sound is synchronized and of high quality.

T8A10: What is the approximate bandwidth of AM fast-scan TV transmissions?

A. More than 10 MHz
B. About 6 MHz
C. About 3 MHz
D. About 1 MHz

Morse Code: Continuous Wave (CW)

Continuous Wave (CW) signals, commonly used for Morse code communication, have the narrowest bandwidth among various types of signals. In CW transmission, a constant-amplitude radio wave is turned on and off to create a series of short and long signals corresponding to the dots and dashes of Morse code.

Morse code comprises dots and dashes representing letters, numbers, and punctuation. CW is the method by which this language is transmitted over the airwaves.

T8D09: What is CW?

A. A type of electromagnetic propagation
B. A digital mode used primarily on 2-meter FM
C. A technique for coil winding
D. Another name for a Morse code transmission

CW signals typically occupy only about 150 Hz of bandwidth, which is significantly narrower than other modes like Single Sideband (SSB) and Frequency Modulation (FM), which are in kilohertz. This narrow bandwidth makes CW very efficient for long-distance communication, especially in crowded or noisy bands where minimizing interference is vital.

Remembering that CW has the narrowest bandwidth is easy if you consider it the most "compact" form of communication. It allows operators to fit more signals into the same frequency space without causing interference.

T8A05: Which of the following types of signal has the narrowest bandwidth?

A. FM voice
B. SSB voice
C. CW
D. Slow-scan TV

T8A11: What is the approximate bandwidth required to transmit a CW signal?

A. 2.4 kHz
B. 150 Hz
C. 1000 Hz
D. 15 kHz

Morse Code

Morse code is one of the oldest and most enduring methods of communication in radio and telegraphy. It was developed in the early 1830s by Samuel Morse and Alfred Vail. This system uses a series of dots (short signals) and dashes (long signals) to represent letters, numbers, and punctuation marks.

A short pause separates each character. In contrast, words are separated by longer pauses, allowing for the transmission of complex messages using simple, binary-like sequences. Initially used for telegraph communication, operators manually key in the dots and dashes to send messages over long distances via telegraph lines. With the advent of radio in the early 20th century, Morse code became a vital tool for ship-to-shore and ship-to-ship communication, military operations, and amateur radio, valued for its simplicity and effectiveness in poor signal conditions or limited bandwidth scenarios.

The simplicity of the equipment needed to send and receive Morse code makes it accessible and cost-effective. Furthermore, Morse code's reliability, even with weak or partially obstructed signals, has made it a popular choice for emergency communication.

Although less commonly used in commercial and military communication today, Morse code remains an essential skill for amateur radio operators. It continues to be used in specific aviation and maritime contexts. It is appreciated for its historical significance and effectiveness in low-signal environments.

Many amateur radio enthusiasts enjoy learning and using Morse code as part of their hobby, maintaining a link to the rich history of radio communication. However, you will not need to know Morse Code for any test.

Bandwidth Summary

Adjusting bandwidth in radio communications involves changing the range of frequencies used to transmit a signal. Depending on the equipment and mode of communication, various methods can be used to accomplish this. Most modern radios have adjustable settings labeled "IF Bandwidth" or "Filter," allowing users to narrow or widen the bandwidth.

Different communication modes, such as Single Sideband (SSB), Frequency Modulation (FM), and Morse code (CW), naturally use different bandwidths, so switching between these modes can also adjust the bandwidth. External filters can be used to restrict or broaden the range of frequencies the radio can handle.

Properly adjusting bandwidth is necessary for minimizing interference and ensuring clear communication, especially in crowded frequency bands.

The Physical Radio Station

SETTING UP YOUR FIRST station is an exciting endeavor. Start with the basics: a transceiver (a device that can transmit and receive communications), a power supply, and an antenna.

The type of equipment you choose should match the operations you intend to perform – and, most importantly, your license. For instance, a simple VHF or UHF setup might suffice if you're interested in local communications. For global communications, you might look into HF radios.

And remember, the antenna is as crucial as the radio itself, if not more so. A well-installed antenna will significantly enhance your ability to send and receive signals.

In this section, we will walk through the physical components of your radio and then discuss its actual use in the next section.

Chapter 13

Electronic And Electrical Components

WELCOME TO THE SECTION on electrical components, where we delve into the fundamental building blocks of radio communication systems. Understanding these components is pivotal for a beginner to troubleshoot, repair, and optimize their equipment. We'll explore essential elements like resistors, capacitors, inductors, and more, explaining their functions, characteristics, and interactions within a circuit.

Electrical Schematic

A schematic is a wiring diagram that represents the elements of a system using abstract, graphic symbols rather than realistic pictures. It illustrates a circuit's electrical connections and functions.

T6C01: What is the name of an electrical wiring diagram that uses standard component symbols?

A. Bill of materials
B. Connector pinout
C. Schematic
D. Flow chart

Electrical schematics focus on accurately representing component connections. These diagrams use standardized symbols to depict various electrical components, such as resistors, capacitors, inductors, and transistors, and show how they are interconnected by lines representing wires. The schematic provides a clear and detailed map of the circuit, illustrating how current flows from one component to another, which is essential for understanding the circuit's functionality and troubleshooting.

Think of an electrical schematic as a blueprint for building or analyzing an electronic device. Each symbol corresponds to a specific component; the lines connecting them indicate electrical current paths. Understanding that the purpose of a schematic is to show these connections will help you recall this concept for your exam and appreciate the importance of schematics in designing and maintaining electronic circuits.

T6C12: Which of the following is accurately represented in electrical schematics?

A. Wire lengths
B. Physical appearance of components
C. Component connections
D. All these choices are correct

Here is an example of an electrical schematic, which, lucky for us, is very similar to the one you will see on the exam.

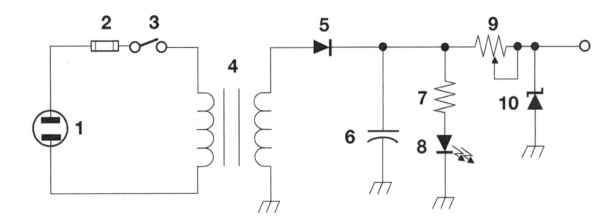

Schematic Components

Here is the identification of each numbered part in the schematic:

1. **AC Power Source**: Provides the electrical energy to the circuit from a wall plug.

2. **Fuse**: Protects the circuit by breaking the connection if the current exceeds a certain level.

3. **Single-Pole Single-Throw Switch**: Controls the flow of electricity, allowing the circuit to be opened or closed.

4. **Transformer**: Changes the voltage level with primary and secondary windings.

5. **Diode**: Allows current to flow in one direction only, used for rectification (the process of converting alternating current (AC) to direct current (DC)).

6. **Capacitor**: Stores electrical energy and releases it when needed.

7. **Resistor**: Limits or opposes the current flow and adjusts signal levels in a circuit.

8. **Light Emitting Diode (LED)**: Emits light when current flows through it.

9. **Variable Resistor (Potentiometer)**: Manually adjusts resistance to control signal levels or other parameters.

10. **Zener Diode**: This device allows current to flow in the reverse direction when a specific voltage is reached, and it is used for voltage regulation.

Together, these components form a circuit that can transform, control, and utilize electrical energy for various purposes. Let's examine each one and prepare for the test. Take some time and begin to memorize the components and symbols.

Resistor

T6A01: What electrical component opposes the flow of current in a DC circuit?

A. Inductor
B. Resistor
C. Inverter
D. Transformer

Don't be fooled by them throwing in the word 'DC circuit.' A resistor (component #7 in the schematic above) is an electrical component that <u>opposes, limits, regulates, or "resists" the flow of electrical current in a circuit</u> by providing resistance (in an

AC or DC circuit). It converts electrical energy into heat, helping to control voltage and current levels within the circuit. I remember the resistor as the zig-zag as it's throwing off heat while limiting the voltage passing through it.

Capacitor

A capacitor is an electrical component that <u>stores energy in an electric field</u>. It consists of two conductive plates separated by an insulating material known as the dielectric. When voltage is applied across these plates, an electric field forms, causing one plate to accumulate a positive charge and another to accumulate a negative charge. This stored energy can be quickly released when needed, making capacitors essential for various applications in electronic circuits.

T6A04: What electrical component stores energy in an electric field?

A. Varistor
B. Capacitor
C. Inductor
D. Diode

And then:

T6C06: What is component 6 in the figure?

A. Resistor
B. Capacitor
C. Regulator IC
D. Transistor

A capacitor (component #6) is an electrical component that stores and releases electrical energy by accumulating charge on its plates when connected to a power source. It is used to smooth out voltage fluctuations, filter signals, and store energy in electronic circuits. I remember this as "storing energy" on the horizontal line and then shooting it out on the curved line. Again, memorize the schematic however you want, but that's what I do.

T6A05: What type of electrical component consists of conductive surfaces separated by an insulator?

A. Resistor
B. Potentiometer
C. Oscillator
D. Capacitor

A capacitor is constructed with <u>two conductive plates separated by an insulating material</u> called the dielectric. The plates can be made of metal, and the dielectric can be composed of ceramic, plastic, or electrolytic substances. When a voltage is applied, electric charge accumulates on the plates, creating an electric field in the dielectric, which allows the capacitor to store energy.

Fuse

T6A09: What electrical component is used to protect other circuit components from current overloads?

A. Fuse
B. Thyratron
C. Varactor
D. All these choices are correct

A fuse (component #2) is a safety device used in electrical circuits to protect against overcurrents and overloads, which can cause damage to equipment or even start a fire. It consists of a metal wire or strip that melts when too much current flows through it, breaking the circuit and stopping the flow of electricity. Once a fuse has blown, it must be replaced to restore the circuit, ensuring that any issues causing the overcurrent are addressed before resuming operation. This one is easy to remember because it looks like a fuse!

Switches

Switches are fundamental components in electrical and electronic circuits. They act as devices that can open or close a circuit, thereby controlling the flow of electrical current. They come in various forms, including toggle, push-button, rotary, and slide switches, each designed for specific applications. By providing a simple means to start or stop current flow, switches are used in virtually every type of electronic equipment, from household appliances to complex industrial machinery.

Understanding how switches work and their different types is key for anyone using electronics. Switches can range from simple single-pole single-throw (SPST) types, which control a single circuit, to more complex configurations like double-pole double-throw (DPDT) switches, which can control multiple circuits.

The Single-Pole Single-Throw (SPST) (component #3) switch is the simplest type of switch, featuring one input (pole) and one output (throw). It acts as an on-off switch that controls a single circuit, allowing current to flow when in the "on" position and interrupting the flow when in the "off" position. Think of this as looking down on two poles. But the switch only touches one – a single pole.

T6A12: What type of switch is represented by component #3 in the schematic?

A. Single-pole single-throw
B. Single-pole double-throw
C. Double-pole single-throw
D. Double-pole double-throw

A Single-Pole Double-Throw (SPDT) switch is a versatile component that allows a single input circuit to be switched between one of two output circuits. It has one common terminal and two output terminals, enabling the user to route the input signal to either of the two outputs. This functionality is helpful in applications where you must toggle between two different circuits or pathways, such as selecting between two audio sources or switching operational modes in a device.

T6A08: What is the function of an SPDT switch?

A. A single circuit is opened or closed
B. Two circuits are opened or closed
C. A single circuit is switched between one of two other circuits
D. Two circuits are each switched between one of two other circuits

It's helpful to think of an SPDT switch as a bridge connecting one path to either of two destinations. When the switch is in one position, the common terminal is connected to the first output terminal; when flipped to the other position, the common terminal connects to the second output terminal.

Relays: Electrically Controlled Switches

A relay is an electrically controlled switch that allows a low-power signal to control a higher-power circuit. It consists of an electromagnet, a set of contacts, and a switching mechanism. When a small current flows through the electromagnet, it generates a magnetic field that either opens or closes the contacts, switching the higher-power circuit on or off. This ability to control large electrical loads with a small input signal makes relays invaluable in various applications, from automotive systems to industrial machinery and home automation.

For beginners, it's helpful to think of a relay as a remote control for electrical circuits. By operating the relay using a small, safe electrical signal, you can manage high-voltage or high-current devices without direct human intervention, ensuring safety and efficiency.

T6D02: What is a relay?

A. An electrically-controlled switch
B. A current controlled amplifier
C. An inverting amplifier
D. A pass transistor

Diode

T6B02: What electronic component allows current to flow in only one direction?

A. Resistor
B. Fuse
C. Diode
D. Driven element

A diode (component #5) is an electronic component that allows current to flow in one direction only, acting as a one-way valve for electric current. It has two terminals: the anode (positive) and the cathode (negative). When a voltage is applied across the diode in the correct direction (forward bias), it conducts electricity; when the voltage is reversed (reverse bias), it blocks the current, providing essential functionality in circuits such as rectification, signal demodulation, and protection against reverse polarity. This one should be easy to remember, as it's an arrow and a bar. Traffic goes only one way.

T6B09: What are the names for the electrodes of a diode?

A. Plus and minus
B. Source and drain
C. Anode and cathode
D. Gate and base

Marking the Cathode Lead of a Semiconductor Diode

A semiconductor diode's (negative) cathode lead is often marked on the package with a distinctive stripe or band. This band is typically located near the cathode end of the diode, making it easy to identify the polarity. The other end of the diode, which is the anode, does not have this marking.

Why does this matter? Recognizing this marking ensures the diode (positive lead) is correctly oriented in the circuit. Installing a diode backward can prevent the circuit from functioning correctly or even damage the diode. Remember that the stripe indicates the cathode will help you correctly install diodes and avoid common mistakes.

T6B06: How is the cathode lead of a semiconductor diode often marked on the package?

A. With the word "cathode"
B. With a stripe
C. With the letter C
D. With the letter K

Understanding Forward Voltage Drop in Diodes

T6B01: Which is true about forward voltage drop in a diode?

A. It is lower in some diode types than in others
B. It is proportional to peak inverse voltage
C. It indicates that the diode is defective
D. It has no impact on the voltage delivered to the load

The forward voltage drop of a diode is the minimum voltage required to allow current to flow through the diode in the forward direction. When the applied voltage exceeds this threshold, the diode conducts electricity, allowing current to pass.

For example, a typical silicon diode has a forward voltage drop of about 0.7 volts, meaning that it needs at least 0.7 volts to start conducting. This voltage drop is due to the energy required to overcome the barrier potential of the diode's semiconductor material, which is essential for its operation in controlling the direction of current flow in electronic circuits.

This voltage drop varies among different types of diodes. For example, a standard silicon diode typically has a forward voltage drop of about 0.7 volts. In contrast, a Schottky diode has a lower forward voltage drop, around 0.2 to 0.3 volts. This lower voltage drop makes Schottky diodes more efficient in applications with low power loss.

For beginners, it's helpful to remember that the forward voltage drop is a characteristic to consider when selecting a diode for a specific application. Knowing that some diodes, like Schottky diodes, have a lower forward voltage drop can help you choose the suitable diode to minimize power loss and improve efficiency in your circuits.

LED (Light Emitting Diode)

T6C07: What is component 8 in Figure T-2?

A. Resistor
B. Inductor
C. Regulator IC
D. Light-emitting diode

Are you thinking, why does a diode sound so familiar? It does because of the 'light emitting diode' we see in component #8 ... yes, the LED, just like your TV screen.

A Light-Emitting Diode (LED) is a semiconductor device that emits light when an electrical current passes through it (otherwise known as a <u>forward current</u>—just like it sounds, current is moving forward through the diode). Unlike traditional incandescent bulbs, which produce light through filament heating, LEDs generate light through electroluminescence, a process in which electrons recombine with holes within the semiconductor material, releasing energy in the form of photons.

T6B07: What causes a light-emitting diode (LED) to emit light?

A. Forward current
B. Reverse current
C. Capacitively-coupled RF signal
D. Inductively-coupled RF signal

LEDs are highly efficient, consuming less power and offering longer lifespans than conventional light sources. <u>They are widely used in various applications</u>, from <u>indicator lights</u> and displays to general illumination. In the schematic, the LED is a visual indicator that shows when the circuit is active.

T6D07: Which of the following is commonly used as a visual indicator?

A. LED
B. FET
C. Zener diode
D. Bipolar transistor

This symbol is precisely like a diode, but it emits light in the form of lightning bolts.

Variable Resistor

T6C08: What is component 9 in the figure?

A. Variable capacitor
B. Variable inductor
C. Variable resistor
D. Variable transformer

This one has the same zig-zag as a resistor but with an extra line arrow, meaning it has some variability. It should now be memorized for you!

A variable resistor, also known as a <u>potentiometer</u> or rheostat, is an adjustable resistor used to <u>control the current or voltage in a circuit</u>. It consists of a <u>resistive</u> element and a <u>sliding or rotating</u> contact (wiper) that moves along the component, changing the resistance value. By adjusting the position of the wiper, you can increase or decrease the resistance, allowing for precise control over the electrical parameters in the circuit. Variable resistors are commonly used for tuning and calibration in electronic devices, such as <u>adjusting the volume on a radio</u> or the brightness of a light.

What was that again? If I listen to my car radio and want to adjust the volume?

Potentiometer

T6A02: What type of component is often used as an adjustable volume control?

A. Fixed resistor
B. Power resistor
C. Potentiometer
D. Transformer

Who knew it had such a fancy name? And what exactly does a potentiometer control?

T6A03: What electrical parameter is controlled by a potentiometer?

A. Inductance
B. Resistance
C. Capacitance
D. Field strength

Hopefully, you remembered that a potentiometer controls current, which is done with a resistor. So, it's resistance we are controlling here (fun how it all comes around full circle).

Transformer

T6C09: What is component 4 in the figure?

A. Variable inductor
B. Double-pole switch
C. Potentiometer
D. Transformer

One of the cooler-looking symbols (component #4), a transformer is an electrical device that transfers electrical energy <u>between two or more circuits</u> through electromagnetic induction.

It consists of two or more wire windings, called coils, wrapped around a common magnetic core. The primary coil receives an alternating current (AC) voltage, which creates a varying magnetic field in the core. This magnetic field induces a voltage in the secondary coil, which can be higher or lower than the primary voltage depending on the ratio of the number of turns in the coils.

Transformers are essential in power distribution. They allow electricity to be transmitted efficiently over long distances by <u>stepping up</u> the voltage to reduce energy loss and then <u>stepping it down</u> for safe use in homes and businesses.

T6D06: What component changes 120 V AC power to a lower AC voltage for other uses?

A. Variable capacitor
B. Transformer
C. Transistor
D. Diode

Here is a practical example. A transformer is essential to convert 120 V AC power to a lower AC voltage suitable for various applications. For beginners, it's helpful to think of a transformer as a device that adapts electrical energy to meet the needs of different devices safely. When you plug in a device that requires less voltage than the standard 120 V AC supply, the transformer ensures that the device receives the appropriate voltage, protecting it from damage and ensuring efficient operation.

Another Schematic to Work Through

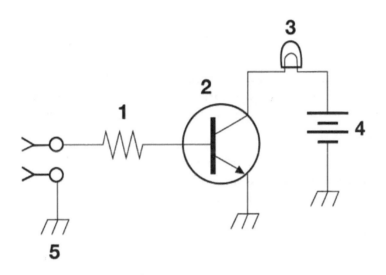

Here is the identification of each numbered part in the schematic:

1. **Resistor**: Limits the current flowing into the base of the transistor.

2. **Transistor (NPN)**: Acts as a switch or amplifier, controlling the current flow through the circuit.

3. **Lamp**: An indicator that lights up when current flows through, showing the circuit is active and functioning correctly.

4. **Battery**: Provides the electrical power for the circuit.

5. **Ground**: Indicates a reference point in the circuit where the voltage is considered to be zero. Ground symbols are essential in circuits to provide a common return path for electric current, prevent electrical shock, and maintain circuit stability.

Let's practice:

> **T6C02: What is component 1 in the figure?**
>
> **A. Resistor**
> B. Transistor
> C. Battery
> D. Connector

Hopefully, you remember this zig-zag from the last section, too.

Transistor

> **T6C03: What is component 2 in the figure?**
>
> A. Resistor
> **B. Transistor**
> C. Indicator lamp
> D. Connector

A transistor (component #2) is a semiconductor device that amplifies or switches electronic signals and electrical power. It has three regions of semiconductor material, which are important for its function as an amplifier or switch in electronic circuits: the base, the collector, and the emitter.

Applying a small current or voltage to the base allows the transistor to control a larger current flowing between the collector and the emitter. This capability makes transistors essential components in many electronic devices, enabling them to perform signal amplification, switching, and voltage regulation functions.

Transistors are essential—-, so they get a fancy symbol (again, how I remember it).

> **T6D10: What is the function of component 2?**
>
> A. Give off light when current flows through it
> B. Supply electrical energy
> **C. Control the flow of current**
> D. Convert electrical energy into radio waves

Because it can switch electronic signals:

> **T6B03: Which of these components can be used as an electronic switch?**
>
> A. Varistor
> B. Potentiometer
> **C. Transistor**
> D. Thermistor

And another one about transistors:

T6B04: Which of the following components can consist of three regions of semiconductor material?

A. Alternator
B. Transistor
C. Triode
D. Pentagrid converter

Transistors come in various types, the most common being bipolar junction transistors (BJTs) and field-effect transistors (FETs).

In BJTs (bipolar junction transistors), the current flowing into the base controls the current between the collector and emitter.

T6B12: What are the names of the electrodes of a bipolar junction transistor?

A. signal, bias, power
B. emitter, base, collector
C. Input, output, supply
D. Pole one, pole two, output

While in FETs (field effect transistors), a voltage applied to the gate controls the current between the drain and source.

T6B05: What type of transistor has a gate, drain, and source?

A. Varistor
B. Field-effect
C. Tesla-effect
D. Bipolar junction

To check if you remember what you read above:

T6B08: What does the abbreviation FET stand for?

A. Frequency Emission Transmitter
B. Fast Electron Transistor
C. Free Electron Transmitter
D. Field Effect Transistor

Power Gain in Transistors

A transistor can provide power gain, which means it can amplify the power of an input signal. This is achieved by controlling a large current flowing through the transistor with a smaller input current or voltage. In a standard configuration like the common-emitter arrangement in bipolar junction transistors (BJTs), a small current at the base controls a much larger current flowing from the collector to the emitter, significantly amplifying the signal's power.

For beginners, it is helpful to think of a transistor as a powerful amplifier. By applying a small input signal to one of its terminals, the transistor can produce a much larger output signal, making it an essential component in audio amplifiers, radio transmitters, and many other electronic devices.

Understanding that a transistor can provide power gain will help you recall this essential function for your exam and recognize its critical role in enhancing signal strength in various applications.

T6B10: Which of the following can provide power gain?-

A. Transformer
B. Transistor
C. Reactor
D. Resistor

The Relationship Between Gain and Transistors

Gain describes a device's ability to amplify a signal, representing the ratio of the output signal to the input signal in an electronic circuit. It is a critical parameter in amplifiers, indicating how much the signal's power, voltage, or current increases.

For beginners, gain measures how much an amplifier boosts a signal's strength. If an amplifier has a high gain, a small input signal will significantly increase the output, making the sound louder in audio systems or boosting weak radio signals.

Gain and transistors are closely related. Transistors are key components in amplifying signals, and their primary function is to provide gain. In a transistor, gain refers to the ratio of the output signal to the input signal, indicating how effectively the transistor can amplify the current, voltage, or power. Transistors, whether they are bipolar junction transistors (BJTs) or field-effect transistors (FETs), utilize their internal properties to control a larger current or voltage with a minor input, achieving amplification.

T6B11: What is the term that describes a device's ability to amplify a signal?

A. Gain
B. Forward resistance
C. Forward voltage drop
D. On resistance

Lamp

T6C04: What is component 3?

A. Resistor
B. Transistor
C. Lamp
D. Ground symbol

Hopefully, this one is easy to memorize, as it looks like a lamp or at least a small light bulb you screw in.

In the context of an electrical circuit, a lamp (component #3) is a device that produces light when electrical current flows through it. It typically consists of a filament or a light-emitting diode (LED) that glows when energized by an electrical current. In the schematic provided, the lamp acts as an indicator, illuminating to show that the circuit is active and the current is flowing correctly. This visual feedback helps confirm the circuit's operation and diagnose any issues with the current flow.

Battery

T6C05: What is component 4 in the figure?

A. Resistor
B. Transistor
C. Ground symbol
D. Battery

A battery (component #4) is a device that stores chemical energy and converts it into electrical energy to provide a steady supply of direct current (DC) to a circuit. It consists of one or more electrochemical cells, each containing positive and negative electrodes immersed in an electrolyte.

When connected to a circuit, a chemical reaction occurs within the battery, generating a flow of electrons from the negative terminal to the positive terminal, providing the necessary power to operate electronic devices. In the schematic, the battery acts as the primary power source, supplying the electrical energy needed for the components, such as the lamp and transistor, to function. In this case, the battery component looks like a battery having multiple polls or cells (again, it's just a way to memorize what it is on a schematic). More on batteries in the power chapter.

One More Schematic to Work Through

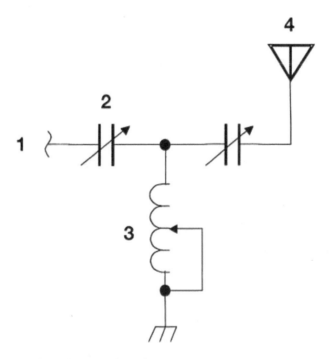

Here is the identification of each numbered part in the schematic:

1. **AC Power Source**: Carries the power to our equipment.

2. **Variable Capacitor**: Allows for capacitance adjustment to tune the circuit for resonance.

3. **Variable Inductor**: Works with the capacitors to form a resonant circuit, which can be tuned to match the antenna's impedance.

4. **Antenna**: Radiates the radio frequency signal into the air or receives signals from the air.

This circuit is an antenna tuner used to match the impedance of the transmission line to the antenna for efficient signal transmission and reception. The chapter on antennas explains this more.

Inductor

An inductor is an electrical component that stores energy in a magnetic field when electric current flows through it. It consists of a coil of wire, and as current passes through it, it generates a magnetic field around it. When the current changes, the magnetic field changes, inducing a voltage that opposes the change in current. This property of inductors makes them helpful in filtering signals, temporarily storing energy, and managing the flow of AC and DC currents in circuits.

For beginners, think of an inductor as a device that resists changes in current, storing energy in the form of a magnetic field when current flows through it. This ability to store and release energy helps smooth out fluctuations in current, making inductors essential in power supplies, radio transmitters, and various other electronic applications.

T6A06: What type of electrical component stores energy in a magnetic field?

A. Varistor
B. Capacitor
C. Inductor
D. Diode

T6A07: What electrical component is typically constructed as a coil of wire?

A. Switch
B. Capacitor
C. Diode
D. Inductor

Variable Inductor

T6C10: What is component 3 in the figure?

A. Connector
B. Meter
C. Variable capacitor
D. Variable inductor

A variable inductor is an electrical component whose inductance can be adjusted. Inductance is the property of a component that opposes changes in current flow and is measured in henries (H).

A variable inductor typically consists of a coil of wire (like the component image in #3), and its inductance can be changed by altering the position of a movable core (often made of ferrite) within the coil or by adjusting the spacing between turns of the coil.

Key Characteristics:

1. **Adjustability**: The ability to fine-tune the inductance allows for precise control of the circuit's characteristics, making variable inductors useful in applications requiring tuning, such as radio frequency (RF) circuits, filters, and oscillators.

2. **Construction**: Variable inductors are usually built with a screw mechanism that moves the core in and out of the coil or changes the coil's geometry. This adjustability affects the magnetic field and, thus, the inductance.

3. **Applications**: They are commonly used in RF tuning circuits, antenna matching networks, and any application where the inductance needs to be varied to achieve optimal performance.

Practical Example:

In an antenna tuning circuit, a variable inductor can be adjusted to match the antenna's impedance with the transmitter's. This matching ensures maximum power transfer and efficient signal transmission.

Understanding the function and use of a variable inductor helps design and optimize circuits requiring precise inductance control, ensuring better performance and flexibility in various electronic applications.

Antenna

T6C11: What is component 4 in the figure?

A. Antenna
B. Transmitter
C. Dummy load
D. Ground

A lot more on antennas later. Just remember this "antenna-looking" thing is meant to illustrate an antenna on a schematic. Makes sense...right!

Other Components

Rectifiers

Converting AC to DC

A rectifier is a device or circuit that <u>converts alternating current (AC) into varying direct current (DC).</u> This conversion is essential in power supplies for electronic devices, which typically require DC power. Rectifiers allow current to flow only in one direction, using components such as diodes. When AC voltage is applied to a rectifier, the diodes block the negative portions of the AC cycle, resulting in a pulsating DC output.

Think of a rectifier as a one-way valve for electrical current. It takes the back-and-forth motion of AC and turns it into a steady flow of DC, which is necessary for powering most electronic circuits.

T6D01: Which of the following devices or circuits changes an alternating current into a varying direct current signal?

A. Transformer
B. Rectifier
C. Amplifier
D. Reflector

Meters

Displaying Electrical Quantities

A <u>meter is a device that displays an electrical quantity as a numeric value,</u> allowing for precise measurement and monitoring of various parameters within a circuit. Common types of meters include voltmeters, which measure voltage; ammeters, which measure current; and ohmmeters, which measure resistance. These devices provide accurate readings essential for diagnosing and troubleshooting electrical issues and ensuring that circuits operate within their specified parameters.

For beginners, think of a meter as the instrument panel for your electrical circuit, much like a speedometer in a car. It provides real-time, numerical data that helps you understand the electrical system's behavior. Whether you are checking the voltage of a power supply, measuring the current draw of a device, or verifying the resistance of a component, meters are indispensable tools for anyone working with electronics.

T6D04: Which of the following displays an electrical quantity as a numeric value?

A. Potentiometer
B. Transistor
C. Meter
D. Relay

Regulators (Voltage)

Controlling Voltage in Circuits

A <u>voltage regulator is a circuit designed to maintain a constant output voltage from a power supply</u>, regardless of variations in input voltage or load conditions. It "regulates" the voltage. This ensures that electronic devices receive a stable and reliable voltage, which is crucial for their proper functioning and longevity. Voltage regulators can be found in various forms, such as linear and switching regulators, each with its own method of controlling and stabilizing the voltage.

Think of a voltage regulator as a manager that ensures the voltage supplied to your electronic components remains steady, much like a thermostat maintains a constant temperature. By keeping the voltage within a specific range, voltage regulators prevent damage to sensitive components and ensure consistent performance of electronic devices.

T6D05: What type of circuit controls the amount of voltage from a power supply?

A. Regulator
B. Oscillator
C. Filter
D. Phase inverter

Circuits

Components like resistors, capacitors, and inductors have unique properties and functions in electronics. However, these components' true power emerges when combined in various configurations.

By strategically connecting different components, we can create circuits with new capabilities and behaviors, such as filtering signals, storing energy, and generating oscillations.

Combining these basic building blocks opens up many possibilities for designing more complex and functional electronic systems. This section will delve into the principles and techniques of combining components, providing a foundation for creating sophisticated circuits with a wide range of practical applications.

Resonant Circuit

A resonant circuit, also known as a tuned circuit, is an electrical circuit that combines inductors and capacitors to create a system capable of oscillating at a specific frequency known as the resonant frequency. At this frequency, the inductive and capacitive reactance are equal in magnitude but opposite in phase, causing them to cancel each other out. This results in the circuit having a high impedance at the resonant frequency, allowing it to store and transfer energy efficiently between the inductor and capacitor.

T6D08: Which of the following is combined with an inductor to make a resonant circuit?

A. Resistor
B. Zener diode
C. Potentiometer
D. Capacitor

At resonance, energy oscillates back and forth between the inductor's magnetic field and the capacitor's electric field, enabling the circuit to store energy effectively.

Resonant circuits are widely used in radio frequency applications, such as tuning radios to specific frequencies, filtering signals, and generating stable frequencies in oscillators.

T6D11: Which of the following is a resonant or tuned circuit?

A. An inductor and a capacitor in series or parallel
B. A linear voltage regulator
C. A resistor circuit used for reducing standing wave ratio
D. A circuit designed to provide high-fidelity audio

Don't let the series or parallel fool you. An inductor and a capacitor is a resonant circuit.

Integrated Circuit

An integrated circuit (IC) is a miniature electronic device comprising a complex assembly of interconnected electronic components, such as transistors, diodes, resistors, and capacitors, all fabricated onto a single piece of semiconductor material, typically silicon. These components are embedded in a tiny chip, which can perform various functions depending on the circuit's design and configuration.

T6D09: What is the name of a device that combines several semiconductors and other components into one package?

A. Transducer
B. Multi-pole relay
C. Integrated circuit
D. Transformer

Integrated circuits have revolutionized electronics by significantly reducing their size, cost, and power consumption while increasing reliability and performance. They are used in virtually all modern electronic equipment, from simple calculators and digital watches to complex computers and communication systems.

Understanding integrated circuits is crucial for anyone involved in electronics. They form the backbone of modern electronic technology and enable the creation of sophisticated and compact devices.

Go back through one more time. Study the schematics and ensure you can name each component.

Chapter 14

Essential Tools and Techniques for Electronics

HAVING THE RIGHT TOOLS and mastering fundamental techniques are crucial for success in electronics. Whether you are a beginner just starting out or an experienced enthusiast, understanding how to use basic test instruments and perform essential tasks like soldering is fundamental. This chapter will guide you through the use of voltmeters, ammeters, and ohmmeters, explaining how these tools help measure and diagnose electrical quantities. Additionally, we will delve into soldering, a critical skill for assembling and repairing electronic circuits.

By the end of this chapter, you will be equipped with the knowledge to accurately measure voltage, current, and resistance and understand the fundamentals of joining components together using soldering techniques. These skills are the building blocks of practical electronic work.

Voltmeter

A voltmeter is a measuring instrument used to measure the electrical potential difference, or voltage, between two points in an electrical circuit. It is an essential tool for anyone working with electronics, as it helps ensure that circuits operate correctly and safely. Voltmeters can be analog or digital, with digital voltmeters providing numerical readings on a display and analog voltmeters using a needle to indicate the voltage on a scale.

T7D01: Which instrument would you use to measure electric potential?

A. An ammeter
B. A voltmeter
C. A wavemeter
D. An ohmmeter

Voltmeters are typically connected in parallel with the component or section of the circuit being measured. This parallel connection allows the voltmeter to measure the voltage without significantly affecting the circuit's operation. Using a voltmeter, you can diagnose issues, verify circuit functionality, and ensure that your electronic devices receive the correct voltage. Understanding how to use a voltmeter is fundamental for troubleshooting and maintaining electronic systems.

T7D02: How is a voltmeter connected to a component to measure applied voltage?

A. In series
B. In parallel
C. In quadrature
D. In phase

Precautions When Measuring High Voltages

When measuring high voltages with a voltmeter, it is vital to ensure that the voltmeter and its leads are rated for the voltages you intend to measure. Using equipment not rated for high voltage can lead to inaccurate readings, damage to the equipment, or even personal injury. High voltage can cause arcs, which might damage the voltmeter or create hazardous conditions for the operator.

T0A12: Which of the following precautions should be taken when measuring high voltages with a voltmeter?

A. Ensure that the voltmeter has very low impedance
B. Ensure that the voltmeter and leads are rated for use at the voltages to be measured
C. Ensure that the circuit is grounded through the voltmeter
D. Ensure that the voltmeter is set to the correct frequency

Always check the voltmeter's maximum voltage rating and probes to measure high voltages safely. This rating should be clearly marked and must exceed the voltage you plan to measure. Additionally, appropriate personal protective equipment, such as insulated gloves and eye protection, should be used to reduce the risk of electric shock. Understanding and following these precautions is essential for ensuring accurate measurements and safety during high-voltage testing.

Ammeter

An ammeter is a measuring instrument used to measure the electric current flowing through a circuit. It is a tool for anyone working with electronics, as it allows for monitoring and troubleshooting of current flow to ensure that circuits operate within their intended parameters. Ammeters can be analog or digital.

T7D04: Which instrument is used to measure electric current?

A. An ohmmeter
B. An electrometer
C. A voltmeter
D. An ammeter

To measure current accurately, an ammeter is connected in series with the component or section of the circuit being measured. This series connection allows the entire current flowing through the circuit to pass through the ammeter. Using an ammeter, you can detect issues such as excessive current that might indicate a short circuit or insufficient current that could suggest a poor connection or high resistance.

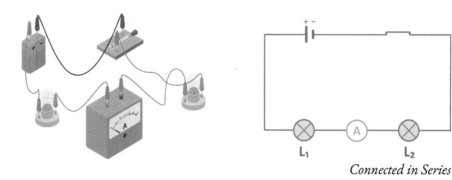

Connected in Series

T7D03: When configured to measure current, how is a multimeter connected to a component?

A. In series
B. In parallel
C. In quadrature
D. In phase

Ohmmeter

An ohmmeter is an instrument used to <u>measure the electrical resistance</u> of a component or a circuit. Resistance measures how much a component opposes the flow of electric current and is typically measured in ohms (Ω).

To measure resistance, an ohmmeter is connected across the component or section of the circuit being tested, with the <u>circuit power turned off</u> to avoid damaging the meter or the circuit.

The <u>ohmmeter applies a small known voltage to the component</u>. It measures the resulting current flow, using Ohm's Law to calculate the resistance. Using an ohmmeter, you can check for open and short circuits and ensure that components have the correct resistance values.

T7D11: Which of the following precautions should be taken when measuring in-circuit resistance with an ohmmeter?

A. Ensure that the applied voltages are correct
B. Ensure that the circuit is not powered
C. Ensure that the circuit is grounded
D. Ensure that the circuit is operating at the correct frequency

---

Understanding Ohmmeter Readings Across a Discharged Capacitor

When an ohmmeter is connected across a large, discharged capacitor, <u>the reading will show an increasing resistance with time.</u> This occurs because the <u>capacitor starts to charge due to the small voltage supplied by the ohmmeter.</u> Initially, the ohmmeter measures a low resistance as the capacitor is uncharged and allows current to flow freely. As the capacitor charges, the current flow decreases, causing the resistance reading on the ohmmeter to increase gradually.

For beginners, it's helpful to visualize this process as the capacitor filling up with electric charge. When fully discharged, the capacitor behaves almost like a short circuit with minimal resistance. As it charges, it starts to resist the current flow more and more, leading to an increasing resistance reading. Understanding this behavior helps identify and verify capacitors in a circuit, ensuring they function correctly. Remembering that a rising resistance reading indicates a charging capacitor will help you recall this concept for your exam and practical applications. Be safe!

T7D10: What reading indicates that an ohmmeter is connected across a large, discharged capacitor?

A. Increasing resistance with time
B. Decreasing resistance with time
C. Steady full-scale reading
D. Alternating between open and short circuit

Multimeter

A multimeter combines the functions of several measurement tools into a single device, typically including the ability to measure voltage (voltmeter), current (ammeter), and resistance (ohmmeter). Multimeters come in analog and digital forms, with digital multimeters (DMMs) being more common due to their ease of use and precision.

Very rarely, in today's world, will you see a separate voltmeter, ammeter, or ohmmeter. Today, they are all combined into one tool – a multimeter.

Functions of a Multimeter

1. **Voltage Measurement (Voltmeter)**: This allows you to measure the electrical potential difference between two points in a circuit. You can measure AC (alternating current) and DC (direct current) voltages.

2. **Current Measurement (Ammeter)**: This function enables you to measure the flow of electric current through a component or section of a circuit. It helps diagnose issues related to current flow.

3. **Resistance Measurement (Ohmmeter)**: This measures the opposition to current flow within a component or circuit. It helps check the integrity of resistors and ensure there are no short circuits or open circuits.

In ham radio, multimeters are indispensable tools for building, testing, and maintaining radio equipment. They help ensure that circuits function correctly, identify faults, and verify the proper operation of various components. For instance, you can use a multimeter to check a power supply's voltage, measure the transmitter's current draw, or test the resistance of a connection. By mastering a multimeter, ham radio operators can ensure their equipment operates efficiently and effectively, leading to better communication and more reliable performance.

T7D07: Which of the following measurements are made using a multimeter?

A. Signal strength and noise
B. Impedance and reactance
C. Voltage and resistance
D. All these choices are correct

Because it's an all-in-one tool, a multimeter can be easily damaged if you attempt to mismeasure components.

For example, suppose you attempt to <u>measure voltage</u> while it is set to <u>measure resistance.</u> In that case, the multimeter applies a small voltage to the circuit in resistance mode to measure the current flow and calculate the resistance. When you connect the multimeter to a voltage source while in this mode, the external voltage can overload the multimeter's internal components, potentially causing permanent damage.

It's wise always to double-check that your multimeter is set to the correct measurement mode before taking any readings. This simple habit can prevent costly mistakes and ensure your multimeter remains in good working condition. Remember, using the wrong setting risks damaging your equipment and can lead to incorrect readings and faulty diagnostics.

T7D06: Which of the following can damage a multimeter?

A. Attempting to measure resistance using the voltage setting
B. Failing to connect one of the probes to ground
C. Attempting to measure voltage when using the resistance setting
D. Not allowing it to warm up properly

One note here. This is one of those tricky questions that you need to make sure you are paying attention to. Answer 'A' might appear valid. It's the opposite of 'C,' the correct answer.

But why is this statement wrong? When you set a multimeter to measure voltage, it is designed to measure the potential difference between two points without sending any current into the circuit. If you attempt to measure resistance while in the voltage setting, the multimeter will not send the necessary small current through the component to measure its resistance, leading to a failed or inaccurate measurement. However, this action does not usually harm the multimeter itself.

Solder

Understanding Solder and Its Importance in Ham Radio

Solder is a fusible metal alloy that creates a permanent bond between metal workpieces. It is commonly composed of tin and lead, although lead-free varieties are also available for health and environmental reasons. The soldering process involves melting the solder and applying it to the joint between two metal surfaces, such as electronic components and circuit board pads, where it cools and solidifies, forming a solid electrical and mechanical connection.

In ham radio, soldering is used to assemble and maintain electronic equipment. Proper soldering ensures reliable electrical connections, which are vital for the performance and longevity of radio circuits. Here are some key reasons why solder is vital in ham radio:

1. **Component Assembly**: Soldering attaches electronic components to printed circuit boards (PCBs), ensuring they stay in place and function correctly.

2. **Signal Integrity**: Good solder joints provide low-resistance connections essential for maintaining signal quality and preventing signal loss or interference.

3. **Durability**: Soldered connections are mechanically robust, which is vital for withstanding the physical stresses that can occur in portable or mobile radio equipment.

4. **Repairs and Modifications**: Soldering skills are necessary for repairing faulty equipment and modifying or upgrading radio gear to improve performance or add new features.

Mastering soldering techniques is essential for any ham radio operator. It enables the construction, maintenance, and repair of radio equipment, ensuring reliable communication and optimal performance. Practice makes perfect. This is a skill you master over time.

The Importance of Using the Right Solder in Electronics

For radio and electronic applications, avoiding acid-core solder is imperative. Acid-core solder contains a flux with an acid-based cleaning agent designed for plumbing and metalwork, not for delicate electronic components. The acid flux can corrode and damage electronic parts, leading to poor electrical connections and potential failure of the circuit over time.

Instead, rosin-core solder should be used for radio and electronic work. Rosin-core solder contains a safe flux for electronic components, providing good cleaning action without the risk of corrosion. Using the correct solder type ensures reliable and long-lasting connections for electronic devices' proper functioning and durability.

T7D08: Which of the following types of solder should not be used for radio and electronic applications?

A. Acid-core solder
B. Lead-tin solder
C. Rosin-core solder
D. Tin-copper solder

Read the question carefully and pick up on the "NOT to be used in radio."

Cold Tin-Lead Solder Joints

A cold tin-lead solder joint is characterized by a rough or lumpy surface, indicating that the solder did not properly melt and flow during the soldering process. This typically occurs when the soldering iron does not reach a high enough temperature or when the joint is disturbed before the solder has thoroughly cooled and solidified. Cold solder joints are weak and unreliable, leading to poor electrical conductivity and potential connection failure.

For beginners, it's essential to recognize that a proper solder joint should have a smooth, shiny, and uniform appearance, ensuring a solid mechanical and electrical connection. Understanding the appearance of cold solder joints helps diagnose and fix soldering issues, ensuring the reliability and performance of your electronic circuits.

T7D09: What is the characteristic appearance of a cold tin-lead solder joint?

A. Dark black spots
B. A bright or shiny surface
C. A rough or lumpy surface
D. Excessive solder

Understanding and mastering essential tools like voltmeters, ammeters, and ohmmeters, along with proper soldering techniques, are foundational skills in electronics. These skills ensure accurate measurements and reliable connections and enhance the overall performance and durability of electronic equipment. As you continue your journey in electronics, remember that these fundamental practices are the building blocks for more advanced projects and successful repairs.

Chapter 15

The Ham Radio Station

WHEN YOU'RE READY TO set up your first ham radio station, it's like preparing to plant a garden. It would help to have the right tools, a good piece of land, and knowledge about what you're about to grow. Similarly, setting up a ham radio station requires a thoughtful selection of equipment, careful setup planning, and a keen eye for safety and operational efficiency. Let's walk through these steps individually to ensure your first foray into setting up a ham radio station is successful and enjoyable.

Transmitter + Receiver = Transceiver

Selecting your first transceiver— <u>a device that transmits and receives radio signals</u>—is akin to picking the seed you will plant. It must suit your environment and the communication you wish to engage in. Start with a clear understanding of your goals. Are you interested in local communications or aiming to reach across continents? This decision will influence whether you should opt for a VHF/UHF transceiver, mainly used for local and regional communication, or an HF transceiver capable of global communication.

> **T7A02: What is a transceiver?**
>
> **A. A device that combines a receiver and transmitter**
> B. A device for matching feed line impedance to 50 ohms
> C. A device for automatically sending and decoding Morse code
> D. A device for converting receiver and transmitter frequencies to another band

Your budget is another factor. Transceivers vary in price from relatively inexpensive to quite costly, depending on their features and capabilities. As a beginner, it might be wise to start with something more fundamental; many entry-level transceivers offer a solid foundation to learn without overwhelming you with too many advanced features. Space is also a consideration—ensure the equipment size matches your available area. A compact, all-in-one transceiver might be ideal if space is limited.

The Theoretical and Practical

Let's recap and start to bring the theoretical and practical together. The science of ham radio begins with radio waves, forms of electromagnetic energy that travel through the air carrying information (remember we covered this already! You do remember it, right?). At its core, the process involves a transmitter converting information into a radio wave, then sending it across distances where a receiver captures it and converts it back into usable information.

Depending on what was initially sent, this might be voice, data, or Morse code. The transmitter begins by taking electrical signals from the microphone or other input device and, using a component called a modulator, alters these signals into a form suitable for transmission - the oscillator generates the radio frequency (RF) carrier wave necessary for carrying the information. This modulation (remember modulation?) can vary; it might involve adjusting the base signal's amplitude

(AM), frequency (FM), or phase (PM) - the carrier wave - to encode the information. Once modulated, the signal is sent to an antenna, converted into a radio wave, and broadcast over the airwaves.

The receiver's job is to capture these radio waves using its antenna and then demodulate them, reversing the modulation process to extract the original information from the carrier wave. The receiver features a mixer, which takes the incoming RF signal and combines it with a locally generated signal to produce an intermediate frequency (IF) signal that is easier to process. The IF stage helps improve selectivity—the ability to discriminate between multiple signals—and sensitivity, the ability to detect weak signals. Following this stage, the signal undergoes filtering and amplification, preparing it for the demodulation stage, where the original audio or data signal is recovered.

This is achieved through a component called the demodulator. After demodulation, the signal is usually weak and needs to be amplified; this is where the receiver's amplifier steps in, boosting the signal to a level suitable for output to speakers, a headset, or other devices. The precision with which these tasks are performed directly affects the quality and clarity of the received transmission, making the design and condition of transmitters and receivers indispensable for effective communication.

Features

Reverse Function

The "reverse" function on a VHF/UHF transceiver listens to a repeater's input frequency rather than its output frequency. Typically, when using a repeater, you transmit on the repeater's input frequency and receive on its output frequency. Your transceiver temporarily switches to listening on the input frequency by activating the reverse function. This lets you hear the station transmitting directly to the repeater, bypassing the repeater's output signal.

T2B01: How is a VHF/UHF transceiver's "reverse" function used?

A. To reduce power output
B. To increase power output
C. To listen on a repeater's input frequency
D. To listen on a repeater's output frequency

This feature is handy for troubleshooting and improving communication. For example, suppose you hear a weak or distorted signal on the repeater's output. In that case, you can use the reverse function to check the input signal's quality. The issue might be with the repeater if the input signal is strong and clear. The reverse function can also help you establish direct contact with other stations during emergencies or high-traffic times, ensuring more reliable communication.

Utilizing Memory Channels and Scanning Functions on FM Transceivers

Many operators utilize memory channels and scanning functions to enhance the convenience and efficiency of operating an FM transceiver. Storing a favorite frequency or channel in a memory channel allows quick and easy access without manually tuning each time. This feature is useful for frequently used frequencies (funny turn of phrase), such as local repeaters, common simplex channels, or emergency communication frequencies. By storing these frequencies in memory, you can instantly switch to them with 'the push of a button,' saving time and ensuring you are always ready to communicate.

T4B04: What is a way to enable quick access to a favorite frequency or channel on your transceiver?

A. Enable the frequency offset
B. Store it in a memory channel
C. Enable the VOX
D. Use the scan mode to select the desired frequency

This is no different than setting your favorite radio stations in your car.

Additionally, the scanning function of an FM transceiver enhances the ability to monitor a range of frequencies. When the scanning function is activated, the transceiver <u>automatically tunes through a preset range of frequencies, pausing whenever it detects activity</u>. This lets operators quickly find active channels without manually tuning through each frequency. Scanning helps identify active conversations, monitor emergency frequencies, or check for open channels in a busy band. Together, memory channels and scanning functions streamline the operation of FM transceivers, making it easier for amateur radio operators to stay connected and informed.

T4B05: What does the scanning function of an FM transceiver do?

A. Checks incoming signal deviation
B. Prevents interference to nearby repeaters
C. Tunes through a range of frequencies to check for activity
D. Checks for messages left on a digital bulletin board

Multimode

<u>Having multiple receive bandwidth choices on a multimode transceiver provides a significant advantage in reducing noise and interference.</u> Each transmission mode, such as SSB, CW, or FM, benefits from a specific bandwidth that optimizes signal clarity and reception quality. For instance, SSB typically uses a narrower bandwidth (around 3 kHz) compared to FM, which uses a wider bandwidth (around 200 kHz). By selecting the appropriate bandwidth for the mode you are operating, you can minimize unwanted noise and interference, improving the overall quality of the received signal.

T4B08: What is the advantage of having multiple receive bandwidth choices on a multimode transceiver?

A. Permits monitoring several modes at once by selecting a separate filter for each mode
B. Permits noise or interference reduction by selecting a bandwidth matching the mode
C. Increases the number of frequencies that can be stored in memory
D. Increases the amount of offset between receive and transmit frequencies

This flexibility is particularly beneficial in crowded or noisy environments, where signals from adjacent channels or other sources can cause interference. By adjusting the receive bandwidth to match the mode, you can effectively filter out these unwanted signals, enhancing your ability to hear the intended transmission clearly.

The Transmitter

<u>The PTT (Push-To-Talk) input on a transceiver is a control that switches the device from receive mode to transmit mode when grounded.</u> When the operator presses the PTT button, it completes a circuit that grounds the PTT input, signaling the transceiver to stop receiving and start transmitting. This function facilitates communication, allowing operators to switch between listening and talking with a simple button push.

Remembering the function of the PTT input is straightforward if you remember it as the "talk button" on your radio. You activate the transmitter by grounding the PTT input, enabling your voice or data to be sent out over the airwaves.

T7A07: What is the function of a transceiver's PTT input?

A. Input for a key used to send CW
B. Switches transceiver from receive to transmit when grounded
C. Provides a transmit tuning tone when grounded
D. Input for a preamplifier tuning tone

An oscillator is a circuit that generates a signal at a specific frequency. It produces a continuous, periodic waveform—typically a sine or square wave—essential for various radio communication and electronics functions. Oscillators are the heart of many devices, providing the stable frequencies needed for signal generation, clock timing in digital circuits, and frequency synthesis in transceivers.

By generating precise and stable frequencies, oscillators ensure that communication systems operate accurately and reliably.

T7A05: What is the name of a circuit that generates a signal at a specific frequency?

A. Reactance modulator
B. Phase modulator
C. Low-pass filter
D. Oscillator

A mixer converts a signal from one frequency to another. It combines two input signals—typically, a signal from the oscillator and the incoming RF signal—to produce new signals at the sum and difference of the original frequencies. This process is known as frequency mixing or heterodyning.

Remember, a mixer's function is to "mix" frequencies to create new ones. This frequency conversion is vital for tuning and demodulating signals in communication systems.

T7A03: Which of the following is used to convert a signal from one frequency to another?

A. Phase splitter
B. Mixer
C. Inverter
D. Amplifier

A transverter is a device that converts the RF (radio frequency) input and output of a transceiver to another band. This allows a transceiver that operates on one frequency band to communicate on different frequency bands. Essentially, the transverter extends the frequency range of a transceiver, enabling it to access bands that it was not originally designed to cover. For example, a transverter can convert a 28 MHz (10-meter band) signal to 144 MHz (2-meter band) and vice versa.

Remembering the term transverter helps understand how amateur radio operators can expand their communication capabilities without needing multiple transceivers. Operators can use a transverter to explore new frequency bands and enhance flexibility in various communication scenarios. This concept is particularly valuable for operators who want to experiment with different bands or who need to adapt their equipment for specific operating conditions.

T7A06: What device converts the RF input and output of a transceiver to another band?

A. High-pass filter
B. Low-pass filter
C. Transverter
D. Phase converter

To enter a transceiver's operating frequency, you can use either the keypad or the VFO (Variable Frequency Oscillator) knob. The keypad allows for direct frequency input by typing in the desired frequency digits, which is particularly useful for quickly setting a specific frequency. This method provides precision and speed, making it easy to switch between frequencies without manually tuning through the band.

T4B02: Which of the following can be used to enter a transceiver's operating frequency?

A. The keypad or VFO knob
B. The CTCSS or DTMF encoder
C. The Automatic Frequency Control
D. All these choices are correct

Alternatively, the VFO knob allows you to adjust the frequency incrementally. By turning the knob, you can fine-tune the operating frequency up or down, which helps find the exact signal or make minor adjustments. The VFO knob is handy during live communication when you need to alter the frequency to improve reception or avoid interference slightly. Understanding how to use both the keypad and VFO knob ensures efficient and accurate frequency management on your transceiver.

The Receiver

Receiver sensitivity refers to a radio receiver's ability to detect the presence of weak signals. It is a critical parameter that determines how well a receiver can pick up signals, especially those faint or distant. A high-sensitivity receiver can detect lower-power signals, making it more effective in various communication scenarios, including long-distance or weak signal operations.

The term sensitivity is essential to remember because it directly impacts the performance of your radio equipment. This highlights the importance of having a sensitive receiver to ensure reliable communication, even under challenging conditions where signals might be weak or subject to interference.

T7A01: Which term describes the ability of a receiver to detect the presence of a signal?

A. Linearity
B. Sensitivity
C. Selectivity
D. Total Harmonic Distortion

Selectivity refers to the ability of a radio receiver to discriminate between multiple signals that are close in frequency. This means that a receiver with high selectivity can effectively isolate and process the desired signal while rejecting nearby unwanted signals or interference. Selectivity is core in crowded radio environments, where many signals are present within a narrow frequency range, such as during contests or in urban areas with numerous transmissions.

A highly selective receiver ensures clear and accurate reception by filtering out adjacent channel interference, allowing operators to focus on the intended communication.

T7A04: Which term describes the ability of a receiver to discriminate between multiple signals?

A. Discrimination ratio
B. Sensitivity
C. Selectivity
D. Harmonic distortion

Electronic Keyer

An electronic keyer is a device designed to assist amateur radio operators in manually sending Morse code. This device simplifies the process of creating the precise timing needed for dots and dashes in Morse code transmissions. When an operator presses the keyer paddles, the electronic keyer generates consistent and accurate Morse code signals, making sending clear and readable messages easier.

T4A12: What is an electronic keyer?

A. A device for switching antennas from transmit to receive
B. A device for voice-activated switching from receive to transmit
C. A device that assists in manual sending of Morse code
D. An interlock to prevent unauthorized use of a radio

Using an electronic keyer can significantly improve the efficiency and accuracy of Morse code communication. It helps to reduce the fatigue associated with manual keying. It ensures that the transmitted code is uniform and easy to decipher. For beginners and experienced operators alike, an electronic keyer is a valuable tool for enhancing Morse code proficiency and ensuring high-quality transmissions.

Power Amplifier

An RF power amplifier is a device that increases the transmitted output power from a transceiver. By boosting the strength of the radio frequency signal generated by the transceiver, an RF power amplifier enables the signal to travel farther and penetrate obstacles more effectively, thereby improving communication range and signal quality. This is particularly useful when higher power is needed to maintain a clear and reliable connection, such as long-distance communication or in environments with significant signal attenuation.

Remembering the role of an RF power amplifier is simple if you think of it as a "signal booster" for your transceiver. It takes the initial signal and amplifies it to a higher power level, making it more robust and capable of overcoming the challenges of distance and interference.

T7A10: What device increases the transmitted output power from a transceiver?

A. A voltage divider
B. An RF power amplifier
C. An impedance network
D. All these choices are correct

An RF preamplifier device will be installed between the antenna and the receiver to amplify weak signals before they enter the receiver. This amplification boosts the signal strength, making it easier for the receiver to process and decode the incoming transmission. By enhancing weak signals, an RF preamplifier improves the overall sensitivity and performance of the receiving system, allowing for clearer and more reliable reception of distant or faint signals.

To remember where an RF preamplifier is installed, consider it the "first stage" in the signal path from the antenna to the receiver. Placing the preamplifier right after the antenna ensures the signal is amplified at the earliest possible stage, minimizing noise and signal degradation.

T7A11: Where is an RF preamplifier installed?

A. Between the antenna and receiver
B. At the output of the transmitter power amplifier
C. Between the transmitter and the antenna tuner
D. At the output of the receiver audio amplifier

At this point, the technician's exam will ask particular questions about VHF.

Understanding the SSB/CW-FM Switch on a VHF Power Amplifier

The SSB/CW-FM switch on a VHF power amplifier allows the user to set the amplifier for proper operation according to the selected mode of transmission: Single Sideband (SSB), Continuous Wave (CW), or Frequency Modulation (FM).

Each mode has different characteristics and power requirements, and this switch ensures that the amplifier adjusts its operating parameters to match the mode being used. For instance, SSB signals require linear amplification to preserve the integrity of the waveform. In contrast, FM signals can benefit from higher power efficiency without distortion.

Think of the SSB/CW-FM switch as a mode selector that optimizes the amplifier's performance for the specific type of signal you are transmitting. Setting the amplifier correctly helps prevent signal distortion and ensures efficient and reliable operation.

T7A09: What is the function of the SSB/CW-FM switch on a VHF power amplifier?

A. Change the mode of the transmitted signal
B. Set the amplifier for proper operation in the selected mode
C. Change the frequency range of the amplifier to operate in the proper segment of the band
D. Reduce the received signal noise

Wiring it Together

Wires for Transceiver's DC Power Connection

Using short, heavy-gauge wires for a transceiver's DC power connection is best for minimizing voltage drop when transmitting. Voltage drop occurs when there is resistance in the wires connecting the power source to the transceiver. This resistance causes a reduction in voltage, which can lead to decreased performance or even malfunction of the transceiver, especially under high current demands during transmission. Heavy-gauge wires have lower resistance than thinner wires, which helps maintain the voltage levels at the transceiver.

T4A03: Why are short, heavy-gauge wires used for a transceiver's DC power connection?

A. To minimize voltage drop when transmitting
B. To provide a good counterpoise for the antenna
C. To avoid RF interference
D. All these choices are correct

In general, when wiring components together in a radio setup, it's essential to consider the quality and specifications of the wiring. Shorter wires reduce resistance and minimize potential interference and signal loss. Additionally, ensuring secure and solid connections between components helps maintain stable and reliable power delivery. Proper wiring practices, such as using suitable wire gauges and lengths, ensure optimal performance and safety in amateur radio operations.

Chapter 16

Antenna Basics

ANTENNAS ARE THE UNSUNG heroes of ham radio; they are the interface that bridges the gap between the electronic world inside your radio and the vast expanse of the airwaves. Understanding how antennas work is akin to understanding how a plant turns sunlight into energy—both are about converting one form of energy into another more usable form.

The Role of Antennas

Antennas are key pieces of equipment in the transmission and reception of radio waves. They come in various shapes and sizes, each designed for specific frequencies and types of operations.

For transmitting, the antenna converts the RF electrical signals into electromagnetic waves, efficiently radiating them into the atmosphere. For receiving, the process reverses, with the antenna capturing electromagnetic waves and converting them back into RF electrical signals for the receiver to process.

The effectiveness of an antenna is often measured by its gain and directivity; gain refers to its ability to focus energy in a particular direction, and directivity is its ability to receive energy from a specific direction. Understanding these properties helps you select a suitable antenna for your needs, whether for local communications on the VHF and UHF bands or for chasing distant contacts on the HF bands.

Types of Antennas

The most common antennas you might encounter or consider as a Technician licensee include dipoles, verticals, and beam antennas. Each type has characteristics suitable for different radio activities and environments.

Several factors should guide your decision when choosing an antenna. The space you have available is one of the most vital constraints. A large beam antenna might offer excellent long-distance capabilities. Still, having only a tiny rooftop or yard will make it impractical. Similarly, your budget is an essential consideration. While spending much on sophisticated antenna systems is possible, many practical antennas can be constructed with inexpensive materials. Your desired communication range also influences your choice; a beam antenna might be necessary for worldwide communications, but a simple dipole might suffice for chatting with fellow hams in your region.

Dipoles

Dipoles are perhaps the most widely used type of antenna in amateur radio. They consist of two conductive elements, usually metal rods or wires, that are equal in length and oriented in a straight line, with the feedline connected to the center. The term "dipole" means "two poles," referring to the two elements of the antenna.

You will also commonly hear the term 'half-wave dipole.' A half-wave dipole is a specific type of dipole antenna where the total length of the antenna is half the wavelength of the frequency it is designed to transmit or receive. "Half-wave" refers to this specific length relative to the wavelength.

For example, a half-wave dipole for a 10-meter band would be approximately 5 meters long, with each element being about 2.5 meters.

In summary, all half-wave dipoles are dipole antennas, but not all dipole antennas are half-wave dipoles.

Dipole antennas are generally popular because of their straightforward design, ease of construction (you need two pieces of wire, some basic tools, and a place to set them up), and effective performance.

They produce a broadside radiation pattern, meaning they radiate most of the signal energy perpendicular to the length of the antenna. This pattern provides good coverage and is ideal for many applications.

Understanding the Radiation Pattern of Dipole Antennas

Dipole antennas produce a broadside radiation pattern, which means they radiate most of the signal energy perpendicular to the length of the antenna. Imagine the dipole antenna as a straight line; the most substantial signal radiation occurs at right angles (90 degrees) to this line, both above and below the antenna, rather than off the ends. This directional pattern is often described as doughnut-shaped when visualized in three dimensions, with the dipole antenna at the center of the doughnut hole.

A simple dipole antenna oriented parallel to the Earth's surface is known as a horizontally polarized antenna. Polarization is a key concept in antenna theory that refers to the orientation of the electric field of the radio waves transmitted or received by an antenna. In the case of a horizontally polarized dipole antenna, the electric field oscillates horizontally, meaning that the electric field oscillation is aligned with the horizon. This orientation is achieved when the dipole elements—usually metal rods or wires—are placed horizontally.

The horizontal polarization of an antenna has specific implications for signal transmission and reception. The most important aspect is the antenna's radiation pattern. A horizontally polarized dipole antenna exhibits a broadside radiation pattern, where the strongest signals are radiated in directions perpendicular to the antenna. This pattern creates two primary lobes of radiation, one on each side of the antenna, with minimal radiation along the axis of the antenna itself. This characteristic makes horizontally polarized dipole antennas highly effective for general communication needs, as they can provide a wide coverage area.

For example, when a dipole antenna is mounted horizontally, it radiates efficiently in all directions perpendicular to its length. This is particularly advantageous for amateur radio operators, broadcasters, and receiving antennas. In amateur radio, horizontal polarization is often used for long-distance communication, as it tends to interact more favorably with the Earth's ionosphere, enabling signals to travel farther distances through a process known as skywave propagation. Additionally, many amateur radio operators prefer horizontally polarized antennas for their ability to reject vertically polarized noise, such as that from electrical equipment, which can interfere with clear communication.

Moreover, understanding the concept of polarization is crucial when designing or selecting an antenna for a specific application. Matching the polarization of the transmitting and receiving antennas maximizes signal strength and clarity, as mismatched polarizations can lead to signal loss. For instance, if a horizontally polarized antenna transmits a signal, a horizontally polarized receiving antenna will pick up that signal more effectively than a vertically polarized one.

To summarize, a horizontally polarized dipole antenna is a versatile and widely used design in radio communications. Its horizontal polarization and broadside radiation pattern make it ideal for various applications, from amateur radio to broadcasting, providing robust signal coverage and enhanced communication effectiveness. By understanding these principles, users can optimize their antenna setups to achieve the best possible performance in their specific use cases.

T9A03: Which of the following describes a simple dipole oriented parallel to the Earth's surface?

A. A ground-wave antenna
B. A horizontally polarized antenna
C. A traveling-wave antenna
D. A vertically polarized antenna

T9A10: In which direction does a half-wave dipole antenna radiate the strongest signal?

A. Equally in all directions
B. Off the ends of the antenna
C. In the direction of the feed line
D. Broadside to the antenna

Resonant Frequency and Dipole Antenna Length

The resonant frequency of a dipole antenna is the frequency at which it naturally resonates and efficiently radiates signals (basically, the frequency at which it works best).

This means an antenna can transmit and receive radio waves most effectively at this frequency, with minimal energy loss. When an antenna operates at its resonant frequency, its electrical length matches the signal's wavelength, allowing optimal energy transfer between the antenna and the air.

In practical terms, if an antenna is designed to have a resonant frequency of 14 MHz, it will perform best when transmitting or receiving signals at that frequency. This concept is fundamental for ensuring effective communication, as using an antenna at its resonant frequency maximizes signal strength and clarity. Understanding resonant frequency helps design and tune antennas to operate efficiently for the desired frequency band.

This frequency is inversely related to the length of the antenna. Remember back: higher frequency = shorter wavelength.

Therefore, shortening a dipole antenna increases its resonant frequency. This happens because the shorter the antenna, the higher the frequency it will resonate, as its physical length becomes more in tune with the shorter wavelength of higher frequencies.

To remember this, think of a guitar string: a shorter string produces a higher pitch. Similarly, a shorter dipole antenna resonates at a higher frequency. Understanding that shortening a dipole antenna increases its resonant frequency will help you recall this concept for your exam, highlighting the importance of antenna length in determining the operating frequency range of your antenna system.

T9A05: Which of the following increases the resonant frequency of a dipole antenna?

A. Lengthening it
B. Inserting coils in series with radiating wires
C. Shortening it
D. Adding capacitive loading to the ends of the radiating wires

Dipole Math Time:

T9A09: What is the approximate length, in inches, of a half-wavelength 6-meter dipole antenna?

A. 6
B. 50
C. 112
D. 236

To calculate the length of a half-wavelength dipole antenna, you can use the formula:

$$Length\ (feet) = \frac{468}{Frequency\ (MHz)}$$

For the curious, the constant 468 is derived from the speed of light and the relationship between wavelength and frequency in free space.

For a 6-meter band, the frequency is typically around 50 MHz. Plugging this into the formula gives:

$$Length\ (feet) = \frac{468}{50} = 9.36\ feet$$

To convert this length to inches:

$$Length\ (feet) = 9.36\ x\ 12 = 112.32\ inches$$

Therefore, the approximate length of a half-wavelength 6-meter dipole antenna is about 112.32 inches. This calculation helps ensure that the antenna is adequately sized to resonate at the desired frequency, providing optimal performance for communication on the 6-meter band.

Ok, but wait. We can do this easier, too. Let's estimate.

First, a 6-meter dipole, and we need "half-wavelength." Half of 6 meters is 3 meters.

Next, we know that 1 meter is approximately equal to 1 yard, 3 feet, or 36 inches.

The question asks for inches, so we multiply 3 meters by 36 inches to get 108.

But 108 isn't the correct answer or even a possible answer on the test. Right, but remembering our study strategy, we look at all the possible answers and eliminate the wrong ones. No other answer is anywhere close to 108 except 112. There you go! There is no hard math involved. But you have also seen the actual formula to figure this out.

Vertical

Vertical antennas are a popular choice in radio communication due to their omnidirectional radiation pattern and compact design. As their name suggests, these antennas stand upright (like a flagpole) and radiate radio waves equally in all horizontal directions. This makes them highly effective for mobile and base station use, especially in areas with limited space, like small backyards or city apartments.

Have you ever seen a skyscraper with protruding vertical antennas on the top? It's that simple!

A common example is the quarter-wavelength vertical antenna. For the 146 MHz frequency band, a quarter-wavelength vertical antenna is approximately 19.2 inches tall (an interesting example; let's look at the math below). These antennas are easy to install and require minimal space, making them ideal for vehicles or locations with limited space. The ground plane or surface on which the antenna is mounted acts as a reflective surface, enhancing the radiation pattern and efficiency of the antenna.

Vertical antennas are favored for their simplicity, efficiency, and ability to provide reliable communication over a wide area. Understanding their operation and applications can help you choose a suitable antenna, ensuring optimal performance and coverage.

Quarter-Wavelength Vertical Antenna Math

T9A08: What is the approximate length, in inches, of a quarter-wavelength vertical antenna for 146 MHz?

A. 112
B. 50
C. 19
D. 12

Start with our favorite formula. It's our favorite formula because it has frequency and length. The test gives us frequency and wanting length (in inches) in the question.

$$\text{meters} = \frac{300}{\text{Frequency (MHz)}}$$

- Step 1) 300 divided by 146 MHZ = 2.05 (let's call it 2.0).

  - We could have also estimated it again by saying 300 divided by 150 MHz (close to 146 MHz), which gives us an estimated answer of 2.

- Step 2) We have 2 meters now, and the question concerns a 'quarter-wavelength' vertical antenna.

  - 2 meters divided by 4 (a quarter equals 4) = 0.5 meters.

- Step 3) We take our 0.5 meters and convert it into inches (because that's what the question wants).

  - 0.5 meters multiplied by 36 inches (1 meter is approximately 1 yard or 36 inches) = 18 inches (half of 36 is 18).

- Step 4) Again, thinking critically about the possible answers, only one is close to our estimate of 18.

  - The correct answer is 'C', 19 inches.

This height ensures the antenna resonates effectively at 146 MHz, allowing for optimal signal transmission and reception. Remembering this calculation helps you design and tune antennas for specific frequencies, ensuring efficient communication.

In summary, the main dimension of concern for a quarter-wave vertical antenna is its height, which is one-quarter of the wavelength at the operating frequency. The width and length are typically not significant factors, as the antenna's functionality is primarily determined by its vertical length.

Beam / Yagi (Directional)

A beam antenna is a directional antenna that concentrates signals in one specific direction, significantly enhancing radio waves' transmission and reception. Compared to omnidirectional antennas, which radiate signals equally in all directions, a beam antenna can achieve higher gain by focusing the signal. This directional focus allows for better long-distance communication and reduced interference from unwanted sources, making beam antennas particularly useful in amateur radio operations, television broadcasting, and other applications where signal clarity and range are critical.

Like the popular Yagi antenna, beam antennas have a central part that sends and receives signals, called the driven element. They also have extra parts that help focus the energy in specific directions. Looking at the image, you see the energy is focused in one direction. This makes them more powerful and able to reach farther distances than simpler antennas. These antennas are highly directional, transmitting and receiving signals in one direction. This focus allows them to go farther than non-directional antennas like dipoles or verticals. However, they are more complex to build and require more space and a rotator to turn them toward the signal you are trying to receive or transmit.

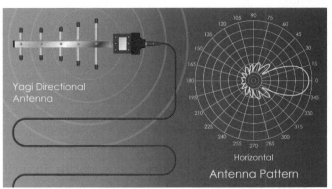
Focused in One Direction

T9A01: What is a beam antenna?

A. An antenna built from aluminum I-beams
B. An omnidirectional antenna invented by Clarence Beam
C. An antenna that concentrates signals in one direction
D. An antenna that reverses the phase of received signals

And because of the greater concentration...

T9A06: Which of the following types of antenna offers the greatest gain?

A. 5/8 wave vertical
B. Isotropic
C. J pole
D. Yagi

Remember that **gain = effectiveness.**

And one more time...

Antenna gain refers to the increase in signal strength that an antenna provides in a specified direction compared to a reference antenna, typically an isotropic radiator or a simple dipole antenna.

This measurement indicates how effective an antenna is at directing radio waves in a particular direction, enhancing both the transmission and reception of signals. Higher gain antennas focus the radio energy more narrowly, similar to how a flashlight concentrates light, which results in stronger signals in the desired direction and improved communication range.

Remembering the concept of antenna gain is simple if you consider it the antenna's ability to "boost" the signal strength in a specific direction. This directed focus makes the antenna more efficient at sending and receiving signals where they are needed most, reducing interference from unwanted directions.

T9A11: What is antenna gain?

A. The additional power that is added to the transmitter power
B. The additional power that is required in the antenna when transmitting on a higher frequency
C. The increase in signal strength in a specified direction compared to a reference antenna
D. The increase in impedance on receive or transmit compared to a reference antenna

Handheld Radios

The short, flexible antennas supplied with most handheld radio transceivers, often referred to as "rubber duck" antennas, have the disadvantage of low efficiency compared to full-sized quarter-wave antennas.

Due to their compact size, these short antennas cannot radiate signals as effectively as longer, quarter-wave antennas, which are better matched to the wavelength of the transmitted signals. This reduced efficiency means less transmitted power is effectively radiated into the air, leading to weaker signal strength and reduced communication range.

Remembering this disadvantage is straightforward if you consider the trade-off between convenience and performance. While the short, flexible antenna is portable and easy to carry, its low efficiency can limit the effectiveness of your handheld radio, especially in challenging communication environments.

T9A04: What is a disadvantage of the short, flexible antenna supplied with most handheld radio transceivers, compared to a full-sized quarter-wave antenna?

A. It has low efficiency
B. It transmits only circularly polarized signals
C. It is mechanically fragile
D. All these choices are correct

For this next question, they are really throwing you a specific situation. But think about the general principles involved. In this exam question, you have a handheld VHF radio and are sitting in a metal or near-metal vehicle.

T9A07: What is a disadvantage of using a handheld VHF transceiver with a flexible antenna inside a vehicle?

A. Signal strength is reduced due to the shielding effect of the vehicle
B. The bandwidth of the antenna will decrease, increasing SWR
C. The SWR might decrease, decreasing the signal strength
D. All these choices are correct

Using a handheld VHF transceiver with a flexible antenna inside a vehicle has the disadvantage of reduced signal strength. This reduction occurs due to the shielding effect of the vehicle's metal body, which can block or reflect radio waves. The vehicle acts like a partial Faraday cage, preventing radio signals from reaching the antenna efficiently. This results in weaker transmissions and reception, making communication less reliable when using the transceiver inside the vehicle.

That's why we use car-mounted, usually magnet, antennas on the outside of our vehicle!

Here is another weirdly specific question. Think about the overall concepts being asked. Compare each answer to the question. What in the world are they getting at?

T9A12: What is an advantage of a 5/8 wavelength whip antenna for VHF or UHF mobile service?

A. It has more gain than a 1/4-wavelength antenna
B. It radiates at a very high angle
C. It eliminates distortion caused by reflected signals
D. It has 10 times the power gain of a 1/4 wavelength whip

Answers B, C, and D make little sense because they say nothing specific about a 5/8 wavelength whip antenna.

Answer 'A' discusses gain. Gain refers to the antenna's ability to focus the radio signal in a particular direction, which enhances the effective radiated power and improves signal strength.

A 5/8 wavelength antenna provides more gain than a 1/4 wavelength antenna <u>because its longer length</u> allows it to <u>focus the radiated energy more effectively in the horizontal plane</u>. This increased focus directs more signal energy outward rather than upward or downward, resulting in a stronger and more efficient signal over longer distances.

In contrast, a 1/4 wavelength antenna has a broader radiation pattern that disperses energy more evenly in all directions, including upward and downward, leading to lower gain and reduced range.

This makes the 5/8 wavelength antenna particularly advantageous for mobile and terrestrial communication, where a robust and horizontally directed signal is necessary for maintaining reliable connections over varying distances and terrain.

Antenna Loading

Antenna loading is a technique for <u>making antennas resonate at desired frequencies without increasing their physical length</u>. This is key when space constraints prevent the use of full-sized antennas. By <u>inserting inductors or capacitors</u>, the electrical properties of the antenna can be modified to achieve resonance at specific frequencies, enhancing performance in limited spaces.

In many practical applications, especially in mobile and portable setups, full-sized antennas are impractical due to their length. "For instance, a half-wave dipole for the 80-meter band must be approximately 40 meters long (using easy math for approximation – as a Technician, you have access to the 80-meter band only for CW from 3.525 to 3.600 MHz). Antenna loading solves this <u>by electrically lengthening the antenna</u>, allowing it to resonate at the desired frequency without needing excessive physical length.

One standard method is inductive loading, where inductors (coils) are inserted into the antenna's radiating elements. This creates reactance, making the antenna behave as if it were longer. Another method is capacitive loading, adding capacitive hats or elements to increase capacitance and <u>effectively lengthen the antenna electrically.</u> These techniques benefit mobile and portable antennas, ensuring they operate efficiently on lower frequencies without requiring large physical sizes.

T9A02: Which of the following describes a type of antenna loading?

A. Electrically lengthening by inserting inductors in radiating elements
B. Inserting a resistor in the radiating portion of the antenna to make it resonant
C. Installing a spring in the base of a mobile vertical antenna to make it more flexible
D. Strengthening the radiating elements of a beam antenna to better resist wind damage

Be careful when answering. You might look at 'B' and consider it.

Inserting a resistor in the radiating portion of an antenna to make it resonant is incorrect because resistors do not create resonance. Resonance in antennas is achieved through reactive components, such as inductors (which provide inductance) or capacitors (which provide capacitance). These <u>reactive components store and release energy</u> to enhance the antenna's ability to resonate at specific frequencies.

<u>Resistors, however, dissipate energy</u> as heat and do not contribute to the reactive properties needed for resonance. Adding a resistor to an antenna would reduce efficiency by converting part of the signal energy into heat, weakening the transmitted or received signal. This would degrade the antenna's overall performance rather than improve it.

In summary, while inductors and capacitors can tune an antenna to the desired resonant frequency, resistors cannot. They serve a different purpose by limiting current and dissipating power, which does not help achieve resonance. Understanding this distinction is key to designing efficient and effective antennas.

Antenna Polarization

Antenna polarization is a fundamental concept in radio communication that refers to the <u>orientation of the electric field of the radio wave radiated by the antenna</u>. An antenna's polarization can significantly affect the performance and clarity of the transmitted and received signals. Understanding and selecting the appropriate polarization for your antenna setup is important for optimizing communication efficiency and reducing signal losses.

This section will explore the different types of antenna polarization, their applications, and how they impact radio communication. Whether setting up a simple dipole antenna or a complex array, knowing how to manage antenna polarization will enhance your ability to establish precise and reliable connections.

Understanding Antenna Polarization

Antenna polarization refers to the orientation of the electric field of the radiated radio wave relative to the Earth's surface. The two primary types of polarization are vertical and horizontal.

- **Vertical Polarization**: The electric field is <u>perpendicular to the Earth's surface</u>. This type of polarization is commonly used for mobile and handheld radio communications because vertically polarized antennas are often more practical for vehicles and portable devices. This type of antenna is straight "up and down" compared to the Earth. So, it's vertically polarized.

- **Horizontal Polarization**: The electric field is <u>parallel to the Earth's surface</u>. This polarization is typically used for fixed-station communications, such as television broadcasting and point-to-point radio links. Horizontal antennas (for example, a dipole) are antennas that are "sideways" compared to the Earth. So, they are horizontally polarized.

  - <u>Horizontal polarization is usually used for long-distance CW (Continuous Wave) and SSB (Single Sideband) contacts on the VHF and UHF bands</u>. This preference arises because horizontally polarized signals tend to suffer less from ground reflections and multipath interference, which can degrade signal quality and reliability over long distances. Horizontal polarization is also advantageous for reducing man-made, vertically polarized noise.

T3A03: What antenna polarization is normally used for long-distance CW and SSB contacts on the VHF and UHF bands?

A. Right-hand circular
B. Left-hand circular
C. Horizontal
D. Vertical

In practical terms, horizontal polarization helps ensure clearer and more stable communication for long-distance contacts, making it the standard choice for serious VHF and UHF operators aiming for maximum range and signal integrity.

Mismatched Polarizations

Choosing the correct polarization for your antenna matters because mismatched polarization between transmitting and receiving antennas can significantly reduce the strength or signal loss. For instance, if a vertically polarized antenna is transmitted to a horizontally polarized receiving antenna, the signal strength can be reduced considerably. Therefore, ensuring that both the transmitting and receiving antennas share the same polarization can greatly enhance signal clarity and strength.

T3A04: What happens when antennas at opposite ends of a VHF or UHF line of sight radio link are not using the same polarization?

A. The modulation sidebands might become inverted
B. Received signal strength is reduced
C. Signals have an echo effect
D. Nothing significant will happen

By understanding and properly implementing antenna polarization, you can optimize your radio communications, ensuring that your signals are transmitted and received with maximum efficiency and minimal interference.

Elliptical Polarization

Elliptical Polarization and Its Impact on Transmission

Elliptical polarization occurs when radio waves are propagated by the ionosphere. The electric field of the waves rotates and traces an elliptical shape as they travel, resulting in a signal that is not purely vertically or horizontally polarized but a combination of both. The key advantage of elliptically polarized signals is their versatility in terms of antenna orientation.

Due to elliptical polarization, vertically or horizontally polarized antennas can be used effectively for transmission or reception. This flexibility simplifies the setup and improves the chances of establishing reliable communication, as the signal can be received by antennas with different polarizations. For amateur radio operators, understanding elliptical polarization helps explain why transmissions via the ionosphere are less dependent on matching the exact polarization between the transmitting and receiving antennas.

T3A09: Which of the following results from the fact that signals propagated by the ionosphere are elliptically polarized?

A. Digital modes are unusable
B. Either vertically or horizontally polarized antennas may be used for transmission or reception
C. FM voice is unusable
D. Both the transmitting and receiving antennas must be of the same polarization

Final Thoughts on Antennas

For those inclined towards DIY projects, building your antenna can be a rewarding endeavor that deepens your understanding of radio physics and propagation. Simple projects like constructing a dipole or a vertical can be accomplished with basic materials like wire, insulators, and some coaxial cables.

These projects save money and offer the satisfaction of communicating through the equipment you have built yourself. Online forums and amateur radio clubs often provide plans and guidance, making these projects accessible even to those with minimal experience building radio equipment.

Chapter 17

Feedline Basics

A FEEDLINE IS A cable or transmission line that connects a radio transmitter or receiver to an antenna.

Its primary function is to transfer radio frequency (RF) signals between the radio equipment and the antenna with minimal power loss. Feedlines are essential in any radio communication system, ensuring that the transmitter's maximum signal power reaches the antenna and that signals received are efficiently delivered to the receiver.

Feedlines come in various types, including coaxial cables (coax), twin-lead, and ladder lines, each with specific characteristics and suitable applications. Coaxial cables, for example, are widely used due to their ease of installation and good shielding properties, which help prevent signal loss and interference.

Standing Waves

A standing wave occurs when two radio waves of the same frequency and amplitude travel in opposite directions along a transmission line, such as a feedline connected to an antenna, and interfere with each other.

These waves interfere with each other, creating points of constructive interference (where the waves add together) and points of destructive interference (where the waves cancel each other out), resulting in a pattern of fixed nodes (points of no movement) and antinodes (points of maximum movement) along the line. This pattern appears stationary, hence the name "standing wave."

Standing Wave Ratio (SWR)

Standing Wave Ratio (SWR) is a measure used to evaluate power transfer efficiency from a radio transmitter to an antenna. It indicates how well the antenna is matched to the transmission line (feedline) and transmitter, which is important for effective communication.

When a radio transmitter sends a signal to an antenna, the goal is to radiate all the power out as radio waves. However, suppose there is a mismatch between the impedance (opposition to the current flow) of the transmission line (feedline) and the antenna. In that case, some of the power gets reflected back toward the transmitter, creating standing waves along the transmission line.

The measurement for standing waves is the <u>standing wave ratio, which measures how well a load is matched to a transmission line.</u>

T9B12: What is the standing wave ratio (SWR)?

A. A measure of how well a load is matched to a transmission line
B. The ratio of amplifier power output to input
C. The transmitter efficiency ratio
D. An indication of the quality of your station's ground connection

A high Standing Wave Ratio (SWR) means that a lot of power is reflected back toward the transmitter instead of being radiated by the antenna, leading to inefficient operation and potential equipment damage. Understanding and minimizing standing waves helps ensure efficient and effective radio communication.

- **Ideal SWR (1:1)**: This means that there is perfect impedance matching, and all the power is transferred to the antenna without reflection.

  - **Now, there are ideals and reality**: any measurement under 2.0:1 is ok to use (you can try to improve it, but it's ok). And if you ever do get a 1:1 reading, take a picture of it and post it online. It's a rare site!

- **High SWR (e.g., 2:1 or higher)**: This indicates an impedance mismatch, meaning some power is being reflected back, resulting in less efficient transmission and potential damage to the transmitter over time.

T7C04: What reading on an SWR meter indicates a perfect impedance match between the antenna and the feed line?

A. 50:50
B. Zero
C. 1:1
D. Full Scale

T7C06: What does an SWR reading of 4:1 indicate?

A. loss of -4 dB
B. Good impedance match
C. gain of +4 dB
D. Impedance mismatch

Measuring the Standing Wave Ratio (SWR) involves using a directional wattmeter. A directional wattmeter measures the power of radio frequency (RF) signals traveling through a transmission line.

T7C08: Which instrument can be used to determine SWR?

A. Voltmeter
B. Ohmmeter
C. Iambic pentameter
D. Directional wattmeter

Unlike a standard wattmeter, a directional wattmeter can differentiate between forward power (the power sent from the transmitter to the antenna) and reflected power (the power that bounces back from the antenna due to impedance mismatches).

Why It Matters

Understanding SWR is vital for beginners because it helps tune and adjust the antenna for optimal performance. A low SWR ensures the antenna radiates most of the transmitted power, improving communication effectiveness (reduced signal loss). Regularly checking and maintaining a good SWR can also prevent potential damage to the radio equipment due to excessive reflected power and heat.

T9B01: What is a benefit of low SWR?

A. Reduced television interference
B. Reduced signal loss
C. Less antenna wear
D. All these choices are correct

T7C07: What happens to power lost in a feed line?

A. It increases the SWR
B. It is radiated as harmonics
C. It is converted into heat
D. It distorts the signal

Simple Explanation

Think of SWR as a health check for your antenna system. A perfect SWR of 1:1 means your antenna system is in great shape, efficiently transmitting all the power it receives. A higher SWR value indicates that your system needs adjustment to minimize power loss, which results in signal loss.

You can maintain an efficient and reliable antenna system by monitoring the SWR and making necessary adjustments.

SWR Meter

When selecting an accessory SWR meter, it's essential to consider the frequency and power level at which the measurements will be made. Different SWR meters are designed to operate optimally within specific frequency ranges, such as HF, VHF, or UHF bands. Using an SWR meter outside its intended frequency range can lead to inaccurate readings, which can affect the efficiency of your antenna system and potentially harm your equipment.

T4A02: Which of the following should be considered when selecting an accessory SWR meter?

A. The frequency and power level at which the measurements will be made
B. The distance that the meter will be located from the antenna
C. The types of modulation being used at the station
D. All these choices are correct

Your transmitter's power level should match the SWR meter's power handling capability. Suppose the SWR meter is not rated for the power level of your transmissions. In that case, it can be damaged or provide unreliable measurements. Therefore, ensuring that your SWR meter is suitable for the frequencies and power levels you intend to use will help maintain accurate readings and protect your SWR meter and radio equipment.

Erratic Changes in SWR

Erratic changes in your Standing Wave Ratio (SWR) are often caused by loose connections in the antenna or feed line (those pesky things!). When connections are not secure, they can introduce intermittent contact or variable resistance, leading to fluctuations in the impedance seen by the transmitter. This causes the SWR to change unpredictably as the match between the antenna system and the transmission line becomes unstable.

For beginners, it's important to remember that maintaining tight and secure connections in your antenna setup is vital for stable and efficient operation. Loose connections can lead to poor performance and potential damage to your equipment due to reflected power. Regularly inspecting and ensuring all connections are secure can prevent erratic SWR changes and provide reliable communication. This concept is important for both practical operation and the exam.

T9B09: What can cause erratic changes in SWR?

A. Local thunderstorm
B. Loose connection in the antenna or feed line
C. Over-modulation
D. Overload from a strong local station

Solid State Transmitters

A solid-state transmitter uses electronic components, such as transistors, diodes, and integrated circuits, instead of vacuum tubes to amplify and generate radio frequency signals. These modern components offer advantages, including greater reliability, efficiency, and compactness.

Key Features of Solid-State Transmitters:

1. **Transistor-Based Amplification**: Solid-state transmitters use transistors for signal amplification. Transistors are more durable and energy-efficient than vacuum tubes. They can handle high power levels and are less prone to failure, making them ideal for continuous operation.

2. **Compact and Lightweight**: Because they rely on solid-state components, these transmitters are generally more compact and lighter than their vacuum tube counterparts. This makes them suitable for mobile and portable applications and environments with limited space.

3. **Efficiency and Performance**: Solid-state transmitters are known for their high efficiency in converting electrical power into radio frequency power, resulting in less heat generation and lower cooling requirements. They also provide consistent performance with fewer maintenance needs.

4. **Protective Features**: These transmitters often come with built-in protective features, such as automatic power reduction when SWR increases, to safeguard the internal components from damage due to impedance mismatches. Most solid-state transmitters automatically reduce the output power when the SWR (Standing Wave Ratio) increases beyond a certain level to protect the output amplifier transistors.

   ○ High SWR indicates a significant impedance mismatch between the transmitter and the antenna, causing a large portion of the transmitted power to be reflected back into the transmitter. This reflected power can generate excessive heat and stress the transistors, potentially leading to damage or failure.

- The transmitter limits the reflected power amount by reducing output power, safeguarding its internal components.

A solid-state transmitter uses modern electronic components to generate and amplify radio signals, offering reliability, efficiency, and size advantages. Understanding the benefits and features of solid-state transmitters highlights their importance in contemporary radio communication, ensuring efficient and dependable operation.

T7C05: Why do most solid-state transmitters reduce output power as SWR increases beyond a certain level?

A. To protect the output amplifier transistors
B. To comply with FCC rules on spectral purity
C. Because power supplies cannot supply enough current at high SWR
D. To lower the SWR on the transmission line

Coaxial Cable

Coaxial cable, commonly called "coax," is a transmission line that carries radio frequency (RF) signals from a transmitter to an antenna or from an antenna to a receiver. Due to its efficiency and ease of use, it is widely used in various communication systems, including amateur radio, television broadcasting, and internet connections.

Structure of Coaxial Cable

1. **Inner Conductor**: The central wire that carries the RF signal. It can be solid or stranded and is typically made of copper for good conductivity.

2. **Dielectric Insulator** surrounds the inner conductor, providing insulation and maintaining the spacing between it and the outer shield.

3. **Outer Conductor (Shield)**: A braided or solid metallic shield surrounding the dielectric insulator. It serves two primary purposes: providing a signal return path and shielding the inner conductor from external electromagnetic interference (EMI).

4. **Outer Jacket**: The protective outer layer that covers the shield. It protects the cable from physical damage and environmental factors.

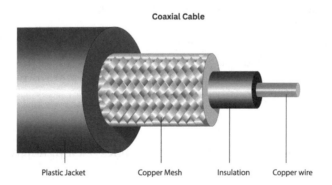

Coaxial Cable

Plastic Jacket   Copper Mesh   Insulation   Copper wire

Advantages of Coaxial Cable

- **Good Shielding**: The outer conductor effectively shields the inner conductor from external interference, ensuring a clean signal.

- ○ Shielded Wire: <u>Shielded wire is used in electrical and electronic systems to prevent the coupling of unwanted signals to or from the wire</u>. This shielding is typically made of a conductive layer surrounding the inner conductor, such as braided copper or aluminum foil. The shield is a barrier against electromagnetic interference (EMI) and radio frequency interference (RFI), which can distort or disrupt the wires' signals. For beginners, consider shielded wire a protective shield for the signals traveling through the wire.

T6D03: Which of the following is a reason to use shielded wire?

A. To decrease the resistance of DC power connections
B. To increase the current carrying capability of the wire
C. To prevent coupling of unwanted signals to or from the wire
D. To couple the wire to other signals

- • **Ease of Installation**: <u>Coax is flexible and relatively easy to install</u>, making it a convenient choice for many applications.

- • **Impedance Consistency**: Standard coaxial cables have a consistent impedance (typically 50 ohms), for minimizing signal reflections and ensuring efficient power transfer.

  - ○ The <u>most common coaxial cable impedance used in amateur radio is 50 ohms.</u> This standard impedance is chosen because it balances power handling capability and low signal loss, making it ideal for various radio frequencies and applications. Using a 50-ohm coaxial cable ensures that the transmission line impedance matches the typical impedance of most radio transmitters and antennas. This is vital for minimizing signal reflections and maximizing power transfer.

  - ○ For beginners, think of impedance as the "resistance" the cable offers to the flow of the radio signal. Matching this impedance correctly helps to ensure that the maximum amount of power reaches the antenna, leading to more efficient transmission and clearer communication.

Understanding coaxial cable is essential for anyone involved in radio communications. It plays a vital role in connecting radios to antennas and ensuring efficient signal transmission.

T9B03: Why is coaxial cable the most common feed line for amateur radio antenna systems?

A. It is easy to use and requires few special installation considerations
B. It has less loss than any other type of feed line
C. It can handle more power than any other type of feed line
D. It is less expensive than any other type of feed line

T9B02: What is the most common impedance of coaxial cables used in amateur radio?

A. 8 ohms
B. 50 ohms
C. 600 ohms
D. 12 ohms

Signal Loss in Coaxial Cables at Higher Frequencies

As the frequency of a signal in coaxial cable increases, the loss also increases. This means that higher frequency signals experience more significant attenuation (the reduction in the strength or amplitude of a signal as it travels through a wire) as they travel through the cable.

The primary reason for this increased loss is the skin effect, where higher-frequency currents tend to flow near the conductor's surface, effectively reducing the cross-sectional area available for current flow and increasing resistance. Dielectric losses in the insulating material between the conductors also contribute to the overall signal loss at higher frequencies.

For beginners, it's helpful to remember that while coaxial cables are efficient for transmitting signals, they are not perfect. As you move to higher frequencies, more of the signal's power is lost as heat within the cable, leading to weaker signals at the other end.

This concept is integral for ensuring efficient signal transmission, especially in applications requiring high-frequency operations, such as VHF and UHF bands.

T9B05: What happens as the frequency of a signal in coaxial cable is increased?

A. The characteristic impedance decreases
B. The loss decreases
C. The characteristic impedance increases
D. The loss increases

Sources of Loss in Coaxial Feed Lines

Several factors can cause loss in coaxial feed lines, including water intrusion into coaxial connectors, high SWR (Standing Wave Ratio), and the use of multiple connectors in the line.

Water intrusion can severely degrade the performance of a coaxial cable by increasing its resistance and causing signal attenuation. Moisture in the connectors can lead to corrosion and create additional pathways for signal loss, causing failure. Water and electricity don't mix! Keep moisture out.

High SWR indicates a poor match between the antenna and the transmission line, resulting in significant power being reflected back toward the transmitter instead of radiating. This reflection not only reduces the efficiency of the transmission but also increases losses in the coaxial cable.

Additionally, having multiple connectors in the line introduces more points where signal degradation can occur due to imperfect connections and increased resistance. Understanding these sources of loss is core to maintaining an efficient and effective communication system, ensuring minimal signal loss and optimal performance.

T9B08: Which of the following is a source of loss in coaxial feed line?

A. Water intrusion into coaxial connectors
B. High SWR
C. Multiple connectors in the line
D. All these choices are correct

T7C09: Which of the following causes failure of coaxial cables?

A. Moisture contamination
B. Solder flux contamination
C. Rapid fluctuation in transmitter output power
D. Operation at 100% duty cycle for an extended period

Coaxial Construction

UV-Resistant Outer Jackets on Coaxial Cables

The outer jacket of the coaxial cable should be resistant to ultraviolet (UV) light because prolonged exposure to UV radiation can degrade the material, making it brittle and prone to cracking. When the outer jacket is damaged, it can no longer effectively protect the inner components of the cable from environmental factors. This damage can allow water to enter the cable, leading to increased attenuation, corrosion of the conductors, and overall signal degradation.

For beginners, it's essential to understand that a UV-resistant jacket ensures the coaxial cable's longevity and reliability, especially when used outdoors. The cable maintains its integrity and performance by preventing UV damage and subsequent water intrusion, ensuring efficient signal transmission, and protecting your communication setup from potential failures.

Simply put, most feedlines go outside. The sun is outside, and UV light damages things over time. It rains outside, and moisture destroys our cables. Protect your feedlines!

T7C10: Why should the outer jacket of coaxial cable be resistant to ultraviolet light?

A. Ultraviolet resistant jackets prevent harmonic radiation
B. Ultraviolet light can increase losses in the cable's jacket
C. Ultraviolet and RF signals can mix, causing interference
D. Ultraviolet light can damage the jacket and allow water to enter the cable

Air Core Coaxial Cable

Air core coaxial cable is a transmission line that uses air as the primary dielectric medium between the inner conductor and the outer shield. This design minimizes signal loss because air has a very low dielectric constant compared to solid or foam dielectrics. The reduced dielectric constant allows for lower capacitance per unit length, resulting in lower signal attenuation, making air core coaxial cables highly efficient for high-frequency and long-distance transmissions.

However, the primary disadvantage of air core coaxial cables is their vulnerability to moisture intrusion. Unlike foam or solid dielectric cables with a more substantial insulating material, air core cables depend on maintaining an air gap. If moisture penetrates this air space, it can drastically degrade the cable's performance by increasing signal loss and causing corrosion of the conductors. Special installation techniques are required to mitigate this, such as using moisture-blocking connectors and ensuring all seals are airtight. These precautions add complexity and cost to the installation process but are necessary to maintain the cable's high performance. Understanding these characteristics of air core coaxial cables highlights the trade-offs between efficiency and environmental vulnerability.

T7C11: What is a disadvantage of air core coaxial cable when compared to foam or solid dielectric types?

A. It has more loss per foot
B. It cannot be used for VHF or UHF antennas
C. It requires special techniques to prevent moisture in the cable
D. It cannot be used at below freezing temperatures

Understanding Air Core Coax and Air-Insulated Hardline

While air core coax and air-insulated hardline both use air as the primary dielectric to reduce signal loss, they are different in their construction and typical applications.

Air Core Coax

- **Construction**: Air core coaxial cable uses air as the dielectric medium between the inner conductor and the outer shield, often supported by spacers or other structures to maintain the air gap.

- **Flexibility**: These cables are generally more flexible than hardlines, making them easier to install in applications where the cable needs to bend or route through tight spaces.

- **Use**: Commonly used in situations where flexibility and lower cost are more important, but they still require careful handling to prevent moisture ingress.

Air-Insulated Hardline

- **Construction**: An air-insulated hardline is a rigid coaxial cable with a solid or semi-rigid outer conductor and an air dielectric. It often includes structural elements to support the inner conductor and maintain the air gap.

- **Durability**: Hardlines are more robust, offer better shielding, and have lower loss than flexible air core coax. They are typically used in professional settings where maximum signal integrity is needed.

- **Use**: It is ideal for long-distance and high-frequency applications, such as VHF and UHF communications, where low signal loss and high durability are essential.

Key Differences

- **Flexibility**: Air core coax is more flexible, while air-insulated hardline is rigid and less flexible.

- **Performance**: Air-insulated hardline offers lower signal loss and better shielding than air core coax.

- **Applications**: Air core coax is used in applications requiring flexibility. In contrast, air-insulated hardline is used in high-performance applications needing minimal signal loss.

Understanding these differences helps select the correct type of feed line for specific needs, ensuring optimal performance in various radio communication scenarios.

Air-insulated hardline feed lines have the lowest loss at VHF and UHF frequencies compared to other feed lines. These cables are designed with an air core as the primary dielectric, significantly reducing signal attenuation. These typically have a robust construction with solid outer conductors, further reducing resistive losses and providing excellent shielding against external interference.

For beginners, it's helpful to remember that air-insulated hardlines are ideal for high-frequency applications because they maintain signal strength over long distances, making them particularly efficient for VHF and UHF communications. While they can be more expensive and require careful installation to prevent moisture intrusion, their superior performance in terms of low signal loss makes them a preferred choice for professional and high-performance amateur radio setups.

T9B11: Which of the following types of feed line has the lowest loss at VHF and UHF?

A. 50-ohm flexible coax
B. Multi-conductor unbalanced cable
C. Air-insulated hardline
D. 75-ohm flexible coax

Understanding "RG" in Coaxial Cables

"RG" stands for "Radio Guide," a designation initially used by the military to classify different types of coaxial cables. Each RG number corresponds to a specific type of coaxial cable with particular characteristics, such as impedance, diameter, and shielding. This system helps users identify the appropriate cable based on standardized specifications.

Key Characteristics of RG Coaxial Cables

- **Impedance**: RG cables typically come with standard impedance values, such as 50 ohms or 75 ohms, which are critical for matching the cable to the transmitter, receiver, and antenna to minimize signal reflection and loss.

- **Diameter**: The physical size of the cable, which affects its flexibility and suitability for different applications.

- **Shielding**: The type and amount of shielding (e.g., braided, foil) that protects the signal from external electromagnetic interference (EMI).

Examples of Common RG Cables

- **RG-58**: A 50-ohm cable commonly used in amateur radio and networking applications.

- **RG-59**: A 75-ohm cable often used for cable television and other video applications.

- **RG-213**: A 50-ohm cable with a larger diameter and better shielding, suitable for higher power applications.

Understanding the "RG" designation helps select the correct coaxial cable for specific requirements, ensuring efficient and reliable signal transmission in various communication systems.

T9B10: What is the electrical difference between RG-58 and RG-213 coaxial cable?

A. There is no significant difference between the two types
B. RG-58 cable has two shields
C. RG-213 cable has less loss at a given frequency
D. RG-58 cable can handle higher power levels

The lower loss in RG-213 is due to its larger diameter and superior shielding, which reduce resistance and minimize the signal's attenuation as it travels through the cable.

For beginners, it's helpful to think of RG-213 as a thicker and more robust cable that maintains signal strength better than the thinner RG-58. This makes RG-213 a preferred choice for applications requiring <u>longer cable runs</u> or <u>higher power transmission</u>, such as in professional and high-performance amateur radio setups.

Plug (PL) Connectors

Whereas the RG designation stands for "Radio Guide" and is used to classify different types of coaxial cables, **PL (plug)** is a type of connector used to terminate coaxial cables. It is commonly used in amateur radio and other communication applications. The PL-259 is designed for connecting coaxial cables to radio equipment and typically mates with an SO-239 socket. It is known for its <u>durability and reliability, particularly in HF (High Frequency) and VHF (Very High Frequency) applications.</u>

The PL-259 connector features a threaded coupling that ensures a secure and stable connection, essential for maintaining signal integrity, especially at higher power levels and frequencies.

The PL-259 connectors are commonly found in many radio setups because they balance mechanical strength and electrical performance well. Their design helps minimize signal loss and reflections, making them suitable for various frequencies typically used in amateur radio.

T9B07: Which of the following is true of PL-259 type coax connectors?

A. They are preferred for microwave operation
B. They are watertight
C. They are commonly used at HF and VHF frequencies
D. They are a bayonet-type connector

Type N (RF Connectors)

Type N connectors are designed for high-frequency applications, typically above 400 MHz. They provide excellent performance with low signal loss and good shielding, making them suitable for UHF and microwave frequencies.

They feature a threaded coupling mechanism that ensures a secure and stable connection, which maintains signal integrity at higher frequencies.

- **Compatibility**: Depending on the application and frequency requirements, Type N and PL-259 connectors can be used with various RG coaxial cables. For example, RG-213 is a thicker, lower-loss cable that can be terminated with either type N or PL-259 connectors, depending on whether the application is at higher frequencies (Type N) or lower frequencies (PL-259).

- **Application**: The right combination of RG cable and connector type depends on the communication system's specific requirements, such as frequency range, power handling, and environmental conditions. <u>Type N connectors are preferred for high-frequency applications</u>, while PL-259 connectors are more commonly used in HF and VHF setups.

- **Signal Integrity**: Correctly matched and installed connectors and cables are crucial for maintaining signal integrity and minimizing loss. For instance, using Type N connectors with RG cables in UHF applications helps achieve better performance and reliability.

Understanding the roles and compatibility of Type N, PL-259 connectors, and RG cables is essential for building effective and efficient coaxial communication systems.

T9B06: Which of the following RF connector types is most suitable for frequencies above 400 MHz?

A. UHF (PL-259/SO-239)
B. Type N
C. RS-213
D. DB-25

In this chapter, we explored the critical role of feedlines in radio communication systems, focusing on their types, functionality, and the importance of minimizing signal loss. Understanding the use of different feedlines, such as coaxial cables and ladder lines, along with concepts like standing wave ratio (SWR), is essential for optimizing signal transmission and protecting equipment. Proper selection and maintenance of feedlines ensure efficient and reliable communication, making it a foundational knowledge area for any radio enthusiast.

Chapter 18

Power Sources and Electrical Safety

Safety, a fundamental core of amateur radio, can often be overlooked. In these next two chapters, we'll delve into the best practices and precautions necessary to ensure the safe installation, maintenance, and operation of antennas and feedlines. From understanding electrical hazards and proper grounding techniques to mitigating risks associated with high-frequency RF exposure and structural safety, this chapter will provide you with the knowledge needed to protect yourself, your equipment, and those around you. Prioritizing safety ensures compliance with regulations and enhances the overall reliability and longevity of your radio setup.

Power Safety

When setting up your radio station, choosing a power source is as important as selecting the transceiver or antenna. It influences not just the functionality but also the safety and portability of your operations. This section will review power sources and, most importantly, the safety of working with electricity.

The station licensee is responsible for ensuring the safety of equipment and power sources and that no person is exposed to RF energy above the FCC exposure limits. Yes, your responsibility is to ensure your setup is safe!

T0C13: Who is responsible for ensuring that no person is exposed to RF energy above the FCC exposure limits?

A. The FCC
B. The station licensee
C. Anyone who is near an antenna
D. The local zoning board

This individual who holds the license for the amateur radio station must ensure that their station operates within the safety guidelines set by the FCC. These guidelines protect both the licensee and the public from potential health risks associated with excessive RF exposure.

To comply with these regulations, the station licensee must evaluate their RF emissions, considering frequency, power level, antenna type, and placement factors. They must take appropriate measures to reduce exposure if it exceeds the permissible limits, such as adjusting power levels, relocating antennas, or implementing barriers to restrict access to high RF areas.

Understanding and adhering to these responsibilities is essential for maintaining a safe operating environment and regulatory compliance.

Power Sources

The three primary power sources you can consider are mains electricity, batteries, and solar power. Each has its unique advantages and considerations.

Mains Electricity

Mains electricity - also known as household power, utility power, or grid power - is the standard electrical power supplied to homes and businesses by the electric utility company; it is the electricity that comes through the outlets in your walls. It is the home-based amateur radio station's most common power source. It's reliable and can handle high-power outputs needed for long-range communications. However, using mains power requires careful handling to avoid electrical hazards. It's key to ensure that all equipment is correctly rated for the voltage and current it will handle and that all connections are secure and insulated. Installing a dedicated circuit for your radio equipment can also prevent circuit overloads and reduce the risk of electrical fires.

Batteries

Batteries are an excellent choice for those who prefer operating their stations in remote locations or prioritize emergency preparedness. They provide a portable and relatively safe power source, making them ideal for amateur radio applications. The most commonly used batteries in amateur radio are sealed lead-acid and lithium-ion batteries. Lead-acid batteries are cheaper and more robust but heavier and require regular maintenance to prevent degradation. Lithium-ion batteries, while more expensive, offer higher energy density and longer life cycles with minimal maintenance. Regularly checking the charge level and ensuring correct recharging is essential to avoid damaging the battery.

Several rechargeable battery chemistries are commonly used in amateur radio, each offering unique advantages. Lithium-ion (Li-ion), Nickel-Metal Hydride (NiMH), and Lead-Acid are the most notable rechargeable battery chemistries. Lithium-ion batteries are known for their high energy density, lightweight design, and long cycle life, making them ideal for portable devices and handheld radios. Nickel-metal hydride batteries are valued for their safety and environmental friendliness, and they are often used in household electronics and portable equipment. Although heavier and with lower energy density, lead-acid batteries are robust, cost-effective, and frequently used in backup power systems and automotive applications. Selecting the right rechargeable battery type ensures reliable power for your equipment and operations.

T6A10: Which of the following battery chemistries is rechargeable?

A. Nickel-metal hydride
B. Lithium-ion
C. Lead-acid
D. All these choices are correct

In contrast, non-rechargeable batteries, also known as primary batteries, are designed for single use and cannot be recharged once depleted. Carbon-zinc batteries are a common type of non-rechargeable battery. They are among the oldest battery chemistries and are often used in low-drain devices such as remote controls, clocks, and flashlights. Carbon-zinc batteries are inexpensive and readily available but typically have a shorter lifespan and lower energy density than alkaline batteries.

POWER SOURCES AND ELECTRICAL SAFETY   139

T6A11: Which of the following battery chemistries is not rechargeable?

A. Nickel-cadmium
B. Carbon-zinc
C. Lead-acid
D. Lithium-ion

Understanding the difference between rechargeable and non-rechargeable batteries is important for amateur radio operators, as it impacts their equipment's choice of power sources. While rechargeable batteries are suitable for repeated use and are more cost-effective over time, non-rechargeable batteries like carbon zinc offer a convenient, ready-to-use power solution for low-drain or infrequently used devices.

Determining Battery Life for Your Equipment

To determine the length of time equipment can be powered from a battery, <u>you need to divide the battery's ampere-hour (Ah) rating by the average current draw of the equipment.</u> A battery's ampere-hour rating indicates the current it can supply over a specific period. For example, a battery with a 10 Ah rating can theoretically supply 10 amps for one hour or 1 amp for ten hours.

T4A09: How can you determine the length of time that equipment can be powered from a battery?

A. Divide the watt-hour rating of the battery by the peak power consumption of the equipment
B. Divide the battery ampere-hour rating by the average current draw of the equipment
C. Multiply the watts per hour consumed by the equipment by the battery power rating
D. Multiply the square of the current rating of the battery by the input resistance of the equipment

To calculate how long your equipment will run on a fully charged battery, first find the average current draw of your equipment in amps. Then, divide the battery's ampere-hour rating by this current draw. For instance, if your radio equipment draws an average of 2 amps and your battery is rated at 20 Ah, the equipment can be powered for approximately 10 hours (20 Ah / 2 A = 10 hours). This calculation helps amateur radio operators plan their operations, especially in the field or during emergencies, ensuring they have adequate power for their needs.

Solar

Solar power's appeal as a renewable energy source is becoming increasingly popular among amateur radio operators, especially those looking to build sustainable and independent stations. Setting up a solar-powered station involves investing in solar panels, charge controllers, and batteries to store the harvested energy. While the initial setup cost can be high, the long-term benefits of reduced energy bills and the ability to operate during power outages make it a worthwhile investment. Solar power systems require minimal maintenance once installed and can provide a reliable power supply, given sufficient sunlight.

Mobile Power

Ham Radios in Vehicles: Power Considerations

Operating ham radios in vehicles involves unique power considerations to ensure reliable performance and safety. Mobile transceivers typically require a stable power supply to function effectively, and vehicles' 12-volt electrical systems provide an ideal power source. However, proper connection and power management are vital to avoiding issues such as voltage drops, interference, or even damage to the radio equipment.

Connecting the Negative Power Return

For a mobile transceiver, the negative power return should be connected to the 12-volt battery chassis ground. This connection ensures a solid and stable ground reference, reducing the risk of electrical noise and interference affecting the transceiver's performance. Connecting directly to the battery chassis ground helps maintain a low-resistance path for the return current, which is essential for reliable operation, especially during high-current conditions such as transmitting.

T4A11: Where should the negative power return of a mobile transceiver be connected in a vehicle?

A. At the 12-volt battery chassis ground
B. At the antenna mount
C. To any metal part of the vehicle
D. Through the transceiver's mounting bracket

Finding the Chassis Ground in a Vehicle

Finding the chassis ground in your vehicle is relatively straightforward. Here's a step-by-step guide to help you locate it:

1. **Locate the Battery**: Find your vehicle's battery, usually under the hood. Identify the negative terminal, typically marked with a minus sign (-) and connected to a black cable.

2. **Follow the Negative Cable**: Trace the black cable from the battery's negative terminal. This cable is usually connected to a large metal part of the car, such as the engine block or frame.

3. **Identify the Ground Point**: The spot where the negative cable attaches to the metal part of the car is your chassis ground. This connection point often has a bolt or clamp securing the cable to the car's body or frame.

4. **Alternative Ground Points**: If you need an additional grounding point, look for other substantial metal parts of the car's frame or body that are clean and free of paint or rust. If they connect well to the vehicle's metal structure, they can serve as effective grounding points.

5. **Check for Existing Grounds**: Many vehicles have designated grounding points for various electrical systems. These are often marked and can be found in the vehicle's manual. They are typically in the engine compartment or near the battery.

Connecting your mobile transceiver's negative power return to this chassis ground ensures a stable and reliable grounding connection, reducing electrical noise and maintaining optimal performance.

Appropriate Power Supply Rating for a Mobile Transceiver

A typical 50-watt output mobile FM transceiver requires a power supply rating of 13.8 volts at 12 amperes. This rating is key because it matches the voltage and current requirements of the transceiver under typical operating conditions. The 13.8 volts is the standard voltage for vehicle electrical systems, ensuring compatibility with the transceiver. The current rating of 12 amperes is necessary to support the power demands during transmission, where the current draw can be substantial. Providing a power supply with these specifications ensures that the transceiver operates efficiently, avoiding problems like voltage drops or overheating that could occur with an inadequate power supply.

T4A01: Which of the following is an appropriate power supply rating for a typical 50-watt output mobile FM transceiver?

A. 24.0 volts at 4 amperes
B. 13.8 volts at 4 amperes
C. 24.0 volts at 12 amperes
D. 13.8 volts at 12 amperes

This can be tricky on its surface, especially when you are new to ham and perhaps electrical equipment.

To understand the appropriate power supply rating for a typical 50-watt output mobile FM transceiver, you can use a basic formula derived from our Power Formula, which we reviewed earlier. Do you remember the Power in Pie? In the question and answers, we have watts (P- Power), volts (E- Voltage) and amperes (I- Current).

Power (P) = Current (I) x Voltage (E)

For a 50-watt transceiver, we want to calculate the required current (I) when the voltage (E) is 13.8 volts, which is a standard operating voltage for mobile transceivers.

Rearrange the formula to solve for current (I):

I = P / E

Substitute the values:

I = 50 watts / 13.8 volts ≈ 3.62 amperes

However, this calculation only considers the power output, not the transceiver's circuitry's efficiency and additional power requirements. Reread and think about the question carefully. It says this mobile FM transceiver has an <u>output</u> of 50 watts (a net or final output of 50 watts). A typical efficiency rating for a mobile transceiver might be around 50-60%, meaning the actual current draw would be <u>higher</u> than this ideal calculation.

Considering inefficiencies and safe operating margins, a general rule of thumb is to double or even triple the calculated current to estimate the required power supply rating. This is why a power supply rating of <u>13.8 volts at 12 amperes</u> is recommended. It accounts for the additional current needed due to inefficiencies and ensures stable operation under various conditions.

So, while the basic formula can help understand the concept, the reader should remember that the final recommended power supply rating (13.8V at 12A) considers practical factors beyond just the power output calculation. This value is typically provided by the manufacturer or can be found in the transceiver's specifications.

Radio Frequency (RF) Safety

As an amateur radio operator, you need to know and understand the guidelines for minimizing RF exposure. Radio Frequency (RF) radiation, at high levels, can pose health risks, which is why the FCC has established specific exposure limits. These guidelines are designed to protect both operators and the general public from potentially harmful RF radiation effects.

<u>Radio signals are a form of non-ionizing radiation.</u> Unlike <u>ionizing radiation, which has enough energy to remove tightly bound electrons from atoms, non-ionizing radiation lacks sufficient energy to ionize atoms or molecules, which could result in chemical changes in cells and even damage DNA.</u> Instead, it primarily causes atoms and molecules to vibrate, which can produce heat but does not cause chemical changes or damage to biological tissues at the atomic level.

T0C01: What type of radiation are radio signals?

A. Gamma radiation
B. Ionizing radiation
C. Alpha radiation
D. Non-ionizing radiation

T0C12: How does RF radiation differ from ionizing radiation (radioactivity)?

A. RF radiation does not have sufficient energy to cause chemical changes in cells and damage DNA
B. RF radiation can only be detected with an RF dosimeter
C. RF radiation is limited in range to a few feet
D. RF radiation is perfectly safe

In amateur radio, understanding that radio signals are non-ionizing radiation is essential for safety and regulatory reasons. This type of radiation is generally considered safe for everyday use, as it does not have the harmful effects of ionizing radiation, such as X-rays or gamma rays.

Factors Affecting RF Exposure

The RF exposure of people near an amateur station antenna is influenced by several key factors: the frequency and power level of the RF field, the distance from the antenna to the person, and the antenna's radiation pattern. Higher frequencies and power levels result in stronger RF fields, which can increase the potential for exposure. For example, antennas transmitting at higher power levels or operating at higher frequencies can generate more intense RF fields, potentially leading to greater exposure.

Distance from the antenna is also important. The intensity of RF radiation decreases rapidly with increased distance from the source. Thus, maintaining a safe distance from the antenna can significantly reduce exposure. Additionally, the antenna's radiation pattern determines the direction and spread of the RF energy.

Directional antennas focus energy in specific directions, leading to higher exposure in those areas. In contrast, omnidirectional antennas distribute energy evenly. Understanding these factors helps operators design their stations to minimize RF exposure and comply with safety regulations, ensuring a safe operating environment for both themselves and the public.

T0C04: What factors affect the RF exposure of people near an amateur station antenna?

A. frequency and power level of the RF field
B. Distance from the antenna to a person
C. Radiation pattern of the antenna
D. All these choices are correct

Duty Cycle

The duty cycle refers to the percentage of time during which a device or signal is active and transmitting, compared to the total time. It is usually expressed as a percentage. For example, suppose a transmitter is on for 1 second and off for 1 second. In that case, the duty cycle is 50% because the transmitter is active for half the total time.

T0C11: What is the definition of duty cycle during the averaging time for RF exposure?

A. The difference between the lowest power output and the highest power output of a transmitter
B. The difference between the PEP and average power output of a transmitter
C. The percentage of time that a transmitter is transmitting
D. The percentage of time that a transmitter is not transmitting

The duty cycle is a parameter in determining safe RF radiation exposure levels because it directly affects the average radiation exposure. Remember, it says average, not necessarily total. A higher duty cycle means the transmitter is on more frequently, increasing the average RF exposure. Conversely, a lower duty cycle reduces the average exposure, as the transmitter is off for a more significant portion of the time. By considering the duty cycle, regulators and operators can assess and manage the potential risks associated with prolonged RF radiation exposure, ensuring that safety guidelines are followed.

T0C10: Why is duty cycle one of the factors used to determine safe RF radiation exposure levels?

A. It affects the average exposure to radiation
B. It affects the peak exposure to radiation
C. It takes into account the antenna feed line loss
D. It takes into account the thermal effects of the final amplifier

During the averaging time for RF exposure, the duty cycle is defined as the percentage of time that a transmitter is transmitting. This metric is used to calculate the overall exposure levels to RF radiation. For instance, if a transmitter operates with a duty cycle of 25%, it means that the transmitter is active and emitting RF signals for 25% of the time and inactive for the remaining 75%. This averaging approach helps evaluate the cumulative exposure and ensure that it stays within safe limits set by regulatory bodies.

In addition to RF exposure, the duty cycle is essential for electronic devices' thermal management and power consumption. A higher duty cycle means the equipment is active for extended periods in high-power applications like radio transmitters. If not properly managed, this leads to increased heat generation and potential overheating. Conversely, a lower duty cycle can help reduce heat build-up and extend the life of the equipment by allowing it to cool down during off periods.

Practical Example

The allowable power density for RF safety depends on the duty cycle of a transmitter. The allowable power density can be doubled (increased by a factor of 2) if the duty cycle decreases from 100 percent to 50 percent. This is because the duty cycle indicates how long the transmitter is actively emitting RF signals. The transmitter is always on at a 100 percent duty cycle, resulting in continuous exposure. However, at a 50 percent duty cycle, the transmitter is only active half the time, effectively halving the average exposure.

By halving the duty cycle, the average power density over time decreases, allowing for a higher instantaneous power density while maintaining safe exposure levels.

T0C03: How does the allowable power density for RF safety change if duty cycle changes from 100 percent to 50 percent?

A. It increases by a factor of 3
B. It decreases by 50 percent
C. It increases by a factor of 2
D. There is no adjustment allowed for lower duty cycle

Frequency

Maximum Permissible Exposure

RF exposure refers to the electromagnetic energy emitted by radio transmitters and its potential effects on human health. Exposure can vary depending on several factors, including frequency.

The maximum permissible exposure (MPE) has the lowest value at 50 MHz. This frequency is particularly significant because it falls within the range where the human body can absorb RF energy most efficiently. The absorption of RF energy by the body is influenced by the wavelength of the signal, and at around 50 MHz, the wavelength is such that it maximizes energy absorption. As a result, the exposure limits are set lower at this frequency to protect against potential health risks.

T0C02: At which of the following frequencies does maximum permissible exposure have the lowest value?

A. 3.5 MHz
B. 50 MHz
C. 440 MHz
D. 1296 MHz

Repetition helps build memorization. 50 MHz lies within the "6-meter band" and is a segment in the VHF (Very High Frequency) spectrum. This band spans from 50 to 54 MHz and is known for its unique propagation characteristics. The 6-meter band is particularly valued by amateur radio operators because it bridges the gap between HF (High Frequency) and VHF, offering local and long-distance communication opportunities under favorable conditions.

Exposure Limits

Exposure limits vary with frequency because the human body absorbs RF energy differently across the spectrum. The body's tissues absorb specific frequencies more efficiently, creating a higher potential for thermal and non-thermal effects. For instance, frequencies around 30-300 MHz are more readily absorbed, which can cause heating of body tissues and potentially lead to harmful biological effects. To mitigate these risks, exposure limits are set lower for these frequencies. By varying the limits according to frequency, regulatory guidelines ensure that RF exposure remains safe, protecting operators and the public from excessive RF energy absorption.

T0C05: Why do exposure limits vary with frequency?

A. Lower-frequency RF fields have more energy than higher-frequency fields
B. Lower frequency RF fields do not penetrate the human body
C. Higher frequency RF fields are transient in nature
D. The human body absorbs more RF energy at some frequencies than at others

---

Antenna RF Safety

The antenna may look like only a big dumb metal pole, but touching an antenna during transmission can result in an RF burn to the skin. RF energy generated during transmission can induce high currents on the surface of the antenna. When someone touches the antenna, these currents can flow through their skin, causing localized heating and potentially painful burns known as RF burns. This is because the human body can act as a conductor, allowing RF energy to pass through and generate heat at the point of contact.

T0C07: What hazard is created by touching an antenna during a transmission?

A. Electrocution
B. RF burn to skin
C. Radiation poisoning
D. All these choices are correct

To prevent RF burns and ensure safety, avoiding touching any part of the antenna system while transmitting is essential. This includes maintaining a safe distance from the antenna and ensuring that any necessary adjustments or repairs are made while the transmitter is off.

One practical action to reduce exposure to RF radiation is to <u>relocate antennas</u>. Positioning antennas farther away from living spaces, work areas, or places where people frequently gather can significantly lower the risk of exposure. By increasing the distance between the antenna and individuals, the intensity of the RF field decreases due to the inverse square law, which states that the strength of the signal diminishes rapidly with distance.

T0C08: Which of the following actions can reduce exposure to RF radiation?

A. Relocate antennas
B. Relocate the transmitter
C. Increase the duty cycle
D. All these choices are correct

Additionally, placing antennas in elevated positions, such as on rooftops or towers, can help direct the RF radiation away from populated areas. This enhances safety by reducing ground-level exposure and improves the antenna's performance by minimizing obstructions and increasing the effective range.

Bonding for Safety

Bonding in electrical systems refers to connecting all metallic parts of an electrical installation to create a continuous conductive path. This process ensures that all components have the same electrical potential, which minimizes the risk of electrical shock and helps effectively manage electrical currents. Bonding is paramount for both safety and the efficient operation of electrical systems, including those used in amateur radio setups.

Importance of Bonding in RF Systems

In RF (radio frequency) systems, bonding is vital for managing RF currents and minimizing interference. Proper bonding helps create a low-impedance path to the ground, which is essential for dissipating unwanted RF energy. This reduces the potential for RF interference that can affect the performance of radio equipment. Additionally, adequate bonding helps in protecting the equipment and the operator from electrical faults and static build-up. Using materials like flat copper straps for bonding ensures efficient current flow. It enhances the overall stability and reliability of the radio station. Understanding the importance of bonding is essential for maintaining a safe and effective amateur radio operation.

Preferred Conductor for RF Bonding: Flat Copper Strap

<u>Flat copper straps are the preferred conductor</u> for bonding at RF (radio frequency). They are chosen because of their low inductance and high surface area, which are key characteristics for effective RF bonding. At high frequencies, RF currents flow along the surface of conductors, a phenomenon known as the skin effect. Flat copper straps provide a larger surface area than round wires, thus minimizing resistance and inductance, ensuring efficient current flow.

T4A08: Which of the following conductors is preferred for bonding at RF?

A. Copper braid removed from coaxial cable
B. Steel wire
C. Twisted-pair cable
D. Flat copper strap

Using flat copper straps for RF bonding helps create a low-impedance path to the ground, which is essential for reducing RF noise and interference. This improves the overall performance of the radio equipment by ensuring stable and reliable connections. Flat copper straps are also flexible and easy to install, making them a practical choice for various bonding and grounding applications in an amateur radio station.

Compliance

You can use several acceptable methods to determine whether your amateur radio station complies with FCC RF exposure regulations. One method is by calculation based on FCC OET Bulletin 65, which provides detailed guidelines and formulas for evaluating RF exposure levels. This bulletin helps operators calculate the potential exposure from their equipment and ensure it falls within safe limits. If you love math and reading government regulations, Google "FCC OET Bulletin 65" and open up the PDF. Enjoy!

Another method is computer modeling. Various software tools can simulate RF exposure levels based on your station's specific parameters, such as antenna type, power output, and operating frequency. These models can provide a detailed analysis of the RF fields around your station, helping you verify compliance with FCC regulations.

Lastly, you can measure field strength using calibrated equipment. This involves using specialized RF measurement devices to measure the RF fields in and around your station directly. Accurate measurements can assess the actual RF exposure levels and compare them to the FCC's safety limits. Understanding and applying these methods ensures that your station operates safely and within regulatory guidelines, an essential aspect of practical operation and exam preparation in amateur radio.

T0C06: Which of the following is an acceptable method to determine whether your station complies with FCC RF exposure regulations?

A. By calculation based on FCC OET Bulletin 65
B. By calculation based on computer modeling
C. By measurement of field strength using calibrated equipment
D. All these choices are correct

Ensuring that your station complies with FCC RF exposure regulations can seem complex. Still, there are straightforward methods and guidelines to help beginners navigate this critical aspect of station operation. Here are some key points and guidance to simplify the process:

Practical Tips for Beginners:

- **Start with FCC OET Bulletin 65:**

  - **Guidance:** Begin by familiarizing yourself with FCC OET Bulletin 65. It provides a solid foundation and step-by-step instructions on how to perform calculations. It's a trusted source directly from the FCC. It's technical, but you should at least look it over once.

- **Use Simple Software Tools:**

  - **Guidance:** Many user-friendly software tools are available for amateur radio operators. These tools can automate much of the calculation process. Look for software that is specifically designed for amateur radio RF exposure assessment.

  - **Start here:** Google 'ARRL RF Exposure Calculator' and it's the first link that comes up. This is a trusted source and relatively simple to use. Just plug in your numbers and the calculator will do the rest.

- **Seek Help from Experienced Operators:**

  - **Guidance:** Don't hesitate to ask for help from more experienced operators or join local amateur radio clubs. Many clubs offer resources and mentorship programs to assist beginners in understanding and applying these regulations.

  - **Recommended:** As a newly minted ham or soon-to-be, this is a great place to start and get some hands-on experience by working with trusted peers.

- **Regularly Review and Update:**

  - **Guidance:** Regularly review your station setup and any changes you make to ensure ongoing compliance. Modifications to your equipment or operating practices can change RF exposure levels.

By following these methods and practical tips, you can confidently ensure your station complies with FCC RF exposure regulations while maintaining safety for yourself and others.

Power Safety

Power safety is a vital aspect of radio operations, encompassing the safe handling and management of electrical power to prevent accidents, equipment damage, and personal injury. Understanding and following proper safety protocols is critical, whether working with low-voltage batteries or high-voltage power supplies. This section will cover key safety practices, including safe measurement techniques, proper grounding, handling of high-voltage equipment, and the importance of appropriately rated tools and protective gear. By adhering to these guidelines, you can ensure a safe and effective radio setup.

Electrical Safety

Electrical current flowing through the body can pose serious health hazards. One significant risk is tissue injury caused by heating, as the electrical energy can generate considerable heat, potentially leading to burns or internal damage. This heating effect is hazardous as it can affect the skin and deeper tissues.

In addition to heating, electrical current can disrupt the body's electrical functions at a cellular level. This disruption can interfere with the regular operation of cells, potentially leading to serious health issues such as heart arrhythmias or neurological damage. Furthermore, electrical currents can cause involuntary muscle contractions. These contractions can be severe enough to cause physical injuries or make it impossible to let go of the source of the current, prolonging exposure and increasing the risk of serious harm.

T0A02: What health hazard is presented by electrical current flowing through the body?

A. It may cause injury by heating tissue
B. It may disrupt the electrical functions of cells
C. It may cause involuntary muscle contractions
D. All these choices are correct

Fuses

The primary purpose of a fuse in an electrical circuit is to <u>remove power in case of an overload,</u> protecting the circuit and connected devices from damage. A fuse is a safety device that contains a thin wire or filament that melts when the current flowing through it exceeds a specific threshold. This melting action breaks the circuit, stopping the flow of electricity and preventing potential damage caused by excessive current.

T0A04: What is the purpose of a fuse in an electrical circuit?

A. To prevent power supply ripple from damaging a component
B. To remove power in case of overload
C. To limit current to prevent shocks
D. All these choices are correct

Fuses are key components in ensuring electrical safety. They help prevent overheating, fires, and damage to sensitive electronic components by automatically disconnecting the power during an overload condition. Fuses safeguard both the equipment and the users by ensuring that circuits operate within safe limits.

Correct Fuse Rating

Using a fuse with the correct rating is for preventing excessive current from causing damage or posing a fire hazard. A fuse ensures that the electrical system operates within safe limits. Exceeding these limits risks serious damage to your equipment and creates significant safety hazards.

For example, a 5-ampere fuse should never be replaced with a 20-ampere fuse because it compromises the safety of the electrical circuit. Fuses are designed to protect circuits by breaking the connection when the current exceeds a specific limit, in this case, 5 amperes. Replacing a 5-ampere fuse with a 20-ampere fuse allows a much higher current to flow through the circuit than it was designed to handle. <u>This can lead to overheating of the wires and components, potentially causing them to melt or catch fire.</u>

T0A05: Why should a 5-ampere fuse never be replaced with a 20-ampere fuse?

A. The larger fuse would be likely to blow because it is rated for higher current
B. The power supply ripple would greatly increase
C. Excessive current could cause a fire
D. All these choices are correct

Standardization of Electrical Components

Understanding Wire Color Coding in the United States

<u>In the United States, the black wire insulation in a three-wire 120 V cable indicates the "hot" or live wire.</u> This wire carries the electrical current from the power source to the load, which is essential for the operation of electrical devices. The hot wire delivers the voltage needed to power appliances, lights, and other equipment.

T0A03: In the United States, what circuit does black wire insulation indicate in a three-wire 120 V cable?

A. Neutral
B. Hot
C. Equipment ground
D. Black insulation is never used

Understanding wire color coding is important for safely working with electrical systems. In a typical three-wire 120 V setup, besides the black hot wire, there is usually a white wire that serves as the neutral conductor and a green or bare wire that acts as the ground. The neutral wire completes the circuit by returning current to the power source. In contrast, the ground wire provides a safe path for electricity in case of a fault. Identifying and using these wires ensures electrical circuits' safe and efficient operation, a fundamental concept for practical electrical work and exam preparation.

Placement of Fuses and Circuit Breakers in a 120V AC Power Circuit

In a 120V AC power circuit, a fuse or circuit breaker should only be installed in series with the hot conductor. The hot conductor is the wire that carries the live current from the power source to the load. Installing the protective device in series with the hot conductor ensures that the circuit will be interrupted in the event of an overload or short circuit, effectively cutting off the flow of electricity and preventing potential damage or fire.

T0A08: Where should a fuse or circuit breaker be installed in a 120V AC power circuit?

A. In series with the hot conductor only
B. In series with the hot and neutral conductors
C. In parallel with the hot conductor only
D. In parallel with the hot and neutral conductors

Placing the fuse or circuit breaker in the hot conductor is crucial because it directly controls the current flow into the circuit. If the protective device were installed in the neutral or ground wire instead, it would not provide the same level of protection. The hot wire is where the electrical energy enters the circuit, so interrupting it with a fuse or circuit breaker ensures that the entire circuit is safely disconnected from the power source in case of a fault.

Guarding Against Electrical Shock at Your Station

Guarding against electrical shock is vital for maintaining a safe amateur radio station. One effective method is to use three-wire cords and plugs for all AC-powered equipment. The three-wire system includes a hot wire, a neutral wire, and a ground wire. The ground wire provides a path for electrical current to return to the ground in case of a fault, thereby reducing the risk of electric shock.

Additionally, connecting all AC-powered station equipment to a common safety ground ensures that any stray electrical currents are safely directed away from the equipment and operator. This grounding practice helps to equalize potential differences between devices, preventing electrical shocks. Another safety measure is to install mechanical interlocks in high-voltage circuits. Mechanical interlocks ensure that high-voltage circuits cannot be accessed; at the same time, they are energized, providing an additional layer of protection.

T0A06: What is a good way to guard against electrical shock at your station?

A. Use three-wire cords and plugs for all AC-powered equipment
B. Connect all AC powered station equipment to a common safety ground
C. Install mechanical interlocks in high-voltage circuits
D. All these choices are correct

Hazard of Stored Charge in Filter Capacitors

A significant hazard in a power supply immediately after turning it off is the charge stored in filter capacitors. Filter capacitors are designed to smooth out fluctuations in the power supply by storing electrical energy. However, even after the power supply is turned off, these capacitors can retain a substantial charge for some time. This stored energy can pose a severe risk of electric shock if someone touches the components connected to the capacitors.

T0A11: What hazard exists in a power supply immediately after turning it off?

A. Circulating currents in the dc filter
B. Leakage flux in the power transformer
C. Voltage transients from kickback diodes
D. Charge stored in filter capacitors

To mitigate this risk, it's essential to safely discharge the capacitors before handling the power supply components. This can be done using a resistor to slowly bleed off the stored charge, ensuring the capacitors are fully discharged. Understanding this hazard and taking appropriate precautions will help prevent accidental shocks and injuries.

Battery Safety

Battery safety is fundamental to operating an amateur radio station, especially when using 12-volt storage batteries. These batteries are commonly used for their reliability and capacity to provide ample power. However, they come with specific safety hazards that operators must be aware of to prevent accidents and ensure safe operation.

One significant safety hazard of a 12-volt storage battery is the risk of shorting the terminals. Suppose the positive and negative terminals are accidentally connected with a conductive material. In that case, a rapid flow of current can cause intense heat. This can result in burns, fire, or even an explosion, posing a severe danger to the operator and surrounding equipment. Always handle batteries carefully to prevent this, ensuring the terminals are covered or insulated when not used.

T0A01: Which of the following is a safety hazard of a 12-volt storage battery?

A. Touching both terminals with the hands can cause electrical shock
B. Shorting the terminals can cause burns, fire, or an explosion
C. RF emissions from a nearby transmitter can cause the electrolyte to emit poison gas
D. All these choices are correct

Another significant hazard is caused by charging or discharging a battery too quickly. Rapid charging or discharging can lead to overheating of the battery. This excessive heat can damage the battery's internal components and reduce lifespan. Additionally, fast charging can cause out-gassing, where the battery releases potentially harmful gases. These gases can create an explosive atmosphere if not adequately ventilated. To mitigate these risks, use appropriate charging equipment designed for your specific battery type and follow the manufacturer's guidelines for safe charging and discharging rates.

> **T0A10: What hazard is caused by charging or discharging a battery too quickly?**
>
> **A. Overheating or out-gassing**
> B. Excess output ripple
> C. Half-wave rectification
> D. Inverse memory effect

Understanding these hazards and implementing proper safety measures ensures the safe use of batteries in your amateur radio operations.

Grounding

Grounding is fundamental to setting up a safe and efficient amateur radio station. Proper grounding ensures protection against electrical faults, lightning strikes, and static build-up, safeguarding both the operator and the equipment. Grounding panels are an essential part of this system, providing a centralized location for all grounding connections. By using a grounding panel, operators can maintain a low-impedance path to the earth, which is needed for adequate grounding.

Bonding External Ground Rods

All external ground rods or earth connections (these are metal rods, typically made of copper or galvanized steel, driven into the ground to provide a direct path to the earth for electrical currents) should be bonded together with heavy wire or a conductive strap to ensure an effective and cohesive grounding system. Bonding these ground connections ensures that they have the same electrical potential, preventing voltage differences that could cause dangerous arcing or reduce the effectiveness of the grounding system. By connecting all ground rods, operators create a more reliable and robust grounding network that enhances overall safety and performance.

> **T0A09: What should be done to all external ground rods or earth connections?**
>
> A. Waterproof them with silicone caulk or electrical tape
> B. Keep them as far apart as possible
> **C. Bond them together with heavy wire or conductive strap**
> D. Tune them for resonance on the lowest frequency of operation

Where to Install a Lightning Arrester

A lightning arrester is a device used to protect electrical equipment from damage caused by lightning strikes or other high-voltage surges. It functions by providing a pathway for the excess electrical energy to be safely diverted to the ground, preventing it from reaching and damaging sensitive equipment. It should be installed in the coaxial feed line on a grounded panel near where the feed lines enter the building. This strategic placement ensures that any surge caused by a lightning strike is safely diverted to the ground before entering the building and damaging the equipment. Installing the arrester on a grounded panel provides a direct path for the electrical surge to follow, minimizing the risk of it traveling through the internal wiring and causing extensive damage. This practice is key for protecting the radio equipment and the operator from the potentially devastating effects of lightning strikes.

> **T0A07: Where should a lightning arrester be installed in a coaxial feed line?**
>
> A. At the output connector of a transceiver
> B. At the antenna feed point
> C. At the ac power service panel
> **D. On a grounded panel near where feed lines enter the building**

Ensuring Compliance

To ensure your station complies with RF safety regulations, it is essential to reevaluate it whenever there are transmitter or antenna system changes. This includes adjusting the power output, changing the antenna type or location, or altering the transmission frequency. Each of these changes can affect the RF exposure levels around your station, potentially bringing it out of compliance with the FCC's safety limits.

> **T0C09: How can you make sure your station stays in compliance with RF safety regulations?**
>
> A. By informing the FCC of any changes made in your station
> **B. By reevaluating the station whenever an item in the transmitter or antenna system is changed**
> C. By making sure your antennas have low SWR
> D. All these choices are correct

Regular re-evaluation involves measuring or calculating the RF field strength to ensure exposure levels are within the permissible limits. This process may include using tools like RF exposure calculators, conducting field measurements, and ensuring that any adjustments do not result in excessive RF exposure. By diligently reevaluating your station after any changes, you can maintain a safe operating environment and adhere to regulatory requirements, thus protecting yourself and the public from potential RF hazards.

Understanding and implementing these safety measures ensures your compliance with legal requirements and secures your well-being and that of others. Whether experimenting with different power sources or fine-tuning your station's setup, keeping safety at the forefront of your activities is essential. This approach prevents accidents and ensures your radio experience is enjoyable and sustainable.

Chapter 19

Antennas, Feedlines and Safety

Antenna Tuner

THE PRIMARY FUNCTION OF an antenna tuner, also known as an antenna coupler, <u>is to match the impedance of the antenna system to the transceiver's output impedance</u>, typically 50 ohms. This matching is important because it ensures that the transceiver's maximum power is transferred to the antenna for efficient radiation.

When the impedances are not matched, significant power can be reflected back to the transceiver, resulting in poor transmission efficiency and potential damage to the equipment.

The tuner then uses adjustable inductors and capacitors to create a matching network. By altering the inductance and capacitance, the tuner changes the impedance seen by the transceiver.

For beginners, it's helpful to think of an antenna tuner as a device that "tunes" the antenna system to make it compatible with the transceiver. By adjusting the impedance, the tuner minimizes signal reflection and maximizes power transfer, leading to clearer and stronger signals.

T9B04: What is the major function of an antenna tuner (antenna coupler)?

A. It matches the antenna system impedance to the transceiver's output impedance
B. It helps a receiver automatically tune in weak stations
C. It allows an antenna to be used on both transmit and receive
D. It automatically selects the proper antenna for the frequency band being used

---

Antenna Analyzer

An antenna analyzer is a specialized device radio operators use to evaluate and optimize the performance of their antennas. It measures impedance, SWR (Standing Wave Ratio), and resonant frequency, providing detailed insights into how well an antenna system functions. This information helps tune and adjust the antenna for optimal performance.

Essential Functions of an Antenna Analyzer:

- **Impedance Measurement**: The analyzer measures the antenna system's impedance across a range of frequencies, helping to identify how closely the antenna's impedance matches the desired value (typically 50 ohms).

- **SWR Measurement**: It provides real-time SWR readings, indicating the power transfer efficiency from the transmitter to the antenna. A low SWR indicates good impedance matching and minimal power loss.

- **Resonant Frequency Identification**: The analyzer identifies the antenna's resonant frequency, which is the frequency at which the antenna operates most efficiently. This helps in tuning the antenna to the desired frequency band and determines if it is resonant at the desired operating frequency.

- **Graphical Displays**: Many modern antenna analyzers include graphical displays that show SWR curves, impedance plots, and other useful data, making it easier to visualize the antenna system's performance.

Think of an antenna analyzer as a diagnostic tool that helps you tune your antenna to its "sweet spot." This ensures that your radio system operates efficiently, with maximum signal strength and clarity.

T7C02: Which of the following is used to determine if an antenna is resonant at the desired operating frequency?

A. A VTVM
B. An antenna analyzer
C. A Q meter
D. A frequency counter

Dummy Loads

A dummy load is an essential tool for radio operators. It is a substitute for an antenna during the testing and calibration of radio equipment.

It provides a non-radiating, resistive load that safely absorbs the transmitter's power, preventing interference with actual broadcasts. By matching the impedance of the radio's output (typically 50 ohms), a dummy load allows operators to test and adjust their equipment under realistic conditions without radiating signals into the air.

This helps ensure transmitters are properly tuned and functioning before being connected to an antenna for real-world communication.

T7C01: What is the primary purpose of a dummy load?

A. To prevent transmitting signals over the air when making tests
B. To prevent over-modulation of a transmitter
C. To improve the efficiency of an antenna
D. To improve the signal-to-noise ratio of a receiver

A dummy load consists of a non-inductive resistor mounted on a heat sink. The non-inductive resistor provides a purely resistive load without introducing inductance, which could affect the accuracy of the testing. This resistor matches the typical impedance of the radio equipment, ensuring that the transmitter operates under normal conditions.

The heat sink is essential as it dissipates the heat the resistor generates when it absorbs the transmitter's power. Without proper heat dissipation, the resistor could overheat and fail.

By safely absorbing the transmitted power and converting it into heat, the dummy load allows radio operators to test and calibrate their equipment without broadcasting signals, ensuring that their transmitters are properly tuned and functioning correctly.

T7C03: What does a dummy load consist of?

A. A high-gain amplifier and a TR switch
B. A non-inductive resistor mounted on a heat sink
C. A low-voltage power supply and a DC relay
D. A 50-ohm reactance used to terminate a transmission line

From the intricate details of antenna resonance and impedance matching to the practical applications of dummy loads and coaxial cables, each component plays a key role in maintaining signal integrity and optimizing performance. Mastering these concepts ensures your radio equipment operates reliably, providing clear and consistent communication in any scenario.

RF Power Meter

An RF power meter is a device used to measure the power level of radio frequency (RF) signals. It is an essential tool for amateur radio operators and professionals working with RF equipment. RF power meters provide accurate measurements of the power being transmitted or received by an antenna, helping operators ensure that their equipment functions correctly and efficiently.

Importance of an RF Power Meter

Using an RF power meter, operators can verify that their transmitters are producing the expected power output and that their antennas are radiating this power effectively. This helps diagnose and troubleshoot issues such as power loss, signal distortion, or mismatched impedance in the transmission line. Accurate power measurements are imperative for maintaining optimal performance, ensuring compliance with regulatory power limits, and protecting the equipment from potential damage due to over-powering or inefficient operation.

Proper Installation of an RF Power Meter

An RF power meter should be installed between the transmitter and the antenna in the feed line. This placement allows the meter to accurately measure the transmitter's power output before it reaches the antenna. By positioning the RF power meter in this location, operators can monitor the transmitted power and ensure it is within the desired range.

T4A05: Where should an RF power meter be installed?

A. In the feed line, between the transmitter and antenna
B. At the power supply output
C. In parallel with the push-to-talk line and the antenna
D. In the power supply cable, as close as possible to the radio

Installing the RF power meter in the transmission line is needed to diagnose and troubleshoot potential transmitter, feed line, or antenna issues. It helps verify that the transmitter is functioning correctly and that the power is effectively delivered to the antenna. Proper installation ensures accurate readings, which is essential for optimizing performance, maintaining regulatory compliance, and protecting the equipment from potential damage.

Antenna Safety

Safety around and with antennas is vital to setting up and maintaining your radio station. While optimizing performance and adhering to RF exposure guidelines are essential, it is equally important to consider the physical safety aspects associated with antenna installation and maintenance. This includes preventing accidents during installation, avoiding hazards related to high structures, and ensuring the antenna system is secure and stable under various weather conditions. In this section, we will explore safety practices and precautions that every amateur radio operator should follow to protect themselves and others from potential physical hazards associated with antennas.

Key Considerations When Setting Up an Antenna

Setting up an antenna involves several fundamental considerations to ensure optimal performance, safety, and regulation compliance. Here are the main factors to take into account:

1. **Location**: Choose an area that provides the best line-of-sight for the antenna, free from obstructions like buildings, trees, and other structures. Elevating the antenna can significantly improve signal reception and transmission.

2. **Height**: The height of the antenna affects its range and performance. Higher placement typically results in better coverage and reduced interference. However, it is essential to comply with local zoning laws and regulations regarding maximum allowable heights.

3. **Safety**: Ensure the installation is safe for both people and property. This includes:

   ○ **Grounding**: Proper grounding protects against lightning strikes and electrical surges.

   ○ **Guy Lines**: Use tension guy lines to stabilize tall masts and towers, especially in windy areas.

   ○ **Clearance**: Maintain a safe distance from power lines and other electrical infrastructure to prevent electrical hazards.

4. **RF Exposure**: To comply with safety regulations, evaluate and minimize RF exposure. This includes ensuring the antenna is placed far enough from areas where people spend time and adjusting power levels as needed.

5. **Structural Integrity**: Use durable materials and mounting hardware suitable for the environmental conditions. Regularly inspect and maintain the antenna and its supporting structures to ensure continued safety and performance.

6. **Regulatory Compliance**: Adhere to all relevant laws, regulations, and guidelines from authorities like the FCC. This includes obtaining necessary permits and ensuring the installation does not interfere with other services.

7. **Environmental Factors**: Consider the local climate and weather conditions. Antennas should withstand wind, rain, snow, and other environmental stresses.

Considering these factors, you can ensure your antenna setup is safe, efficient, and compliant with all relevant standards. This approach not only enhances the performance of your amateur radio station but also safeguards against potential hazards and legal issues.

Constructing the Antenna

One of the most critical safety precautions to observe when installing an antenna tower is to look for and stay clear of any overhead electrical wires. Contact with electrical wires can result in severe injury or even fatality due to electric shock. **It is essential to thoroughly survey the installation site for any nearby power lines** and ensure that the tower and its components are kept at a safe distance.

T0B04: Which of the following is an important safety precaution to observe when putting up an antenna tower?

A. Wear a ground strap connected to your wrist at all times
B. Insulate the base of the tower to avoid lightning strikes
C. Look for and stay clear of any overhead electrical wires
D. All these choices are correct

To ensure safety, maintain a minimum clearance distance as recommended by local electrical codes; typically, though, you **should ensure that if your antenna falls over, no part will ever be closer than 10 feet away from a power line.** Additionally, always assume that power lines are live and potentially dangerous. By taking these precautions, you can prevent accidental contact with electrical wires, safeguarding yourself and others involved in the installation process.

This part is both underlined and bolded – it's that important.

T0B06: What is the minimum safe distance from a power line to allow when installing an antenna?

A. Add the height of the antenna to the height of the power line and multiply by a factor of 1.5
B. The height of the power line above ground
C. 1/2 wavelength at the operating frequency
D. Enough so that if the antenna falls, no part of it can come closer than 10 feet to the power wires

One more piece to add to this. If the above wasn't enough of a warning, the FCC wants to stress one more piece from the test.

Attaching an antenna to a utility pole is highly discouraged because of the significant risk that the antenna or its supporting structures could contact high-voltage power lines. Utility poles often carry wires that transmit electricity at high voltages, posing a severe risk of electric shock or electrocution if touched. Even indirect contact, such as a wire or antenna element coming close to a power line, can lead to dangerous arcing or electrical discharge.

T0B09: Why should you avoid attaching an antenna to a utility pole?

A. The antenna will not work properly because of induced voltages
B. The 60 Hz radiations from the feed line may increase the SWR
C. The antenna could contact high-voltage power lines
D. All these choices are correct

Always choose an installation site well away from utility poles and overhead power lines to ensure safety. This precaution helps prevent accidental contact with high-voltage lines, which can cause severe injury, fatality, or damage to equipment.

Securing the Antenna

Tension Guy Lines

Tension guy lines are essential to stabilize and support tall structures such as antenna masts and towers. They are typically made of strong, durable materials like steel cable or synthetic fiber and designed to withstand significant tension. You've seen them. They are anchored at multiple points around the structure's base and connected to the tower at various heights, forming a supportive framework that resists wind and gravity forces.

- **Stability**: Tension guy lines help maintain the vertical position of the mast or tower by distributing the load and providing counteracting forces, preventing it from swaying or toppling over.

- **Wind Resistance**: Guy lines are crucial in withstanding wind loads, particularly in regions prone to strong winds. They help dissipate the wind force across multiple points, reducing the risk of structural failure.

- **Safety**: Properly installed guy lines ensure the safety of the antenna system and surrounding areas, preventing accidents caused by collapsing structures.

Understanding the importance and correct installation of tension guy lines is vital for ensuring the physical safety and longevity of your antenna setup.

Turnbuckles

A turnbuckle is a device that adjusts the tension or length of cables, ropes, or guy lines in various applications, including antenna installations. It consists of two threaded eye bolts screwed into either end of a metal frame, one with right-hand threads and the other with left-hand threads. The turnbuckle either tightens or loosens by rotating the frame, allowing for precise adjustment of the tension in the guy lines.

Key Features and Uses of Turnbuckles

- **Tension Adjustment**: Turnbuckles are primarily used to adjust the tension in guy lines, ensuring that structures like antenna masts and towers remain stable and secure. Proper tension helps prevent swaying and structural failure, particularly in windy conditions.

- **Versatility**: They are used in various applications, from construction and marine settings to amateur radio installations, where precise line tension control is essential.

- **Safety Enhancement**: Turnbuckles help maintain the integrity of the support system. They allow you to easily adjust and maintain the necessary tension in the guy lines, contributing to the overall safety and reliability of the installation.

Example of Use

Turnbuckles are attached to the guy lines that stabilize the antenna mast in an antenna installation. By tightening or loosening the turnbuckles, the operator can ensure that each guy line is evenly tensioned, maintaining the mast's vertical position and stability. This is critical for preventing the mast from leaning or collapsing, especially in adverse weather conditions.

For additional safety, a wire is put through the turnbuckle. The purpose of a safety wire through a turnbuckle used to tension guy lines is to prevent the turnbuckle from loosening inadvertently. Over time, vibrations from wind, weather changes, or other environmental factors can cause turnbuckles to rotate and loosen, potentially compromising the stability of the antenna structure.

By threading a safety wire through the turnbuckle and securing it, you ensure it remains adjusted, maintaining the necessary tension on the guy lines. This added security helps prevent structural failure and enhances the overall safety and reliability of the antenna installation.

T0B05: What is the purpose of a safety wire through a turnbuckle used to tension guy lines?

A. Secure the guy line if the turnbuckle breaks
B. Prevent loosening of the turnbuckle from vibration
C. Provide a ground path for lightning strikes
D. Provide an ability to measure for proper tensioning

Crank-Up Tower

A crank-up tower is a telescoping tower used in amateur radio and other applications to support antennas at varying heights. The tower consists of multiple nested sections that can be extended and retracted using a manual or motorized crank mechanism. This design allows for flexibility in raising the antenna to a desired height for optimal performance while enabling the tower to be lowered for maintenance, transport, or to reduce exposure to severe weather.

Key Features and Uses of Crank-Up Towers

- **Adjustable Height**: The primary feature of a crank-up tower is its ability to adjust the height of the antenna. Operators can elevate their antennas by cranking the tower up to improve signal reception and transmission. Conversely, the tower can be lowered to protect the antenna during storms or for easy maintenance access.

- **Ease of Use**: Crank-up towers are relatively easy to operate. The crank mechanism, which can be manual or motorized, allows for smooth raising and lowering of the tower sections. This makes it convenient for operators to adjust the antenna height as needed without requiring extensive effort or equipment.

- **Safety Considerations**: While crank-up towers offer convenience and flexibility, they also have specific safety considerations. The tower should only be climbed if fully retracted or equipped with mechanical safety locks to prevent unintended movement. Ensuring the tower is stable and secure is vital to avoid accidents and injuries.

Practical Applications

Crank-up towers are widely used by amateur radio enthusiasts who need to optimize their antenna performance by adjusting their height. They are also beneficial for other applications requiring temporary or adjustable equipment elevation, such as temporary broadcasting setups or emergency communication systems.

T0B07: Which of the following is an important safety rule to remember when using a crank-up tower?

A. This type of tower must never be painted
B. This type of tower must never be grounded
C. This type of tower must not be climbed unless it is retracted, or mechanical safety locking devices have been installed
D. All these choices are correct

Climbing an Antenna Tower

Climbing a tower is often necessary for amateur radio operators and technicians who install, maintain, or adjust antennas and other equipment. However, it is also one of the most hazardous activities associated with radio operations. Ensuring safety while climbing towers requires a thorough understanding of proper techniques, appropriate safety equipment, and adherence to established protocols. This section will cover the essential safety practices and precautions to follow when climbing towers, helping you minimize risks and perform your tasks effectively and safely. Whether you are a seasoned climber or new to tower work, these guidelines are to protect you and ensure a secure working environment.

Essential Requirements for Climbing an Antenna Tower

Climbing an antenna tower safely requires adhering to several safety measures. First and foremost, <u>climbers must have sufficient training in safe tower climbing techniques</u>. This is not training you get from a book but real-life training that ensures climbers understand the risks involved and are proficient in using climbing equipment and techniques to minimize these risks. Proper training is essential for developing the skills and knowledge necessary to navigate the complexities of tower climbing safely.

In addition to training, using an approved climbing harness and <u>appropriate tie-off methods</u> are mandatory. An <u>approved climbing harness</u> is designed to provide support and security, preventing falls and reducing the risk of injury. The harness must be properly fitted and secured before climbing. Furthermore, climbers must use appropriate tie-off techniques always to remain connected to the tower. This continuous connection ensures that the harness and tie-off system prevent a fall if a climber loses their grip or footing.

> **T0B02: What is required when climbing an antenna tower?**
>
> A. Have sufficient training on safe tower climbing techniques
> B. Use appropriate tie-off to the tower at all times
> C. Always wear an approved climbing harness
> **D. All these choices are correct**

<u>Climbing a tower without a helper or observer is never safe</u>. Having a second person present is essential for several reasons. A helper or observer can immediately assist in an emergency, such as a fall or medical issue. They can also help manage climbing equipment, ensure safety lines are correctly secured, and communicate with the climber to monitor their status throughout the climb.

Additionally, a helper or observer acts as an extra set of eyes to spot potential hazards the climber might overlook. This added vigilance enhances overall safety by ensuring all safety protocols are followed, and any issues are promptly addressed.

> **T0B03: Under what circumstances is it safe to climb a tower without a helper or observer?**
>
> A. When no electrical work is being performed
> B. When no mechanical work is being performed
> C. When the work being done is not more than 20 feet above the ground
> **D. Never**

Understand the importance of never climbing a tower alone. This will help maintain safety and prevent accidents. This principle is vital for both practical tower work and exam preparation, emphasizing the necessity of teamwork and proper safety measures in tower climbing activities.

Grounding the Antenna

Grounding the antenna is fundamental to setting up and maintaining a safe and effective amateur radio station. Proper grounding provides several benefits, including protection from lightning strikes, reduced electrical noise, and enhanced overall signal performance.

Establishing a reliable grounding system can safeguard your equipment from damage, improve communication clarity, and ensure compliance with safety regulations. This section will explore the principles and practices of grounding antennas, offering essential guidelines to help you implement a robust and effective grounding solution for your radio setup.

Grounding Requirements

Local electrical codes establish ground requirements for an amateur radio tower or antenna. These codes provide specific guidelines and regulations designed to ensure the safety and effectiveness of the grounding system. Adhering to local electrical codes is important because they are tailored to address the area's unique environmental and infrastructural conditions, such as soil conductivity and regional weather patterns.

Following local electrical codes helps prevent electrical hazards, such as lightning strikes and electrical surges, by properly designing and installing the grounding system. Compliance with these codes protects your equipment, enhances its performance, and ensures that your installation meets legal and safety standards.

> **T0B11: Which of the following establishes grounding requirements for an amateur radio tower or antenna?**
>
> A. FCC Part 97 rules
> **B. Local electrical codes**
> C. FAA tower lighting regulations
> D. UL recommended practices

Proper Grounding Method for a Tower

A proper grounding method for a tower involves using separate eight-foot ground rods for each tower leg, which are then bonded to the tower and each other. This setup provides a robust grounding system that effectively disperses electrical currents, such as those from lightning strikes, into the earth. By installing a ground rod at each tower leg and connecting these rods together, you create a low-resistance path to the ground that helps protect both the tower and any connected equipment from electrical surges.

> **T0B08: Which is a proper grounding method for a tower?**
>
> A. A single four-foot ground rod, driven into the ground no more than 12 inches from the base
> B. A ferrite-core RF choke connected between the tower and ground
> C. A connection between the tower base and a cold water pipe
> **D. Separate eight-foot ground rods for each tower leg, bonded to the tower and each other**

Bonding the ground rods to the tower and each other ensures the grounding system works as a unified structure, providing consistent protection throughout the installation. This method not only enhances safety by reducing the risk of electrical shocks and equipment damage but also helps improve the overall performance of the antenna system by minimizing electrical noise and interference.

Best Practices for Installing Ground Wires for Lightning Protection

When installing ground wires on a tower for lightning protection, it is good practice to ensure that the connections are short and direct. Short, direct ground connections provide the most efficient path for lightning-induced electrical currents to travel into the ground, minimizing the potential for damage to the tower and connected equipment. Long or convoluted ground paths can increase resistance and the likelihood of side-flash, where the lightning current jumps to nearby objects, potentially causing damage or injury.

T0B01: Which of the following is good practice when installing ground wires on a tower for lightning protection?

A. Put a drip loop in the ground connection to prevent water damage to the ground system
B. Make sure all ground wire bends are right angles
C. Ensure that connections are short and direct
D. All these choices are correct

Direct connections help maintain a low-impedance path to the ground, which is essential for quickly dissipating the high-energy surge from a lightning strike. This practice enhances the installation's safety and the grounding system's overall effectiveness.

Importance of Avoiding Sharp Bends in Grounding Conductors

Sharp bends must be avoided when installing grounding conductors used for lightning protection. Sharp bends can create points of high impedance, which hinder the efficient flow of lightning-induced electrical currents to the ground. This impedance can cause the electrical energy to slow or even arc at the bend, potentially damaging the grounding system, the tower, or connected equipment.

Ensuring that grounding conductors have smooth, gradual bends instead of sharp angles provides a more direct and low-resistance path for the electrical currents. This practice enhances the overall effectiveness of the grounding system, allowing it to dissipate the energy from a lightning strike quickly and safely into the earth.

T0B10: Which of the following is true when installing grounding conductors used for lightning protection?

A. Use only non-insulated wire
B. Wires must be carefully routed with precise right-angle bends
C. Sharp bends must be avoided
D. Common grounds must be avoided

As we conclude our discussion on safety, it should be clear that a thorough understanding of these principles will not only keep your equipment safe and in top operating condition but will also ensure the safety of you and others from the potential harm of operating an amateur radio station.

Operating Your Radio

Now that you have a solid understanding of the science behind radio and have familiarized yourself with the physical setup and components, it's time to start operating your radio. This section will guide you through the basics of getting on the air, from tuning and selecting frequencies to making your first contact. Whether using a handheld transceiver, a mobile unit in your vehicle, or a base station at home, learning how to operate your equipment effectively is fundamental to enjoying all that amateur radio offers. We'll cover essential skills such as setting up your radio, choosing the right modes and bands, and following proper operating procedures. With these foundational skills, you'll be ready to communicate with other hams, participate in nets, and explore exciting amateur radio communication.

Chapter 20

Decoding Ham Radio Jargon

IN HAM RADIO, EVERY term and abbreviation carries weight, serving as a bridge to more efficient communication. For instance, a "QSO," one of the most commonly heard terms, refers simply to a conversation between two or more amateur radio operators.

Each interaction you have on the air is a QSO, the basic building block of your ham radio experience. Another term, "DX," stands for "distance" and is a nod to the thrill of long-distance communication, often crossing international borders. "CQ," pronounced in a way like "'seek you," is an invitation for any operator who hears the call to respond, typically used when you want to initiate a new conversation without a specific individual in mind. Understanding these terms is your first step in feeling at home among seasoned operators.

Are you already feeling overwhelmed and concerned about keeping all these terms straight? Don't worry. An extensive glossary is provided at the end of the book.

Phonetic Alphabet

The phonetic alphabet is a standardized set of words used to represent each letter of the alphabet in voice communication. This system ensures clear and precise communication, especially when audio quality may be poor or misunderstandings due to similar-sounding letters are to be avoided. Each word in the phonetic alphabet uniquely corresponds to a letter, making it easier to spell words and prevent confusion.

Here is the NATO phonetic alphabet, commonly used in aviation, military, and amateur radio communications:

Phonetic Alphabet

A- Alfa	**G-** Golf	**M**- Mike	**S**- Sierra	**Y**- Yankee
B- Bravo	**H**- Hotel	**N**- November	**T**- Tango	**Z**- Zulu
C- Charlie	**I**- India	**O**- Oscar	**U**- Uniform	
D- Delta	**J**- Juliet	**P**- Papa	**V**- Victor	
E- Echo	**K**- Kilo	**Q**- Quebec	**W**- Whiskey	
F- Foxtrot	**L**- Lima	**R**- Romeo	**X**- X Ray	

Importance in Ham Radio

In ham radio, the phonetic alphabet is essential for ensuring clear communication, especially when conveying call signs, coordinates, or other critical information. It minimizes the risk of errors caused by mishearing. It helps operators exchange information accurately and efficiently, even in noisy or challenging conditions.

Although helpful and a common practice, officially, the FCC rules state that using a phonetic alphabet for station identification in the Amateur Radio Service is encouraged—not mandated, not required, but encouraged.

T1A03: What do the FCC rules state regarding the use of a phonetic alphabet for station identification in the Amateur Radio Service?

A. It is required when transmitting emergency messages
B. It is encouraged
C. It is required when in contact with foreign stations
D. All these choices are correct

Q-Codes

Q-codes are a standardized set of three-letter codes used in radio communications to convey complex information quickly and efficiently. Developed originally for commercial radiotelegraph communication and later adopted by amateur radio operators, Q codes simplify and standardize the communication process, particularly when language barriers or signal conditions might make verbal communication difficult.

Learning these codes is not just about efficiency; it's about fluency in a language that speeds up exchanges and builds camaraderie among operators who might be continents apart. The use of Q-codes dates back to the early 20th century, making them a tradition carried forward by today's digital-age hams.

Each Q code represents a specific question or statement, allowing operators to convey detailed information using short, universally understood codes. Here are a few examples of commonly used Q codes in amateur radio:

- **QRM**: Are you experiencing interference? / I am experiencing interference.

- **QRN**: Are you troubled by static? / I am troubled by static.

- **QRO**: Should I increase power? / Increase power.

- **QRP**: Should I decrease power? / Decrease power.

- **QRS**: Should I send more slowly? / Send more slowly.

- **QRT**: Should I stop sending? / Stop sending.

- **QRZ**: Who is calling me? / You are being called by _____.

- **QSB**: Are my signals fading? / Your signals are fading.

- **QSL**: Can you acknowledge receipt? / I acknowledge receipt.

- **QSY**: Should I change the frequency? / Change frequency to _____.

- **QTH**: What is your location? / My location is _____.

A printable version of Q-codes and the Phonetic Alphabet can be found here: **www.MorseCodePublishing.com/TechExam**

Printable Copy

Scan the QR code or click the link to receive 'Your Ham Packet,' which includes a formatted and printable copy of Q-Codes and the Phonetic Alphabet. Print and keep close to your radio.

A couple of these will be on the test. So let's practice.

T2B10: Which Q signal indicates that you are receiving interference from other stations?

A. QRM
B. QRN
C. QTH
D. QSB

QRM: Are you experiencing interference? / I am experiencing interference.

T2B11: Which Q signal indicates that you are changing frequency?

A. QRU
B. QSY
C. QSL
D. QRZ

QSY: Should I change the frequency? / Change frequency to _____.

My recommendation: You will learn these as you gain experience. Go get the printable Q-Codes linked above and print them out. Keep them by your radio. Over time, you will memorize them all.

For now, for today, just memorize the two for the test.

Common Words and Terms

Beyond the structured codes and official terms, ham radio is rich in slang and common phrases that color the conversations. "Rag chew" refers to a long, casual conversation, usually without any specific agenda other than enjoying good company over the airwaves. "Elmer," another endearing term, describes an experienced ham who mentors newer enthusiasts, helping them navigate their initial amateur radio adventures.

As you become more familiar with these terms, abbreviations, and phrases, you'll become an integral part of the ham radio community, ready to share your stories and experiences across the airwaves. Each term learned is a step closer to confident transmissions and enriched interactions, ensuring that each QSO you engage in is as rewarding as it is educational.

See the glossary for more common terms!

Operational Terms

Understanding operational terms is important for effective communication and smooth operation in amateur radio. These terms describe various modes, methods, and protocols used during radio operations, providing a common language that all operators can understand and use.

This section will introduce you to essential operational terms, such as simplex, duplex, and more, that you will encounter frequently in your ham radio activities. By familiarizing yourself with these terms, you will be better equipped to navigate and participate in radio communications, ensuring you can successfully operate your equipment and confidently engage with other operators.

Simplex

The term "simplex" describes an amateur station transmitting and receiving on the same frequency. In simplex communication, both stations take turns transmitting and receiving on a single frequency, allowing for a straightforward exchange of information. This method is commonly used for local line-of-sight communication, where both stations can hear each other clearly without additional infrastructure.

Simplex operation is easy to set up and use, making it ideal for casual conversations, field operations, and emergency communication scenarios. Using the same frequency for transmission and reception, simplex communication ensures that all participating stations are on the same channel, simplifying the process of making contact and maintaining a conversation.

T2A11: What term describes an amateur station that is transmitting and receiving on the same frequency?

A. Full duplex
B. Diplex
C. Simplex
D. Multiplex

Duplex

Duplex communication is a method where transmission and reception occur on different frequencies. This setup allows simultaneous two-way communication, as each station can transmit and receive simultaneously without interference. There are two types of duplex communication: half-duplex and full-duplex.

1. **Half-Duplex**: In half-duplex systems, communication can occur in both directions but not simultaneously. One station transmits while the other receives, and then they switch roles. An example of half-duplex communication is using a repeater, where the repeater receives a signal on one frequency and retransmits it on another.

2. **Full-Duplex**: In full-duplex systems, both stations transmit and receive simultaneously at different frequencies. This type of communication is commonly used in telephone networks and some advanced radio systems, allowing for continuous and uninterrupted conversation.

Duplex communication is essential when continuous and simultaneous two-way communication is needed, such as in extended-range repeaters or complex communication systems.

Squelch

Squelch is a feature in radio receivers <u>that mutes the audio output when the received signal is below a certain threshold or not present.</u> This helps eliminate background noise and static, ensuring that only signals strong enough to be intelligible are heard. By adjusting the squelch control, users can set the minimum signal strength required to open the audio path, allowing for a better listening experience.

T2B13: What is the purpose of a squelch function?

A. Reduce a CW transmitter's key clicks
B. Mute the receiver audio when a signal is not present
C. Eliminate parasitic oscillations in an RF amplifier
D. Reduce interference from impulse noise

For beginners, think of squelch as a noise gate for your radio. Without squelch, you would constantly hear static and weak signals, making it difficult to discern important communications. Setting the squelch level appropriately allows you to filter out these unwanted sounds, ensuring that only strong, clear signals come through.

Squelch in Action

Squelch is a feature in FM receivers that mutes the audio output when the received signal falls below a certain threshold, effectively reducing background noise when no signal is present. The squelch threshold must be adjusted appropriately to hear a weak FM signal. The squelch control can be set so that the <u>receiver's audio output is always on</u>, even when the signal is weak.

To adjust the squelch for weak signals, you turn the squelch knob until the background noise stops. This setting allows the receiver to produce audio output for even the faintest signals, ensuring you can hear weak transmissions. Setting the squelch threshold low ensures that the receiver remains open to any incoming signal, no matter how weak, which is essential for receiving distant or low-power stations.

T4B03: How is squelch adjusted so that a weak FM signal can be heard?

A. Set the squelch threshold so that receiver output audio is on all the time
B. Turn up the audio level until it overcomes the squelch threshold
C. Turn on the anti-squelch function
D. Enable squelch enhancement

Continuous Tone-Coded Squelch System (CTCSS)

CTCSS, which stands for Continuous Tone-Coded Squelch System, is a method used in radio communication to <u>control a receiver's squelch function. It involves transmitting a sub-audible tone,</u> typically between 67 and 254 Hz, along with the regular voice audio signal. The receiver is set to open its squelch and allow the audio to be heard only when it detects the correct tone, effectively reducing interference from unwanted signals on the same frequency.

For beginners, think of CTCSS as a selective gatekeeper for your radio communications. This system ensures that your receiver only picks up transmissions intended for you, filtering out background noise and transmissions from other users, not sending the specific tone. This is particularly useful in environments with heavy radio traffic or shared frequency scenarios.

T2B02: What term describes the use of a sub-audible tone transmitted along with normal voice audio to open the squelch of a receiver?

A. Carrier squelch
B. Tone burst
C. DTMF
D. CTCSS

Digital Coded Squelch (DCS)

DCS, which stands for Digital Coded Squelch, is an advanced method of controlling the squelch function in radio communication systems. Unlike CTCSS, which uses sub-audible analog tones, DCS employs digital codes to achieve the same purpose. When a radio transmits a signal, it includes a specific digital code and the voice or data. The receiving radio will only open its squelch and allow the audio to be heard if it detects the correct digital code.

Key Features of DCS:

- **Digital Encoding**: DCS uses a series of digital bits as the squelch code, offering a larger number of unique codes compared to CTCSS tones. This reduces the chances of interference from other users who do not use the correct DCS code at the same frequency.

- **Interference Reduction**: Using digital codes, DCS provides more precise control over which signals are allowed through the squelch, further minimizing unwanted noise and enhancing communication clarity.

- **Flexibility**: DCS is widely used in commercial and amateur radio systems, offering flexibility and enhanced privacy for users needing reliable communication in busy radio environments.

Consider DCS as a digital key unlocking your radio's audio only when the correct digital code is received. This ensures that you only hear transmissions intended for you.

The 'Your Ham Packet' link above also has a full list of all the CTCSS and DCS codes in printable format.

Now that you know some of the terms and common language. Let's try putting it into action.

Chapter 21

Making Your First Contact

Choice of Frequencies and Time of Day

SELECTING THE CORRECT FREQUENCY and time for making contacts is much like choosing the right time and place for planting seeds in a garden. It would help if you considered the conditions to maximize the chance of success. For example, trying to connect with people in the United States at 10am on a Tuesday might be more difficult because a lot of us work during the day. But at 8:30 pm, when the routine housework is done, the kids are in bed, and now it's time to relax, offers you a greater chance of success.

National Calling Frequency for FM Simplex on the 2-Meter band

The national calling frequency for FM simplex operations in the 2-meter band is **146.520 MHz**. This frequency is designated for initial contact between amateur radio operators before moving to another frequency to continue their conversation. It is a standard frequency where hams can reach out and establish communication, especially in unfamiliar areas or trying to contact new stations.

For beginners, it's important to remember 146.520 MHz as the primary frequency for calling and making initial contact on the 2-meter band (VHF). This helps make connecting with other operators and participating in the ham radio community easier.

> **T2A02: What is the national calling frequency for FM simplex operations in the 2 meter band?**
>
> **A. 146.520 MHz**
> B. 145.000 MHz
> C. 432.100 MHz
> D. 446.000 MHz

Handling Nerves

It's natural to feel nervous when making your first few contacts. The key to overcoming this is preparation and practice. Begin by listening to other exchanges to get a feel for the typical flow of a conversation. To build your confidence, you might also try simulated QSOs with a friend or mentor. Remember, every ham was once a beginner, and the community is known for being welcoming and helpful. Most operators will be patient and supportive, understanding the jitters of being new to the hobby.

Steps to Take Before Calling CQ

Before calling CQ on a frequency, it is essential to ensure that you are not interfering with ongoing communications and that you are authorized to use that frequency. <u>The first step is to listen carefully to the frequency for a short period to ensure it is clear and not already used by another station.</u> This helps avoid interrupting any ongoing conversations or activities.

Next, it is good practice <u>to ask if the frequency is in use</u> by transmitting a brief message such as, "Is this frequency in use?" and waiting for a response. This courteous step ensures that you are not inadvertently causing interference. <u>Finally, verify that you can use the frequency based on your license class and the regulations governing that band.</u> Following these steps, you help maintain orderly and respectful use of the airwaves. Understanding and remembering these practices will help you prepare for your exam and ensure proper etiquette in real-world communications.

T2A12: What should you do before calling CQ?

A. Listen first to be sure that no one else is using the frequency
B. Ask if the frequency is in use
C. Make sure you are authorized to use that frequency
D. All these choices are correct

QSO Etiquette

Just as there are rules of etiquette in social settings, there are unwritten rules that govern the conduct of QSOs. These include identifying yourself correctly with your call sign, listening more than you talk to ensure you're not interrupting ongoing communications, and being clear and concise in your transmissions. Always be polite and considerate, thank the other operator for the contact, and sign off appropriately with your call sign.

QSO Basics

A QSO, or a radio contact, is the fundamental interaction in the ham radio community. It begins with the simple yet profound act of reaching out through the ether and connecting with another person. This process involves several key steps: initiating the contact, conducting the conversation, and logging the interaction details.

To initiate a QSO, you first need to find a clear frequency that is available for use. This involves tuning your radio while listening for ongoing conversations to avoid interference. Once you've found a clear frequency - you can always start at 146.520 MHz - you call "<u>CQ</u>," followed by your call sign, inviting others to respond.

The procedural signal "<u>CQ" is used in amateur radio to indicate that a station is calling for any station that might be listening.</u> When an operator transmits "CQ," they are essentially sending out an open invitation for a conversation with anyone who can hear the signal. It's a way for operators to initiate contact and make new connections, whether for casual chatting, exchanging information, or seeking specific communication partners.

T2A08: What is the meaning of the procedural signal "CQ"?

A. Call on the quarter hour
B. Test transmission, no reply expected
C. Only the called station should transmit
D. Calling any station

Managing a QSO requires a delicate balance of listening and speaking. It's like a dance, where participants move in sync, respecting each other's space and pace. This exchange serves the practical purpose of testing and enjoying your radio setup and fosters a sense of community and shared interest.

After the exchange, log the details of your QSO. This log should include the call sign of the station contacted and the frequency, mode, date, and time of the QSO. Logging serves as a personal record and is also a requirement in many aspects of the hobby, especially if you wish to apply for awards or participate in contests.

Transmit Frequency Placement

When tuning an FM receiver, accurately set it to the signal's exact frequency. <u>The audio signal will become distorted if the receiver is tuned slightly above or below the intended frequency.</u> This distortion occurs because FM (Frequency Modulation) receivers are designed to demodulate signals at a specific frequency. Deviating from this frequency disrupts the proper demodulation process, resulting in poor audio quality, including static, hissing, or muffled sounds.

T4B12: What is the result of tuning an FM receiver above or below a signal's frequency?

A. Change in audio pitch
B. Sideband inversion
C. Generation of a heterodyne tone
D. Distortion of the signal's audio

One note about setting a frequency. Setting your transmit frequency precisely at the edge of an amateur band or sub-band can lead to several issues that might result in unintentional non-compliance with FCC regulations. One primary reason to avoid this practice is to account for <u>calibration errors in your transmitter's frequency</u> display. Even minor inaccuracies in calibration can cause your signal to extend beyond the permissible frequency range, leading to potential violations.

Additionally, when transmitting, the <u>modulation sidebands</u> of your signal can extend beyond your set frequency. If your transmit frequency is right at the edge of a band, these sidebands might spill over into frequencies that are not allocated for your use, causing interference with other services. Lastly, transmitter <u>frequency drift</u>, which can occur due to temperature changes or component aging, can shift your signal outside the intended band. Setting your transmit frequency slightly away from the band edge ensures that your entire signal, including any sidebands, remains within the authorized frequency range, thus maintaining compliance and avoiding interference with adjacent frequencies.

T1B09: Why should you not set your transmit frequency to be exactly at the edge of an amateur band or sub-band?

A. To allow for calibration error in the transmitter frequency display
B. So that modulation sidebands do not extend beyond the band edge
C. To allow for transmitter frequency drift
D. All these choices are correct

Example First Contact

Let's look at an example of a typical QSO (contact) between two amateur radio operators. Here's a simplified version of how it might go:

Operator 1: "CQ CQ CQ, this is November Alpha One Charlie Charlie, NA1CC, calling CQ and standing by."

Operator 2: "November Alpha One Charlie Charlie, this is Kilo Bravo Nine Romeo Echo Mike, KB9REM responding. Your signal is 5 and 9 into Chicago."

Operator 1: "Kilo Bravo Nine Romeo Echo Mike, thanks for the 5 and 9. You're also 5 and 9 into Boston. The name here is John. How do you copy?"

Operator 2: "Roger, John. Good copy. You're loud and clear. My name is Mike. It's a pleasure to make the QSO with you today. What's the weather like over there?"

Operator 1: "Thanks, Mike. The weather here is sunny and warm, and it is a beautiful day for radio. How about there?"

Operator 2: "It's pretty much the same here, John. Great conditions for a chat. Are you running any special equipment today?"

Operator 1: "I'm using an Icom 7300 with a dipole antenna about 20 feet up. Power is set to 100 watts. How about yourself, Mike?"

Operator 2: "I'm on a Yaesu FT-991 with a vertical antenna. Also running about 100 watts. It's working well, as you can hear!"

Operator 1: "Sounds great, Mike. Your setup is doing a fine job. I won't hold it too long since I know others want to make contact. Thanks for the QSO and 73!"

Operator 2: "73, John. Thanks for the contact, and have a great day. KB9REM clear."

Operator 1: "NA1CC clear."

In this example, "CQ" means a general call to any operators who might be listening. "5 and 9" refers to the signal report: "5" means perfectly readable, and "9" indicates a strong signal. "73" is a standard ham radio shorthand for "best regards" or "goodbye."

Now, let's pretend you are 'operator 2.'

Responding to a Station Calling CQ

When you hear a station calling CQ, it indicates they are looking to contact any listening station. To respond correctly, you should transmit the calling station's call sign followed by your call sign.

From the example above, if you hear NA1CC calling CQ, you would respond by saying, " NA1CC, this is KB9REM," where NA1CC is the station calling CQ and KB9REM is your call sign.

This method ensures the calling station knows precisely who is responding and can acknowledge your call. Keeping your response clear and concise helps maintain efficient communication on the airwaves, allowing both stations to establish contact quickly and begin their conversation.

T2A05: How should you respond to a station calling CQ?

A. Transmit "CQ" followed by the other station's call sign
B. Transmit your call sign followed by the other station's call sign
C. Transmit the other station's call sign followed by your call sign
D. Transmit a signal report followed by your call sign

As you begin making your first contacts in amateur radio, remember that the choice of frequency and time, coupled with proper etiquette and technical knowledge, plays a pivotal role in your enjoyment.

Now that you've learned the basics of initiating QSOs and ensuring clear communication, you're ready to explore the next exciting aspect of amateur radio: repeaters. In the upcoming chapter, we'll delve into how repeaters work, their benefits, and how to use them to extend your communication range and connect with other operators.

Chapter 22

Repeaters

IN AMATEUR RADIO, REPEATERS play a vital role in extending the range and reliability of communications. These powerful systems are strategically placed to receive and retransmit signals, allowing operators to communicate over much greater distances than possible with direct radio-to-radio contact. Understanding how repeaters work and how to use them is essential for any ham radio enthusiast.

A repeater is an electronic device that receives a radio signal and then retransmits it at a higher power level, extending the signal's range. Repeaters are typically located on high towers, buildings, or mountains, giving them a wide coverage area. They consist of a receiver, a transmitter, and an antenna, all tuned to specific frequencies. The components of a repeater include:

1. **Receiver**: Captures the incoming signal on one frequency.

2. **Transmitter**: Amplifies and rebroadcasts the signal on a different frequency.

3. **Duplexer**: A single antenna can receive and transmit without interference.

4. **Antenna**: Positioned at a high location to maximize coverage.

How Repeaters Work

When a radio operator transmits a signal, the repeater's receiver picks it up. It immediately retransmits it at a higher power on a different frequency. This process effectively boosts the original signal, allowing it to cover a much larger area. The standard frequency offset used in repeaters ensures that the transmitted and received signals do not interfere with each other.

T1F09: What type of amateur station simultaneously retransmits the signal of another amateur station on a different channel or channels?

A. Beacon station
B. Earth station
C. Repeater station
D. Message forwarding station

Repeater Offset

Repeater offset is the difference between a repeater's transmit and receive frequencies. Repeaters extend the communication range by receiving a signal at one frequency and retransmitting it at another. This frequency separation, known as the offset, prevents the repeater from interfering with its own signal. For example, in the 2-meter band, a standard repeater offset is 600 kHz. If the repeater receives 146.940 MHz, it might transmit 146.340 MHz. Offsets can be either positive or negative.

T2A07: What is meant by "repeater offset"?

A. The difference between a repeater's transmit and receive frequencies
B. The repeater has a time delay to prevent interference
C. The repeater station identification is done on a separate frequency
D. The number of simultaneous transmit frequencies used by a repeater

Benefits of Using Repeaters

Repeaters offer several advantages:

- **Extended Range**: They significantly increase the communication range, allowing contacts over distances that would be impossible with direct communication.

- **Improved Signal Quality**: Repeaters improve signal clarity and reduce interference by retransmitting signals with higher power and from elevated locations.

- **Emergency Communication**: Repeaters are crucial in emergencies, providing reliable communication channels for coordinating rescue and relief efforts.

Understanding repeaters and how to effectively use them is a fundamental aspect of ham radio operation. Whether for everyday communication, participating in local nets, or handling emergency traffic, repeaters enhance the functionality and reach of amateur radio systems.

Repeaters in Action

2 Meter Band (VHF Repeater)

To be repetitive, because that is how we learn, the 2-meter band is also commonly called the "VHF (Very High Frequency) band." This band (2-meter) covers frequencies from 144 MHz to 148 MHz. It is a popular range for amateur radio operators due to its favorable propagation characteristics and the availability of repeaters.

The VHF band allows for reliable communication over relatively long distances, especially when using repeaters to extend the signal range.

A standard repeater frequency offset in the 2-meter band is 600 kHz. This offset means that the repeater's transmit frequency is either 600 kHz higher or 600 kHz lower than its receive frequency. For example, if a repeater receives signals on 146.240 MHz, it might transmit on 146.340 MHz (600 kHz lower) or 147.540 MHz (600 kHz higher). This separation of transmit and receive frequencies allows the repeater to listen for incoming signals and retransmit them without interference simultaneously.

T2A01: What is a common repeater frequency offset in the 2-meter band?

A. Plus or minus 5 MHz
B. Plus or minus 600 kHz
C. Plus or minus 500 kHz
D. Plus or minus 1 MHz

70 cm Band (UHF Repeater)

The 70-centimeter band is called the "UHF (Ultra High Frequency) band." This band covers frequencies from 420 MHz to 450 MHz. Amateur radio operators widely use it for various types of communication, including local and regional contacts and repeater operations. The UHF band is known for penetrating buildings and other obstacles more effectively than lower frequencies, making it ideal for urban environments and mobile operations.

A standard repeater frequency offset in the 70-centimeter band is 5 MHz. This means the repeater's transmit frequency is either 5 MHz higher or 5 MHz lower than its receive frequency. For instance, if a repeater receives signals on 444.000 MHz, it might transmit on 449.000 MHz (5 MHz higher) or 439.000 MHz (5 MHz lower). This offset allows the repeater to receive and transmit signals simultaneously without interference, facilitating clear and effective communication over extended distances.

T2A03: What is a common repeater frequency offset in the 70 cm band?

A. Plus or minus 5 MHz
B. Plus or minus 600 kHz
C. Plus or minus 500 kHz
D. Plus or minus 1 MHz

Test time. Remember that some of these questions require you to think critically if you forgot or didn't memorize the answer. Let's say you forget the offset. By remembering the band range, you should eliminate some potential wrong answers. The 2m band is from 144 to 148 MHz. Only 4 MHz wide. So, having an offset in the MHz range would be unrealistic. Therefore, the likely answer would be in kilohertz (kHz).

The same applies to the UHF range (70 cm), which covers the band from 420 to 450 MHz. The wide 30 MHz range allows for a larger offset. An offset of kilohertz would be too small, so the answer is one of the MHz answers.

When you start to connect to repeaters, you will most often be given the repeater offset by looking them up in a directory, such as Repeater Book. Which can be found by a simple Google search for Repeater Book.

Listening in on a Repeater

When a station is listening on a repeater and looking for a contact, it typically announces its call sign, followed by the word "monitoring." For example, an operator might say, "This is K1ABC monitoring." This phrase indicates that K1ABC is actively listening and open to contacting any other station on the same repeater frequency. It's a way for operators to make themselves available for communication without initiating a specific call to another station.

For beginners, it's essential to recognize and use this standard practice to facilitate effective and courteous communication on repeaters. By announcing that you are "monitoring," you signal to other operators that you are ready and willing to engage in a conversation.

T2A09: Which of the following indicates that a station is listening on a repeater and looking for a contact?

A. "CQ CQ" followed by the repeater's call sign
B. The station's call sign followed by the word "monitoring"
C. The repeater call sign followed by the station's call sign
D. "QSY" followed by your call sign

Calling a Station on a Repeater

When you know the call sign of the station you want to contact on a repeater, the appropriate way to call them is first to say their call sign, followed by your own call sign. For example, if you want to call station K1ABC and your call sign is N1XYZ, you would say, "K1ABC, this is N1XYZ." This method clearly identifies both the calling and the receiving stations, facilitating smooth and efficient communication.

This practice helps ensure that the other station knows who is trying to contact them and can respond accordingly. It also maintains the standard communication protocol within the ham radio community, promoting orderly and respectful use of the repeater.

T2A04: What is an appropriate way to call another station on a repeater if you know the other station's call sign?

A. Say "break, break," then say the station's call sign
B. Say the station's call sign, then identify with your call sign
C. Say "CQ" three times, then the other station's call sign
D. Wait for the station to call CQ, then answer

Linked Repeaters

Linked repeaters are a network of repeaters connected to extend the range and coverage of radio communications. It is a system where multiple repeaters are interconnected, allowing signals received by one repeater to be transmitted by all the repeaters in the network.

By linking multiple repeaters, operators can communicate over much greater distances than possible with a single repeater. This is achieved through various methods, such as using the internet, dedicated radio links, or other communication technologies to interconnect repeaters.

Link Methods: Repeaters can be linked using different technologies. Some common methods include:

- **Internet Linking**: Systems like IRLP (Internet Radio Linking Project) or EchoLink use the internet to connect repeaters globally.

- **Dedicated Radio Links**: Microwave or UHF/VHF links directly connect repeaters without relying on the internet.

- **Satellite Links**: Satellites can be used to connect repeaters across vast distances.

Imagine you are a ham radio operator in New York City and want to communicate with a friend in Los Angeles. If both cities have repeaters that are part of a linked network, your transmission in New York can be relayed through the linked repeaters all the way to Los Angeles. This allows you to have a real-time conversation with your friend as if you were both on the same local repeater.

T2B03: Which of the following describes a linked repeater network?

A. A network of repeaters in which signals received by one repeater are transmitted by all the repeaters in the network
B. A single repeater with more than one receiver
C. Multiple repeaters with the same control operator
D. A system of repeaters linked by APRS

Simplex Channels & Repeaters in VHF/UHF

Simplex channels are designated in the VHF/UHF band plans to <u>facilitate direct communication between stations within range of each other without relying on repeaters.</u> This practice helps ensure that repeaters, which are valuable community resources, remain available for situations where they are truly needed, such as extending the communication range over greater distances or through obstacles. Operators can communicate directly by using simplex channels (remember: where you transmit and receive on the same frequency), reducing the load on repeaters and preventing unnecessary congestion.

T2B09: Why are simplex channels designated in the VHF/UHF band plans?
A. So stations within range of each other can communicate without tying up a repeater
B. For contest operation
C. For working DX only
D. So stations with simple transmitters can access the repeater without automated offset

Using simplex channels is especially beneficial during events, emergencies, or casual conversations where direct line-of-sight communication is sufficient. It promotes efficient use of the radio spectrum by allowing multiple simultaneous conversations in different areas without overburdening the repeater infrastructure.

Chapter 23

Space (Satellites and Stations)

SATELLITE COMMUNICATION REPRESENTS ONE of the most thrilling aspects of amateur radio, offering a unique blend of technical challenges and the sheer joy of making contacts that travel through space. In amateur radio, the control operator is responsible for ensuring that all transmissions follow the rules. When communicating through an amateur satellite or space station, <u>the important thing to remember is that anyone with a valid amateur radio license who can transmit on the satellite's uplink frequency can be the control operator.</u>

So yes, as a Technician licensee, you can engage with satellites specifically designed for amateur radio. Essentially, these satellites act as repeaters in space; they receive signals transmitted from the Earth and then rebroadcast them back down to other global locations. This ability to communicate via satellite opens up intercontinental QSOs (contacts) even with the relatively limited power and antenna systems permissible under a Technician license.

T1E02: Who may be the control operator of a station communicating through an amateur satellite or space station?

A. Only an Amateur Extra Class operator
B. A General class or higher licensee with a satellite operator certification
C. Only an Amateur Extra Class operator who is also an AMSAT member
D. Any amateur allowed to transmit on the satellite uplink frequency

---

Embarking on satellite communications requires specific equipment, but getting started can be practical and affordable. The most basic setup includes:

- A dual-band handheld transceiver (VHF / UHF).

- A simple handheld directional antenna.

- A means to track satellite passes.

Software applications, many of which are free, can predict when and where satellites will be visible over your location. These apps provide essential data like azimuth and elevation of each pass, helping you point your antenna accurately. A popular choice among beginners for your antenna is a handheld Yagi, which is relatively inexpensive and provides sufficient gain to make successful satellite contacts.

Preparation is vital when you're ready to make your first satellite QSO. Begin by selecting a suitable satellite. Choose a pass high enough over the horizon (usually more than 30 degrees) to ensure clear line-of-sight communication. Before the pass begins, set up your station—this includes adjusting your transceiver to the appropriate uplink frequency (for transmitting) and downlink frequency (for receiving) and preparing your antenna. As the satellite approaches, start listening to the downlink frequency. You might hear other operators making contacts; listen to these exchanges to get a sense of the rhythm and pace of satellite communication.

Initiating contact involves transmitting your call sign and listening for responses during the satellite pass. Remember, satellite passes typically last only about 10 minutes, so operations need to be efficient. Adjust your antenna position regularly to maximize signal strength, a process that can be challenging but becomes easier with practice. Making your first contact through a satellite is an exhilarating experience, often accompanied by a sense of achievement that bolsters your enthusiasm for further explorations in this high-tech area of amateur radio.

Websites like AMSAT (The Radio Amateur Satellite Corporation) offer information, including tutorials, operational news, and details of current and upcoming satellite missions. These resources are invaluable for both novices and experienced satellite operators. Engaging with these communities can provide practical advice, troubleshooting tips, and the camaraderie of shared interest.

Space Stations

According to the FCC Part 97 regulations, a space station is an amateur radio station located more than 50 kilometers (about 31 miles) above the Earth's surface. Remembering this definition is straightforward if you consider a space station as any equipment operating in the "space" above our atmosphere.

SPACE STATION

These stations facilitate global communications, allowing amateur radio operators to communicate over vast distances by relaying signals through these space-based stations.

T1A07: What is the FCC Part 97 definition of a space station?

A. Any satellite orbiting Earth
B. A manned satellite orbiting Earth
C. An amateur station located more than 50 km above Earth's surface
D. An amateur station using amateur radio satellites for the relay of signals

---

One of the most exciting and unique aspects of amateur radio is the ability to communicate with the International Space Station (ISS). This capability opens up a new frontier for ham radio enthusiasts, allowing unique opportunities to interact directly with astronauts aboard the ISS, bringing a thrilling dimension to the hobby.

Contacting the International Space Station (ISS)

Any amateur radio operator with a Technician class or higher license can contact the International Space Station (ISS) on VHF bands – no NASA approval needed! The ISS operates an amateur radio station that can be accessed by licensed amateurs worldwide, providing a unique and thrilling opportunity to communicate with astronauts in space. Typically, these contacts are made on the 2-meter band (144-148 MHz), a frequency range that Technician class licensees are authorized to use.

T1B02: Which amateurs may contact the International Space Station (ISS) on VHF bands?

A. Any amateur holding a General class or higher license
B. Any amateur holding a Technician class or higher license
C. Any amateur holding a General class or higher license who has applied for and received approval from NASA
D. Any amateur holding a Technician class or higher license who has applied for and received approval from NASA

Contacting the ISS involves using a VHF radio and a suitable antenna, often with a clear line of sight to the sky. Operators need to know the ISS's orbit and timing as it passes overhead quickly. This is where your software comes into play. This capability is one of the many privileges of holding a Technician class or higher license.

Why VHF Bands are Specifically Called Out for ISS Contacts

VHF bands are specifically called out to contact the International Space Station (ISS) because the ISS's amateur radio equipment primarily operates on the 2-meter band, which falls within the VHF frequency range (144-148 MHz). The VHF frequencies are well-suited for this purpose due to their ability to support clear, long-distance communication without being significantly affected by atmospheric conditions. Additionally, the VHF band balances range and equipment size, making it accessible for many amateur radio operators.

The 2-meter band is also widely available to amateur radio operators holding a Technician class license, making it an ideal choice for ISS contacts. Using VHF frequencies allows for reliable communication with the ISS as it orbits the Earth, enabling operators to take advantage of the relatively low power requirements and ease of antenna construction compared to higher frequency bands.

Receiving Telemetry from a Space Station

Telemetry from a space station, such as data on its health, status, and scientific measurements, <u>can be received by anyone with the appropriate equipment</u>. You do not need a specific license to receive and interpret these signals. Telemetry data is often broadcasted openly to provide valuable information to scientists, engineers, and amateur radio enthusiasts interested in space exploration and satellite technology.

T8B11: Who may receive telemetry from a space station?

A. Anyone
B. A licensed radio amateur with a transmitter equipped for interrogating the satellite
C. A licensed radio amateur who has been certified by the protocol developer
D. A licensed radio amateur who has registered for an access code from AMSAT

For amateur radio operators and space enthusiasts, receiving telemetry offers a fascinating glimpse into the operations of space missions and the functioning of satellites. With a suitable receiver and software, <u>anyone can decode these signals</u>, including information on the satellite's power levels, temperature, and other fundamental parameters. This accessibility encourages widespread interest and participation in space science, making it an engaging and educational aspect of amateur radio.

Satellite Communications

A Low-Earth Orbit (LEO) satellite orbits the Earth at relatively low altitudes, typically between 160 and 2,000 kilometers (100 to 1,240 miles) above the Earth's surface. These satellites move quickly, completing an orbit in about 90 to 120 minutes. LEO satellites are commonly used for various applications, including communications, Earth observation, and scientific research. Their proximity to Earth allows for lower communication latency and better imaging resolution.

T8B10: What is a LEO satellite?

A. A sun-synchronous satellite
B. A highly elliptical orbit satellite
C. A satellite in low energy operation mode
D. A satellite in low earth orbit

A satellite beacon is a <u>transmission from a satellite containing status information about the satellite's health</u>, operational status, and other data. These beacons are essential for tracking the satellite and ensuring it functions correctly. They provide valuable information (telemetry) to amateur radio operators and satellite controllers, including battery levels, temperature, and signal strength (the health and status of the satellite). By decoding these beacon signals, operators can monitor the satellite's condition and performance, making satellite beacons an important element in satellite communication and management.

T8B05: What is a satellite beacon?

A. The primary transmit antenna on the satellite
B. An indicator light that shows where to point your antenna
C. A reflective surface on the satellite
D. A transmission from a satellite that contains status information

---

T8B01: What telemetry information is typically transmitted by satellite beacons?

A. The signal strength of received signals
B. Time of day accurate to plus or minus 1/10 second
C. Health and status of the satellite
D. All these choices are correct

Common Modes of Transmission Used by Amateur Radio Satellites

Amateur radio satellites commonly use several transmission modes, including Single-Sideband (SSB), Frequency Modulation (FM), and Continuous Wave (CW) or data modes. Each serves a different purpose and offers unique advantages for satellite communication.

Single Sideband (SSB) is widely used for voice communications. It provides efficient bandwidth use, making it suitable for long-distance communication with minimal power. Frequency Modulation (FM) is popular for its simplicity and clear audio quality, making it ideal for voice contacts, especially for beginners. Continuous Wave (CW) involves Morse code, and various digital data modes are used for more robust communication, especially in weak signal conditions. These modes are also efficient regarding bandwidth and power usage, making them ideal for telemetry and control signals.

T8B04: What mode of transmission is commonly used by amateur radio satellites?

A. SSB
B. FM
C. CW/data
D. All these choices are correct

Satellite Signals

Spin Fading

Satellite signal spin fading is caused by the rotation of the satellite and its antennas as it orbits the Earth. As the satellite spins, the orientation of its antennas relative to the receiving station on Earth changes continuously. This variation in orientation affects the polarization and signal strength, leading to fluctuations in the received signal. These fluctuations are perceived as fading, where the signal strength periodically increases and decreases.

> **T8B09: What causes spin fading of satellite signals?**
>
> A. Circular polarized noise interference radiated from the sun
> **B. rotation of the satellite and its antennas**
> C. Doppler shift of the received signal
> D. Interfering signals within the satellite uplink band

Understanding spin fading is vital for amateur radio operators to optimize satellite communication. It highlights the need for circularly polarized antennas or signal diversity techniques to mitigate the effects of spin fading. By knowing this phenomenon, operators can better prepare for and manage the challenges of maintaining a stable communication link with orbiting satellites.

Doppler Shift

Doppler shift refers to the observed change in signal frequency caused by the <u>relative motion between the satellite and the Earth station</u>. As a satellite moves toward the observer, its signal frequency increases; conversely, as it moves away, the frequency decreases. This phenomenon is similar to the change in pitch of a passing siren.

> **T8B07: What is Doppler shift in reference to satellite communications?**
>
> A. A change in the satellite orbit
> B. A mode where the satellite receives signals on one band and transmits on another
> **C. An observed change in signal frequency caused by relative motion between the satellite and Earth station**
> D. A special digital communications mode for some satellites

Understanding and compensating for the Doppler shift will aid in maintaining clear satellite communication. The frequency changes can be significant, especially for higher frequency bands like VHF and UHF, and operators need to adjust their transmit and receive frequencies accordingly to keep the signal clear. Many modern transceivers and satellite tracking software can automatically adjust for Doppler shifts, simplifying the process.

Satellite Tracking

Satellite tracking programs are essential for radio operators engaged in satellite communications. These programs provide valuable real-time information that helps operators predict and track satellite positions. One of the key features of satellite tracking programs is the ability to <u>display maps showing the satellite's real-time position</u> and track over the Earth. This visual representation allows operators to see where the satellite is and where it will be, facilitating better planning for communication attempts.

Additionally, satellite tracking programs provide detailed <u>information on a satellite pass's time, azimuth, and elevation</u>. This includes the start, maximum altitude, and end of a pass, enabling operators to align their antennas accurately for optimal signal reception. Furthermore, these programs account for the Doppler shift, showing the <u>apparent frequency of the satellite transmission</u> as it changes due to the relative motion between the satellite and the Earth station.

T8B03: Which of the following are provided by satellite tracking programs?

A. Maps showing the real-time position of the satellite track over Earth
B. The time, azimuth, and elevation of the start, maximum altitude, and end of a pass
C. The apparent frequency of the satellite transmission, including effects of Doppler shift
D. All these choices are correct

Understanding Azimuth in Satellite Tracking

Azimuth is a term used in satellite tracking and navigation to describe an object's horizontal angle or direction, such as a satellite, from a specific observation point. It is measured in degrees, with 0 degrees representing true north. The angle increases clockwise, with 90 degrees corresponding to the east, 180 degrees to the south, and 270 degrees to the west. Essentially, azimuth helps to pinpoint the direction along the horizon from which the satellite will appear or disappear, allowing operators to align their antennas correctly.

For amateur radio operators, azimuth is a key parameter when tracking satellites. By knowing the azimuth angle, operators can adjust their antennas to accurately follow the satellite's path as it moves across the sky. This ensures optimal signal reception and transmission, making establishing and maintaining satellite communication easier. Understanding azimuth and how to use it in conjunction with elevation and other tracking data is essential for successful satellite operations.

Keplerian Elements

To function effectively, satellite tracking programs require specific inputs known as Keplerian elements. Keplerian elements are sets of parameters that describe the orbits of satellites. They include information such as the satellite's inclination, eccentricity, and mean anomaly, which are used to calculate its position and velocity at any given time. By regularly updating the Keplerian elements, tracking programs can provide accurate predictions and real-time tracking of satellite movements. Understanding how to input and utilize these elements ensures amateur radio operators can maximize their satellite communication endeavors, maintaining precise monitoring and effective communication with satellites in orbit.

T8B06: Which of the following are inputs to a satellite tracking program?

A. The satellite transmitted power
B. The Keplerian elements
C. The last observed time of zero Doppler shift
D. All these choices are correct

Satellite Uplink and Downlink Operations

In satellite communications, you need to ensure your uplink power is neither too low nor too high. One way to determine whether your satellite uplink power is appropriate is to compare your signal strength on the downlink to the satellite's beacon signal. Your signal strength should be about the same as the beacon. This balance ensures that your transmission is strong enough to be received clearly without overpowering other signals, maintaining optimal operation for all satellite users.

T8B12: Which of the following is a way to determine whether your satellite uplink power is neither too low nor too high?

A. Check your signal strength report in the telemetry data
B. Listen for distortion on your downlink signal
C. Your signal strength on the downlink should be about the same as the beacon
D. All these choices are correct

Using excessive effective radiated power (ERP) – remember, ERP is the measure of the power output of the radio transmitter - on a satellite uplink can have a significant negative impact. When one user's signal is too strong, it can block access for other users, preventing them from successfully transmitting and receiving signals through the satellite. This behavior, known as "hogging" the satellite, disrupts the shared nature of amateur satellite operations and diminishes the experience for the broader amateur radio community. By keeping your uplink power at an appropriate level, you help ensure that the satellite remains accessible to all operators.

T8B02: What is the impact of using excessive effective radiated power on a satellite uplink?

A. Possibility of commanding the satellite to an improper mode
B. Blocking access by other users
C. Overloading the satellite batteries
D. Possibility of rebooting the satellite control computer

Understanding satellite operating modes is also essential. When a satellite is described as operating in U/V mode, the uplink frequency is in the 70-centimeter band (UHF), and the downlink frequency is in the 2-meter band (VHF). This mode designation helps operators know which bands to transmit to and receive from the satellite. Familiarity with these modes is essential for effective satellite communication, as it ensures that operators use the correct frequencies and maximize the utility of the satellite for all users.

T8B08: What is meant by the statement that a satellite is operating in U/V mode?

A. The satellite uplink is in the 15-meter band, and the downlink is in the 10-meter band
B. The satellite uplink is in the 70-centimeter band, and the downlink is in the 2-meter band
C. The satellite operates using ultraviolet frequencies
D. The satellite frequencies are usually variable

Satellite and space station communication offers a new frontier for those with a Technician license, providing an engaging mix of technical challenges and the exciting opportunity to communicate through space.

As you delve deeper into this hobby, keep in mind that each new skill you learn and every boundary you push enriches your personal experience and contributes to the vibrant global community of amateur radio operators, even reaching the final frontier of space!

Chapter 24

Exploring Other Modes

Computers & the Internet

COMBINING COMPUTERS WITH RADIO equipment has opened many possibilities for amateur radio operators. Digital mode operations involve using computer software to encode and decode digital signals, which enables more efficient and varied forms of communication.

In digital mode operation, specific signals are used in a computer-radio interface: receive audio, transmit audio and transmitter keying. Receive audio is the signal from the radio that the computer needs to process. Transmit audio is the signal generated by the computer that needs to be sent to the radio for transmission. Transmitter keying is used to switch the transceiver between receive and transmit modes. Understanding these signals is essential for setting up a functional digital mode station.

> **T4A06: What signals are used in a computer-radio interface for digital mode operation?**
>
> A. Receive and transmit mode, status, and location
> B. Antenna and RF power
> **C. Receive audio, transmit audio, and transmitter keying**
> D. NMEA GPS location and DC power

When connecting a computer to a transceiver for digital operations, one essential connection is between the computer's "line in" port and the transceiver's speaker connector. This connection allows the computer to receive audio signals from the transceiver, which can then be processed by digital software. This setup ensures the signals are correctly received and transmitted, enabling smooth digital communication.

> **T4A07: Which of the following connections is made between a computer and a transceiver to use computer software when operating digital modes?**
>
> A. Computer "line out" to transceiver push-to-talk
> B. Computer "line in" to transceiver push-to-talk
> **C. Computer "line in" to transceiver speaker connector**
> D. Computer "line out" to transceiver speaker connector

You need to read carefully here. Did you see that answer 'D' was thrown in there to potentially catch you off guard?

Additionally, digital hot spots have become a popular tool for ham operators. A digital mode hotspot is a device that connects to the internet and allows for communication using digital voice or data systems. By linking a transceiver to a digital hot spot, operators can extend their communication reach via the internet, accessing a broader network of digital systems. This capability enhances the flexibility and utility of amateur radio, making it easier to connect with other operators worldwide. This is the same thing as using your phone as a hotspot!

T4A10: What function is performed with a transceiver and a digital mode hot spot?

A. communication using digital voice or data systems via the internet
B. FT8 digital communications via AFSK
C. RTTY encoding and decoding without a computer
D. High-speed digital communications for meteor scatter

Digital

Understanding Digital Communications Modes

Digital communications modes transmit data using digital signals rather than analog ones. Examples of digital modes include packet radio, IEEE 802.11 (Wi-Fi), and FT8. Packet radio sends data in packets over radio frequencies, commonly used for amateur radio networking and message forwarding. IEEE 802.11, more widely known as Wi-Fi, is a standard for wireless local area networking, enabling devices to communicate wirelessly over short distances. FT8 is a digital mode used in amateur radio for weak signal communication. It is known for its efficiency in low-bandwidth conditions and ability to decode signals barely above the noise level.

These digital modes offer various advantages, such as improved signal clarity, efficient bandwidth use, and the ability to transmit data reliably over long distances or through challenging conditions. These digital communication modes expand the possibilities for experimentation and practical communication in the field. Recognizing the differences and applications of these modes will help you in your exam preparation and practical amateur radio activities.

T8D01: Which of the following is a digital communications mode?

A. Packet radio
B. IEEE 802.11
C. FT8
D. All these choices are correct

To get started with digital modes like FT8 and DMR, you'll need a basic setup:

- A transceiver capable of the mode.

- A computer with suitable software.

- An interface to connect your transceiver to your computer.

There are numerous advantages to using digital modes. They allow communication across vast distances with minimal equipment, provide clear audio unaffected by the static and noise typically associated with analog modes, and offer new ways to interact and exchange information. Additionally, digital modes like FT8 are particularly useful in crowded band conditions, as their signals are much narrower than typical voice transmissions, allowing more communications to occur within the same frequency spectrum.

Numerous resources are available for those looking to dive deeper into digital modes. Online tutorials, many of which are free, can offer step-by-step guides on setting up and operating digital modes. Websites like the "ARRL" (American Radio Relay League) provide extensive documentation and forums where experienced amateurs share their knowledge and advice.

FT8

FT8, named after its creators Franke and Taylor and the "8" denoting mode's 8-frequency keying format, operates <u>under weak or low signal-to-noise operating</u> conditions and primarily makes quick, long-distance contacts. Its ability to work under challenging conditions where other modes might fail makes it particularly appealing to amateurs who enjoy making international contacts without needing elaborate setups.

T8D13: What is FT8?

A. A wideband FM voice mode
B. A digital mode capable of low signal-to-noise operation
C. An eight channel multiplex mode for FM repeaters
D. A digital slow-scan TV mode with forward error correction and automatic color compensation

---

Starting with FT8, the first step is installing <u>WSJT-X software</u>, explicitly designed for weak-signal communication by radio amateurs. Once installed, you'll configure the software to recognize your radio's settings, which involves selecting the correct port, <u>audio input, and output settings</u>. The true magic begins when you tune your radio to an FT8 frequency (commonly 14.074 MHz for the 20m band) and start decoding signals. Observing the software automatically decode transmissions and even auto-reply based on your settings is practical and thrilling.

T4A04: How are the transceiver audio input and output connected in a station configured to operate using FT8?

A. To a computer running a terminal program and connected to a terminal node controller unit
B. To the audio input and output of a computer running WSJT-X software
C. To an FT8 conversion unit, a keyboard, and a computer monitor
D. To a computer connected to the FT8converter.com website

Operating Activities Supported by WSJT-X Software

The WSJT-X software is renowned for supporting various specialized digital modes that facilitate unique operating activities in amateur radio. These activities include Earth-Moon-Earth (EME) communication, weak signal propagation beacons, and meteor scatter communication.

<u>Earth-Moon-Earth (EME) communication</u>, also known as moonbounce, involves transmitting a signal to the moon and receiving the reflected signal back on Earth. This mode allows for long-distance communication by leveraging the moon as a passive reflector. <u>Weak signal propagation</u> beacons are used to monitor and study propagation conditions. These beacons transmit low-power signals that can be received over great distances under the right conditions, providing valuable data on the behavior of radio waves. <u>Meteor scatter</u> communication takes advantage of ionized trails left by meteors entering the Earth's atmosphere. These trails reflect radio signals, allowing brief communication windows as the meteor trails dissipate.

These activities and how WSJT-X facilitates them help to illustrate amateur radio's advanced capabilities and innovative techniques.

T8D10: Which of the following operating activities is supported by digital mode software in the WSJT-X software suite?

A. Earth-Moon-Earth
B. Weak signal propagation beacons
C. Meteor scatter
D. All these choices are correct

Digital Mobile Radio (DMR)

On the other hand, DMR is a digital voice mode that offers clear audio communication and the ability to share data alongside voice messages. It uses time-division multiple access (TDMA) technology, allowing multiple users to share the same frequency channel, which increases efficiency and reduces interference.

DMR requires a different approach. First, you'll need a DMR-capable transceiver and a registration for a Radio ID from the DMR network. Setting up involves programming your radio with talkgroups and repeaters, which can be a complex process for beginners. Software tools like Tytera MD-380 are commonly used for programming DMR radios. These tools allow you to input different channels and talkgroups corresponding to your local DMR repeater settings. Once set up, using DMR can be as simple as selecting a channel and talking, with the technology handling the complexities of digital communication in the background.

A DMR (Digital Mobile Radio) "code plug" is a file that <u>contains all the access information</u> needed to operate a DMR radio. It is the programming file for your DMR radio, setting up frequencies, color codes, time slots, and talkgroups to enable seamless communication. Without a properly configured code plug, your DMR radio won't know how to connect to the network or communicate effectively.

Think of a code plug as the instruction manual for your DMR radio, telling it exactly how to access various repeaters and participate in different talkgroups. This setup ensures you can easily switch between different communication channels and networks.

T4B07: What does a DMR "code plug" contain?

A. Your call sign in CW for automatic identification
B. Access information for repeaters and talkgroups
C. The codec for digitizing audio
D. The DMR software version

DMR Repeaters

The DMR repeater system enhances communication by allowing multiple users to share the same frequency channel through time-division multiple access (TDMA). This effectively doubles the capacity of a single repeater, enabling more efficient use of available frequencies.

Key Features of the DMR Repeater System

- **Time-Division Multiple Access (TDMA)**: DMR uses TDMA to split a single frequency into two-time slots, allowing two separate conversations to co-occur on the same frequency. This increases the repeater system's efficiency and capacity.

- **Enhanced Audio Quality**: DMR provides superior audio quality to analog systems, especially in noisy environments. Digital signal processing helps reduce background noise and interference, resulting in clearer communications.

- **Advanced Features**: DMR supports a range of advanced features, including text messaging, GPS location services, and data transmission, making it a versatile tool for both amateur and professional users.

- **Network Connectivity**: DMR repeaters can be connected via the internet to form wide-area networks, allowing users to communicate across great distances beyond the reach of a single repeater. This connectivity enables global communication and linking multiple repeaters into a seamless network.

Relevance to Amateur Radio

DMR has become increasingly popular in amateur radio due to its efficiency and advanced capabilities. Operators use DMR repeaters to extend their communication range, improve audio quality, and access digital features.

Time-Division Multiple Access (TDMA)

DMR allows two separate voice signals to be transmitted on a single 12.5 kHz repeater channel through a technique called time-multiplexing. This method divides the channel into two timeslots, enabling two conversations to occur simultaneously without interference. Each time slot alternates between the two voice signals, effectively doubling the repeater channel's capacity.

By using time-multiplexing, DMR allows more users to communicate over the same channel.

T8D07: Which of the following describes DMR?

A. A technique for time-multiplexing two digital voice signals on a single 12.5 kHz repeater channel
B. An automatic position tracking mode for FM mobiles communicating through repeaters
C. An automatic computer logging technique for hands-off logging when communicating while operating a vehicle
D. A digital technique for transmitting on two repeater inputs simultaneously for automatic error correction

---

Color Codes in DMR Repeater Systems

In DMR (Digital Mobile Radio) repeater systems, the color code functions similarly to CTCSS tones or DCS codes in analog systems. The primary purpose of the color code is to ensure that only authorized users can access the repeater. For a radio to communicate through a DMR repeater, its color code must match the repeater's color code. This helps to prevent interference from other nearby repeaters operating on the same frequency and maintains organized and secure communication channels.

T2B12: What is the purpose of the color code used on DMR repeater systems?

A. Must match the repeater color code for access
B. Defines the frequency pair to use
C. Identifies the codec used
D. Defines the minimum signal level required for access

For beginners, it's important to remember that the color code acts as a digital key. The repeater will only accept your transmission with the correct color code, even if you are on the right frequency and time slot.

Wait a minute. I still don't understand "color codes." For example, is this repeater "blue?" The term "color code" refers to a digital identifier rather than an actual color. These codes differentiate between different repeaters and networks operating on the same frequency. Each DMR repeater is assigned a color code, which is a number from 0 to 15. This code must be programmed into the user's radio to allow access to the repeater.

For example, if you want to use a DMR repeater with the frequency 445.500 MHz and it has a color code of 1 (the code is provided by the repeater owner or in the directory), you would set your radio to 445.500 MHz and program the color code to 1. Only then will your radio be able to communicate through that repeater.

Talkgroups

Talkgroups in Digital Mobile Radio (DMR) systems are a way to organize and manage communication channels. They function like virtual groups within the DMR network, allowing groups of users to communicate without interference from other groups. Each talkgroup is assigned a unique identifier, and users can switch between talkgroups to join different conversations or activities.

T8D02: What is a "talkgroup" on a DMR repeater?

A. A group of operators sharing common interests
B. A way for groups of users to share a channel at different times without hearing other users on the channel
C. A protocol that increases the signal-to-noise ratio when multiple repeaters are linked together
D. A net that meets at a specified time

Key Features of Talkgroups

1. **Organized Communication**: Talkgroups help organize communications by categorizing users into specific groups based on their interests, activities, or operational needs. For instance, there can be talkgroups for local chat, regional communication, emergency response, or specific clubs and events.

2. **Selective Calling**: By selecting a talkgroup, users ensure that their transmissions are only heard by other users in the same talkgroup. This prevents the network from becoming overloaded with unrelated conversations and keeps communications relevant to each group's purpose.

3. **Efficient Use of Resources**: Talkgroups use the available frequency spectrum and network infrastructure efficiently. Multiple talkgroups can share the same frequency without interfering with each other, as they are digitally separated within the DMR system.

How to Use Talkgroups

To use a talkgroup, you must program your DMR radio with the correct talkgroup ID. When you switch to a talkgroup, your radio will transmit and receive only within that group. For example, if you want to participate in a regional discussion, you would switch to the corresponding regional talkgroup ID.

Example Scenario

Imagine you are part of a ham radio club that uses a DMR repeater. The club might have a general talkgroup for everyday conversation, an emergency talkgroup for urgent communications, and a special events talkgroup for coordinating activities during club events. By selecting the appropriate talkgroup, you can communicate with fellow club members without disturbing other groups using the same repeater.

T2B07: How can you join a digital repeater's "talkgroup"?

A. Register your radio with the local FCC office
B. Join the repeater owner's club
C. Program your radio with the group's ID or code
D. Sign your call after the courtesy tone

Digital Voice Transceiver

A digital voice transceiver selects a specific group of stations by <u>entering the group's identification code</u>. This talkgroup ID allows the transceiver to filter and communicate with only the stations that are part of that designated group.

T4B09: How is a specific group of stations selected on a digital voice transceiver?

A. By retrieving the frequencies from transceiver memory
B. By enabling the group's CTCSS tone
C. By entering the group's identification code
D. By activating automatic identification

Using these identification codes, digital voice transceivers can ensure that communications are directed to the intended recipients without interference from other users on the same frequency.

D-Star

D-STAR, which stands for Digital Smart Technologies for Amateur Radio, is a digital voice and data protocol designed for amateur radio by the Japan Amateur Radio League (JARL). It provides advanced features and capabilities compared to traditional analog radio, including improved voice clarity, efficient use of the radio spectrum, and the ability to transmit data such as text messages, images, and GPS information.

Key Features of D-STAR:

- **Digital Voice and Data Communication:** D-STAR allows for clear digital voice communications and can also transmit data, which is beneficial for sending text messages, GPS coordinates, and other types of digital information.

- **Call Sign Routing:** One of D-STAR's unique aspects is its ability to route communications based on call signs. This means you can communicate with other amateur radio operators worldwide by simply entering their call sign, and the D-STAR network will handle the signal routing.

- **Internet Connectivity:** D-STAR repeaters can be linked via the internet, enabling worldwide communication. This is particularly useful for amateur radio operators who wish to connect with others beyond the range of local repeaters.

- **Automatic Repeater Linking:** D-STAR repeaters can automatically link to other repeaters, creating a wide-area communications network. This allows for greater coverage and the ability to participate in larger communication networks.

- **Data Transmission:** In addition to voice, D-STAR supports digital data transmission, which can include everything from short text messages to more complex data packets.

How D-STAR Works:

D-STAR uses digital modulation techniques, specifically GMSK (Gaussian Minimum Shift Keying), to transmit information. When you speak into a D-STAR radio, your voice is digitized and compressed, then transmitted as a digital signal. This signal can include your voice and additional data, such as your call sign and location.

Repeaters and gateways in the D-STAR network play a role in extending the range of communications. D-STAR repeaters receive digital signals and retransmit them, while gateways connect these repeaters to the internet, facilitating global communication.

Before transmitting with a D-STAR digital transceiver, it is essential to program your call sign into the device. D-STAR (Digital Smart Technologies for Amateur Radio) is a digital voice and data protocol explicitly developed for amateur radio. One of its key features is using call signs to identify and route digital communications. By entering your call sign, the transceiver can correctly identify you to other stations and ensure your transmissions are routed correctly through repeaters and digital networks.

> **T4B11: Which of the following must be programmed into a D-STAR digital transceiver before transmitting?**
>
> **A. Your call sign**
> B. Your output power
> C. The codec type being used
> D. All these choices are correct

Programming your call sign into the D-STAR transceiver is a straightforward process typically done through the radio's menu system. This step is not only for compliance with FCC regulations, which require identification of the transmitting station but also for the proper functioning of the D-STAR network.

Packet Radio

Packet radio is a digital communication mode that transmits data over radio frequencies. It allows the exchange of text messages, telemetry data, and even internet traffic by breaking the data into small packets. Each packet contains not only the data itself but also addressing and error-checking information to ensure the accurate delivery of the message.

How Packet Radio Works

- **Data Packaging**: Information is divided into packets, which include headers with addressing and control information and a payload with the actual data.

- **Transmission**: Packets are transmitted over the radio frequency using protocols such as AX.25, specifically designed for amateur radio use.

- **Receiving**: The receiving station collects the packets, checks for errors, and reassembles them into the original message. Error-checking information in the packets ensures that only accurate data is processed.

Benefits of Packet Radio

- **Error Correction**: The built-in error-checking mechanisms help ensure the accuracy of transmitted data, making packet radio highly reliable.

- **Efficient Use of Bandwidth**: By transmitting data in packets, the system can efficiently use the available bandwidth, allowing multiple users to share the same frequency.

- **Automatic Repeat Request (ARQ)**: If a packet is received with errors, the receiving station can request a retransmission, ensuring data integrity.

Practical Applications

Packet radio is used for various purposes in the amateur radio community:

- **Messaging**: Sending text messages between operators, similar to email.

- **Telemetry**: Transmits data from remote sensors or stations, which is helpful for weather stations, balloon experiments, and satellite communications.

- **Emergency Communications**: Providing a reliable and robust method for data transmission during emergencies when other communication systems may be down.

Components of Packet Radio Transmissions

Packet radio transmissions include several components that ensure the accuracy and reliability of data communication. One essential element is the checksum, which permits error detection. The checksum is a calculated value based on the data in the packet, allowing the receiving station to verify the integrity of the received information. If the data doesn't match the checksum, it indicates an error occurred during transmission.

Additionally, packet radio transmissions feature a header containing important control information, such as the station's call sign to which the data is being sent. This header ensures that the packet is correctly routed to its intended recipient. Another component is the automatic repeat request (ARQ). In case of an error detected by the checksum, the ARQ mechanism enables the receiving station to request a retransmission of the faulty packet, ensuring the data is received correctly.

Remembering the roles of the checksum, header, and ARQ will help you understand how packet radio maintains data integrity and accurate communication.

T8D08: Which of the following is included in packet radio transmissions?

A. A check sum that permits error detection
B. A header that contains the call sign of the station to which the information is being sent
C. Automatic repeat request in case of error
D. All these choices are correct

ARQ Transmission Systems

An ARQ (Automatic Repeat reQuest) transmission system is an error correction method used in digital communications. In an ARQ system, the receiving station continuously checks the incoming data for errors. If an error is detected, the receiving station requests the transmitting station to resend the erroneous data. This process ensures that the data received is accurate and error-free, providing reliable communication even over noisy or unstable channels.

> **T8D11: What is an ARQ transmission system?**
>
> A. A special transmission format limited to video signals
> B. A system used to encrypt command signals to an amateur radio satellite
> **C. An error correction method in which the receiving station detects errors and sends a request for retransmission**
> D. A method of compressing data using autonomous reiterative Q codes prior to final encoding

ARQ in Amateur Radio

In amateur radio, ARQ transmission systems benefit digital modes where accurate data transmission is critical. For example, modes like PACTOR and some implementations of RTTY (Radio Teletype) use ARQ to maintain data integrity. PACTOR is commonly used for email, file transfers, and text communication, particularly in situations where other forms of communication might be unreliable or unavailable.

By automatically correcting errors, ARQ systems enable hams to communicate more effectively, reducing the need for manual intervention and retransmission requests. This error correction method ensures messages are received as intended, making ARQ a valuable tool for amateur radio operators engaged in digital communication.

Automatic Packet Reporting System (APRS)

APRS, or Automatic Packet Reporting System, is a digital communication protocol used in amateur radio to provide real-time tactical data and location information. One of the primary applications of APRS is to facilitate digital communications combined with a mapping system that shows the locations of participating stations. This feature is particularly useful in emergencies, public service events, and other scenarios where real-time tracking and information sharing is important.

> **T8D05: Which of the following is an application of APRS?**
>
> **A. Providing real-time tactical digital communications in conjunction with a map showing the locations of stations**
> B. Showing automatically the number of packets transmitted via PACTOR during a specific time interval
> C. Providing voice over internet connection between repeaters
> D. Providing information on the number of stations signed into a repeater

How APRS Enhances Communication

By transmitting data packets that include GPS coordinates and other relevant information, APRS allows operators to visualize the positions and movements of stations on a map. This capability enhances situational awareness and coordination among operators, making it an invaluable tool for search and rescue operations, disaster response, and large-scale event management.

Types of Data Transmitted by APRS

APRS can transmit various data types to enhance real-time communication and situational awareness. The primary data transmitted by APRS includes GPS position data, which allows operators to track the locations of stations and moving objects on a map. This feature is handy for emergency response, search and rescue operations, and public service events where precise location tracking is critical.

In addition to GPS data, APRS can transmit text messages, enabling operators to exchange short, real-time messages. This capability supports efficient coordination and information sharing during events or operations. APRS also transmits weather data, providing real-time weather conditions from stations equipped with weather sensors. This information is valuable for monitoring and responding to changing weather conditions during outdoor and emergency activities.

T8D03: What kind of data can be transmitted by APRS?

A. GPS position data
B. Text messages
C. Weather data
D. All these choices are correct

Phase Shift Keying (PSK)

The abbreviation "PSK" stands for Phase Shift Keying, a digital modulation technique that transmits data over radio waves. In PSK, the carrier signal's phase is varied according to the digital data being sent. This phase variation represents the binary data, making it an efficient method for transmitting information, especially in noisy environments. There are different types of PSK, including Binary Phase Shift Keying (BPSK) and Quadrature Phase Shift Keying (QPSK), each differing in how the phase changes to encode data.

T8D06: What does the abbreviation "PSK" mean?

A. Pulse Shift Keying
B. Phase Shift Keying
C. Packet Short Keying
D. Phased Slide Keying

PSK in Amateur Radio

In amateur radio, PSK is commonly used in digital communication modes, particularly PSK31. PSK31 is a popular mode because it uses narrow bandwidth, allowing for effective communication even with low power and under poor conditions. It is especially favored for keyboard-to-keyboard communications, where operators can type messages to each other in real-time.

Voice Over Internet Protocol (VoIP)

Voice Over Internet Protocol (VoIP) is a technology that allows you to make voice calls using a broadband internet connection instead of a regular phone line. VoIP converts your voice into digital signals and transmits them over the internet. This method uses digital techniques to deliver clear and efficient voice communications, making it a popular choice for personal and business use.

Remembering VoIP is easy if you consider it the technology behind internet-based phone calls, like those made with services such as Skype, Zoom, or WhatsApp. VoIP leverages the internet instead of relying on traditional telephone infrastructure, offering advantages like lower costs, flexibility, and integration with other Internet services. Knowing that VoIP delivers voice communications over the internet using digital techniques will help you quickly recall this concept for your exam and understand its growing importance in modern communication.

T8C07: What is Voice Over Internet Protocol (VoIP)?

A. A set of rules specifying how to identify your station when linked over the internet to another station
B. A technique employed to "spot" DX stations via the internet
C. A technique for measuring the modulation quality of a transmitter using remote sites monitored via the internet
D. A method of delivering voice communications over the internet using digital techniques

A gateway in amateur radio is a station that connects other amateur radio stations to the internet. This allows radio signals to be transmitted over the internet, extending the reach of communication far beyond the traditional range of radio waves. Gateways bridge the radio frequency spectrum and the internet, enabling seamless communication between operators in different parts of the world.

Think of it as a station that provides the "gate" to the internet. This setup enhances amateur radio's capabilities by allowing operators to connect globally, regardless of geographic limitations.

T8C11: What is an amateur radio station that connects other amateur stations to the internet?

A. A gateway
B. A repeater
C. A digipeater
D. A beacon

Mesh Network

An amateur radio mesh network is a data network designed for amateur radio operators. It utilizes commercial Wi-Fi equipment modified with specialized firmware to enable its use within amateur radio bands. This adaptation allows amateur radio operators to create a flexible and decentralized network where data can be transmitted over long distances without relying on traditional internet infrastructure. The mesh network structure means that each node can communicate with multiple other nodes, creating a robust and resilient communication system that can be particularly useful in emergencies or for extending internet connectivity in remote areas.

T8D12: Which of the following best describes an amateur radio mesh network?

A. An amateur-radio based data network using commercial Wi-Fi equipment with modified firmware
B. A wide-bandwidth digital voice mode employing DMR protocols
C. A satellite communications network using modified commercial satellite TV hardware
D. An internet linking protocol used to network repeaters

Understanding how to set up and operate an amateur radio mesh network can significantly enhance an operator's ability to participate in and contribute to various amateur radio activities.

Internet Radio Linking Project (IRLP)

The Internet Radio Linking Project (IRLP) is a technique that connects amateur radio systems, like repeaters, via the internet using Voice Over Internet Protocol (VoIP). This allows amateur radio operators to communicate with each other over long distances, far beyond the normal range of their radio equipment, by linking their local repeaters to other repeaters worldwide through the internet.

Think of IRLP as a bridge between traditional radio communication and the internet. By using VoIP, IRLP enables clear and reliable voice communication between radio operators in different regions, enhancing the versatility and reach of amateur radio networks. Knowing that IRLP connects repeaters via the internet using VoIP will help you recall this concept for your exam, highlighting its role in expanding the capabilities of ham radio communication.

T8C08: What is the Internet Radio Linking Project (IRLP)?

A. A technique to connect amateur radio systems, such as repeaters, via the internet using Voice Over Internet Protocol (VoIP)
B. A system for providing access to websites via amateur radio
C. A system for informing amateurs in real time of the frequency of active DX stations
D. A technique for measuring signal strength of an amateur transmitter via the internet

---

Directly accessing IRLP (Internet Radio Linking Project) nodes over the air is accomplished by using Dual-Tone Multi-Frequency (DTMF) signals. DTMF signals are the audio tones you hear when pressing keys on a telephone keypad (digital tones). In the context of IRLP, these tones send commands from your radio to the IRLP node, instructing it to connect to other nodes or perform specific functions.

DTMF are signals that "dial" into the IRLP system using your radio. You can control the IRLP node and link with other repeaters worldwide by pressing the appropriate keys on your radio's keypad.

T8C06: How is over the air access to IRLP nodes accomplished?

A. By obtaining a password that is sent via voice to the node
B. By using DTMF signals
C. By entering the proper internet password
D. By using CTCSS tone codes

And...

T2B06: What type of signaling uses pairs of audio tones?

A. DTMF
B. CTCSS
C. GPRS
D. D-STAR

EchoLink

EchoLink is a protocol that allows an amateur station to transmit through a repeater without needing a traditional radio to initiate the transmission. Instead, EchoLink uses Voice Over Internet Protocol (VoIP) to connect amateur radio operators over the internet. This means you can use your computer or smartphone to access and transmit through repeaters anywhere worldwide, as long as they are connected to the EchoLink network. How cool is that!

EchoLink is like a modern bridge between internet technology and traditional ham radio. It enables greater flexibility and convenience, allowing operators to participate in amateur radio communication from virtually any location with internet access. Knowing that EchoLink allows transmission through repeaters using VoIP without a physical radio will help you quickly recall this concept for your exam, emphasizing its role in expanding the accessibility and reach of ham radio operations.

T8C09: Which of the following protocols enables an amateur station to transmit through a repeater without using a radio to initiate the transmission?

A. IRLP
B. D-STAR
C. DMR
D. EchoLink

Before using the EchoLink system, you must register your call sign and provide proof of your amateur radio license. This process ensures that only licensed radio operators can access the system, maintaining the integrity and security of the EchoLink network. Registration typically involves submitting your call sign and a copy of your license to the EchoLink administrators, who will verify your credentials.

Think of this registration step as a way to authenticate and validate your identity within the EchoLink community. Once registered, you can use your computer or smartphone to connect to repeaters and other stations worldwide.

T8C10: What is required before using the EchoLink system?

A. Complete the required EchoLink training
B. Purchase a license to use the EchoLink software
C. Register your call sign and provide proof of license
D. All these choices are correct

National Television System Committee (NTSC)

The term "NTSC" stands for National Television System Committee and refers to a type of analog fast-scan color TV signal. NTSC is a standard for analog television used predominantly in North America and parts of South America before the transition to digital broadcasting. This system encodes color video signals and synchronizes them for display on television screens, providing the capability to transmit moving images and sound over radio frequencies.

NTSC in Amateur Radio

In the context of amateur radio, NTSC transmissions can be used for Amateur Television (ATV) operations, where enthusiasts transmit live video signals. These transmissions allow for sharing video content such as public service announcements, live events, or technical demonstrations.

T8D04: What type of transmission is indicated by the term "NTSC?"

A. A Normal Transmission mode in Static Circuit
B. A special mode for satellite uplink
C. An analog fast-scan color TV signal
D. A frame compression scheme for TV signals

Now, that was a lot to take in and remember. But don't let it overwhelm you. Like any hobby, it's best to start with the basics and build your skills with the fundamentals. As you grow and gain experience, you'll naturally start to branch out into these other operating modes, adding depth and versatility to your radio operation.

Chapter 25

Troubleshooting

TROUBLESHOOTING ISSUES IS ESSENTIAL for any ham radio enthusiast. We'll cover common troubleshooting techniques to help you identify and resolve issues that may arise during operation. Mastering these skills will ensure smooth and reliable communication as a beginner, enhancing your overall ham radio experience. Let's dive into the essentials of radio operation and problem-solving to keep your equipment running optimally.

On the Air Issues

Radio Frequency Interference

Radiofrequency interference (RFI) can significantly impact the quality of communications in amateur radio. It can be caused by various factors, including fundamental overload, harmonics, and spurious emissions. Understanding each of these sources of interference and knowing how to address them is essential for maintaining clear and reliable transmissions.

> **T7B03: Which of the following can cause radio frequency interference?**
>
> A. Fundamental overload
> B. Harmonics
> C. Spurious emissions
> **D. All these choices are correct**

Fundamental Overload: This occurs when a strong signal overwhelms the receiver's front end, causing it to malfunction. Fundamental overload can be mitigated by improving the receiver's selectivity or using an attenuator to reduce the strength of the incoming signal. Ensuring your equipment is calibrated correctly and not operating excessively high power levels can also help prevent this issue.

Harmonics: Harmonics are unwanted frequencies that are multiples of the fundamental frequency. They can cause interference on other bands and frequencies. To reduce harmonics, use low-pass filters on transmitters and ensure all equipment is properly shielded and grounded. Regularly checking your equipment for proper operation and maintenance can also help minimize harmonic emissions.

Spurious Emissions are unintended signals that are not harmonic but can still cause interference. They can result from faulty equipment or improper adjustments. Band-pass filters and maintaining your equipment in good working order can help eliminate these emissions. Additionally, ensuring your transmitter is tuned correctly and not operating beyond its designed parameters can reduce spurious emissions.

By understanding these causes of RFI and taking appropriate measures to mitigate them, amateur radio operators can ensure their transmissions are clear and free from interference.

Radio Frequency Interference with Consumer Electronics

Amateur radio transmissions can sometimes unintentionally interfere with consumer electronics, such as AM/FM radios and television sets. This interference is often due to the consumer device's inability to reject strong signals outside its intended frequency band. Knowing the causes and solutions to these issues is key to maintaining harmony between amateur radio operations and other electronic devices.

Unintentional Reception by AM/FM Radios

When a broadcast AM or FM radio unintentionally receives an amateur radio transmission, it is usually because the receiver cannot reject strong signals outside its intended band. This problem can be widespread in areas with strong amateur transmissions. Improving the receiver's ability to filter out unwanted signals through better internal filtering or external band-pass filters can help mitigate this issue.

> **T7B02: What would cause a broadcast AM or FM radio to receive an amateur radio transmission unintentionally?**
>
> **A. The receiver is unable to reject strong signals outside the AM or FM band**
> B. The microphone gain of the transmitter is turned up too high
> C. The audio amplifier of the transmitter is overloaded
> D. The deviation of an FM transmitter is set too low

Reducing VHF Transceiver Overload

VHF transceivers can experience overload from nearby commercial FM stations. This type of interference can be reduced by installing a band-reject filter, also known as a notch filter, which attenuates the specific frequency range of the commercial FM signals, thereby preventing them from overwhelming the transceiver.

> **T7B07: Which of the following can reduce overload of a VHF transceiver by a nearby commercial FM station?**
>
> A. Installing an RF preamplifier
> B. Using double-shielded coaxial cable
> C. Installing bypass capacitors on the microphone cable
> **D. Installing a band-reject filter**

Fundamental Overload in Non-Amateur Devices

Strong amateur signals might cause fundamental overload in non-amateur radios or TV receivers. This problem can often be resolved by installing a filter at the antenna input of the affected device. The filter blocks the amateur signal before it can enter the receiver, eliminating the interference.

T7B05: How can fundamental overload of a non-amateur radio or TV receiver by an amateur signal be reduced or eliminated?

A. Block the amateur signal with a filter at the antenna input of the affected receiver
B. Block the interfering signal with a filter on the amateur transmitter
C. Switch the transmitter from FM to SSB
D. Switch the transmitter to a narrow-band mode

TV Interference Solutions

One common issue is interference with non-fiber optic cable TV systems caused by amateur transmissions. The first step in resolving this type of interference is to <u>ensure that all TV feed line coaxial connectors are correctly installed</u>. Poorly installed connectors can act as entry points for unwanted signals, causing interference. Adequately secured and shielded connectors help maintain signal integrity and reduce the chances of interference.

T7B09: What should be the first step to resolve non-fiber optic cable TV interference caused by your amateur radio transmission?

A. Add a low-pass filter to the TV antenna input
B. Add a high-pass filter to the TV antenna input
C. Add a preamplifier to the TV antenna input
D. Be sure all TV feed line coaxial connectors are installed properly

By understanding these types of interference and implementing the appropriate solutions, amateur radio operators can minimize the impact of their transmissions on nearby consumer electronics. This ensures better operation of their equipment and helps maintain good relations with neighbors and the broader community.

Addressing Interference Issues with Neighbors

Interference between amateur radio stations and nearby consumer electronics can be a common issue. Knowing how to handle these situations responsibly and diplomatically is essential for maintaining good relations with your neighbors and ensuring your station operates within legal and technical standards.

When Your Station Causes Interference

If a neighbor informs you that your station's transmissions are interfering with their radio or TV reception, <u>the first step is to ensure that your station is functioning properly</u>. Check your equipment to verify that it does not cause interference to your own radio or television when tuned to the same channel. This self-check helps you confirm that your transmissions are clean and within acceptable parameters. Additionally, consider installing low-pass filters, ferrite chokes, or other interference mitigation devices on your equipment to reduce the possibility of causing unintended interference.

T7B06: Which of the following actions should you take if a neighbor tells you that your station's transmissions are interfering with their radio or TV reception?

A. Make sure that your station is functioning properly and that it does not cause interference to your own radio or television when it is tuned to the same channel
B. Immediately turn off your transmitter and contact the nearest FCC office for assistance
C. Install a harmonic doubler on the output of your transmitter and tune it until the interference is eliminated
D. All these choices are correct

When a Neighbor's Device Causes Interference

If you experience harmful interference to your amateur station from something in a neighbor's home, it is important to approach the situation politely and cooperate. First, work with your neighbor to <u>identify the offending device</u>. Once identified, <u>explain that FCC rules prohibit the use of devices that cause harmful interference</u> to licensed radio services. Offer practical solutions, such as using better-quality cables or adding ferrite chokes to the interfering device. At the same time, <u>ensure that your station meets the standards of good amateur practice</u> by maintaining proper grounding, using well-shielded equipment, and operating within legal power limits.

T7B08: What should you do if something in a neighbor's home is causing harmful interference to your amateur station?

A. Work with your neighbor to identify the offending device
B. Politely inform your neighbor that FCC rules prohibit the use of devices that cause interference
C. Make sure your station meets the standards of good amateur practice
D. All these choices are correct

You are committed to resolving interference issues amicably and responsibly by taking these steps. This helps maintain a good relationship with your neighbors and ensures that your amateur radio station operates smoothly and within FCC regulations.

Understanding RF Feedback

RF feedback, or radio frequency feedback, can significantly impact the quality of voice transmissions. A common symptom of RF feedback in a transmitter or transceiver is receiving <u>reports of garbled, distorted, or unintelligible voice transmissions from other operators</u>. This issue occurs when transmitted RF energy re-enters the transmitter's audio circuits, causing unwanted feedback that distorts the transmitted audio signal.

T7B11: What is a symptom of RF feedback in a transmitter or transceiver?

A. Excessive SWR at the antenna connection
B. The transmitter will not stay on the desired frequency
C. Reports of garbled, distorted, or unintelligible voice transmissions
D. Frequent blowing of power supply fuses

To mitigate RF feedback, ensure your station is grounded correctly, and all connections are secure. Using ferrite chokes on microphone cables and other audio lines can help prevent RF energy from coupling into the audio path. Additionally, keeping antenna feed lines away from the radio equipment and audio cables can reduce the likelihood of RF feedback.

Distorted or Unintelligible Audio Signals

Suppose you receive a report that your audio signal through an FM repeater is distorted or unintelligible. In that case, several factors could be causing the problem. One common issue is that your transmitter might be slightly off frequency. Even a slight deviation can result in poor signal quality, making your audio sound distorted or unclear. Ensuring your transmitter is calibrated correctly and operating on the correct frequency is needed for clear communication.

Another potential problem could be that your batteries are running low. Low battery power can lead to reduced transmitter output and poor audio quality. Always check your battery levels before operating, especially in portable or mobile setups, and replace or recharge them as necessary. Additionally, being in a poor location, such as an area with heavy obstructions or poor signal coverage, can cause audio issues. Moving to a higher or more open area often improves signal strength and clarity. Addressing these factors ensures your audio signal remains clear and intelligible when using FM repeaters.

T7B10: What might be a problem if you receive a report that your audio signal through an FM repeater is distorted or unintelligible?

A. Your transmitter is slightly off frequency
B. Your batteries are running low
C. You are in a bad location
D. All these choices are correct

Distorted FM Transmission Audio

If your FM transmission audio is distorted on voice peaks, one likely cause is that you are talking too loudly into the microphone. Speaking too loudly can overdrive the microphone input, causing the audio signal to become clipped and distorted. This distortion occurs because the microphone and transmitter circuits are designed to handle a specific range of audio levels, and excessive volume exceeds this range, resulting in poor sound quality.

To avoid this issue, speaking at a normal volume and maintaining an appropriate distance from the microphone is essential. Additionally, adjusting the microphone gain setting on your transceiver can help ensure that your audio levels remain within the optimal range for clear transmission.

T2B05: What would cause your FM transmission audio to be distorted on voice peaks?

A. Your repeater offset is inverted
B. You need to talk louder
C. You are talking too loudly
D. Your transmit power is too high

FM, or Frequency Modulation, is mentioned explicitly in the question because the nature of FM transmission makes it particularly sensitive to audio input levels. In FM, the frequency of the carrier wave is varied by the amplitude of the input audio signal. When you speak too loudly, the microphone captures a high-amplitude audio signal, which causes significant variations in the carrier frequency. This can lead to over-modulation, resulting in distortion, especially on voice peaks where the audio signal is strongest.

In other modulation methods like AM (Amplitude Modulation), the amplitude of the carrier wave is varied, and it has different characteristics and tolerances for audio input levels. FM's inherent sensitivity to input volume makes it essential for operators to manage their speaking levels carefully to avoid distortion. By highlighting FM, the question emphasizes the importance of maintaining proper audio levels, specifically in FM transmissions, to ensure clear and distortion-free communication.

Over-Deviating

Over-deviation in FM transceivers occurs when the transmitted signal's modulation exceeds the specified frequency deviation limits. Frequency deviation refers to the extent to which the carrier frequency varies in response to the transmitted audio signal. FM transceivers operate within certain deviation limits to ensure clear communication and avoid interference with adjacent channels.

This results in a too-wide signal for the designated channel, causing distortion and interference with adjacent channels. Talking farther from the microphone is a simple and effective solution if you are told your transceiver is over-deviating.

Increasing the distance between your mouth and the microphone reduces the audio input level, decreasing the modulation depth. This adjustment helps ensure your signal stays within the proper deviation limits, leading to clearer and more reliable communication.

T7B01: What can you do if you are told your FM handheld or mobile transceiver is over-deviating?

A. Talk louder into the microphone
B. Let the transceiver cool off
C. Change to a higher power level
D. Talk farther away from the microphone

Distorted Audio Caused by RF Current

Suppose you experience distorted audio due to RF current on the shield of your microphone cable. In that case, one effective solution is to use a ferrite choke. A ferrite choke, also known as a ferrite bead, is a passive electronic component that suppresses high-frequency noise and interference. When placed on the microphone cable, the ferrite choke helps to block or absorb the unwanted RF currents that can cause distortion in your audio signal.

T7B04: Which of the following could you use to cure distorted audio caused by RF current on the shield of a microphone cable?

A. Band-pass filter
B. Low-pass filter
C. Preamplifier
D. Ferrite choke

The ferrite choke impedes the RF current, reducing the amount of RF energy that travels along the cable shield. This simple addition can significantly improve audio quality by eliminating interference and ensuring clear and intelligible communication.

Single Side Band

Excessive microphone gain on SSB (Single Sideband) transmissions can result in distorted transmitted audio. When the microphone gain is set too high, the audio signal becomes too strong, causing the transmitter to over-modulate. This over-modulation leads to audio distortion, making the transmission sound unclear and challenging to understand. Additionally, excessive gain can cause splatter, where the signal spreads into adjacent frequencies, potentially causing interference to other stations. Setting the microphone gain at an appropriate level is essential to maintain clear and intelligible audio quality.

T4B01: What is the effect of excessive microphone gain on SSB transmissions?

A. Frequency instability
B. Distorted transmitted audio
C. Increased SWR
D. All these choices are correct

Suppose the voice pitch of a single-sideband signal returning to your CQ call seems too high or too low. You can use the RIT (Receiver Incremental Tuning) or Clarifier control in that case. The RIT or Clarifier allows you to fine-tune the receiver frequency without changing the transmitter frequency. This adjustment helps correct any slight frequency mismatches between your transmitter and the responding station, ensuring the audio pitch is accurate. Proper use of the RIT or Clarifier enhances communication clarity, making it easier to understand the incoming signal.

T4B06: Which of the following controls could be used if the voice pitch of a single-sideband signal returning to your CQ call seems too high or low?

A. The AGC or limiter
B. The bandwidth selection
C. The tone squelch
D. The RIT or Clarifier

Repeater Issues

Unable to Access, But can Hear

If you can hear a repeater's output but cannot access it, several factors could be causing the issue. One common reason is an improper transceiver offset. Repeaters receive signals on one frequency and transmit on another, typically with a standard offset. If your transceiver is not set to the correct offset, your signal won't reach the repeater's input frequency, preventing access.

Another possible reason is using the wrong CTCSS tone or DCS code. Repeaters often require a specific sub-audible tone (CTCSS) or digital code (DCS) to open the squelch and allow your signal to be retransmitted. If your transceiver is not programmed with the correct CTCSS tone or DCS code, the repeater will not recognize your signal, even though you can hear its output. Ensuring that your transceiver settings match the repeater's requirements is essential for successful communication.

T2B04: Which of the following could be the reason you are unable to access a repeater whose output you can hear?

A. Improper transceiver offset
B. You are using the wrong CTCSS tone
C. You are using the wrong DCS code
D. All these choices are correct

Communicating with a Distant Repeater Using a Directional Antenna

When buildings or other obstructions block the direct line of sight to a distant repeater, a directional antenna can help overcome this challenge by finding a path that reflects signals to the repeater. Instead of aiming your antenna directly at the repeater, you can point it towards a nearby surface, such as a building, hill, or other large structure, that can reflect the radio waves. This reflection can create an indirect path for the signals to reach the repeater, bypassing the obstruction.

T3A05: When using a directional antenna, how might your station be able to communicate with a distant repeater if buildings or obstructions are blocking the direct line of sight path?

A. Change from vertical to horizontal polarization
B. Try to find a path that reflects signals to the repeater
C. Try the long path
D. Increase the antenna SWR

This approach requires critical thinking and experimentation. As a ham operator, you should consider the environment and identify potential reflective surfaces. Adjust the direction of your antenna and monitor the signal strength and quality. By methodically testing different angles and positions, you can find the optimal reflection path that allows clear communication with the repeater. This troubleshooting technique enhances problem-solving skills and ensures reliable communication even in challenging environments.

As with any skill or hobby, real-life troubleshooting will be your best teacher. Don't hesitate to lean on mentors and peers for guidance and support as you navigate challenges and expand your knowledge.

Chapter 26

Privacy and Ethics

IN AMATEUR RADIO, WHERE the airwaves are open and accessible to anyone with the right equipment, privacy and ethics have a unique significance. While ham radio operates on a foundation of openness and community, specific legal and ethical standards are designed to protect the privacy of communications and ensure all operators engage with honesty and respect. You will need to understand these nuances in order to maintain the integrity and camaraderie that define the amateur radio community.

Privacy Laws

Unlike traditional forms of communication like telephony or emailing, where privacy can often be tightly controlled, the nature of amateur radio means that transmissions are inherently public. However, legal boundaries still govern what is considered acceptable regarding listening to and sharing the content of transmissions. It's important to note that the FCC prohibits using amateur radio frequencies for personal or commercial gain, and there are specific rules against broadcasting music, obscene content, or transmissions intended to facilitate a crime.

Eavesdropping, or listening to private transmissions without the consent of those involved, falls into a legal gray area in amateur radio. Since transmissions are technically public, listening in is not illegal unless the information is used for criminal or harmful purposes. However, the ethical implications of eavesdropping can be significant. It's considered poor practice and contrary to the spirit of amateur radio to use information gleaned from private conversations inappropriately. Moreover, the deliberate interception and sharing of encrypted transmissions are strictly illegal, emphasizing the balance between open communication and privacy.

Ethical Communication

Ethics in amateur radio extend beyond mere legal compliance; they touch upon how operators interact. Ethical communication is founded on honesty and integrity. This means identifying oneself accurately with a call sign, engaging in truthful and respectful exchanges, and providing help or advice in good faith. The amateur radio community prides itself on a spirit of friendship and support, often called the "ham spirit," which encourages seasoned operators to assist newcomers and promotes mutual respect among all participants, regardless of their level of expertise or geographical location.

In practical terms, ethical communication involves more than adhering to regulations; it's about fostering a positive, supportive environment. For instance, if you notice a fellow operator making a mistake in frequency use or protocol, the ethical approach would be to gently and privately correct them rather than publicly criticizing or shaming them. This helps maintain the individual's dignity and supports the broader community ethos of learning and improvement.

Handling Interference

Intentional or accidental interference can be one of the most challenging aspects of ham radio operation. Ethically handling interference involves first determining whether the interference is malicious or unintentional. If it's the latter, reaching out to the interfering station with a polite request to adjust their practices, such as changing frequency or modifying transmission power, can often resolve the issue. Keeping a calm and cooperative demeanor during these interactions is necessary, as it reflects respect and understanding, fostering a more amicable resolution.

Avoiding direct confrontation is advisable if interference is suspected to be intentional, which is rare but can occur. Instead, documenting the instances of interference and reporting them to the appropriate authorities or amateur radio organizations can ensure that the issue is addressed formally and fairly without escalating the conflict or disrupting the broader community harmony.

Managing Interference on the Same Frequency

When two stations transmit on the same frequency and interfere with each other, the <u>recommended course of action is for the stations to negotiate continued use of the frequency</u>. This involves operators communicating respectfully and collaboratively to decide how to share or alternate frequency use. Such negotiations help prevent ongoing interference and ensure that both stations can operate effectively without disrupting each other.

T2B08: Which of the following applies when two stations transmitting on the same frequency interfere with each other?

A. The stations should negotiate continued use of the frequency
B. Both stations should choose another frequency to avoid conflict
C. Interference is inevitable, so no action is required
D. Use subaudible tones so both stations can share the frequency

Public Service and Privacy

Amateur radio operators often play a fundamental role during emergencies, providing critical communication links when other systems fail. Balancing this commitment to public service with respect for individual privacy is essential. Handling all transmitted information sensitively during public service operations, such as emergency or disaster communications, is vital. Operators should avoid disclosing sensitive personal details over the airwaves. They should be cautious about sharing information about the situation that could lead to panic or misinformation.

Moreover, when handling emergency communications, maintaining operational security by restricting sensitive operational details to those who need to know them is a fundamental practice. This protects the privacy of those affected by the emergency and ensures the effectiveness and integrity of the response efforts.

Navigating the intricate balance between open communication, privacy, and ethics in amateur radio is about following rules and embracing a culture of respect, support, and responsibility. Adhering to these principles helps maintain the amateur radio community as a welcoming and valuable space for all who join. Whether communicating across towns or continents, your approach to privacy and ethics shapes your experience and the broader perception and effectiveness of the amateur radio community worldwide.

Rules & Regulations

NAVIGATING RADIO IS AKIN to learning the rules of the road before taking the wheel. Just as drivers must understand and adhere to traffic laws to ensure safety and order on the streets, amateur radio operators must familiarize themselves with specific regulations and operating procedures.

This chapter aims to demystify the regulatory landscape governed by the Federal Communications Commission (FCC), clarify the process of obtaining your Technician license, and discuss the importance of ethical operation, all of which form the backbone of responsible and enjoyable use of the amateur radio spectrum.

Chapter 27

Understanding the FCC's Role

Regulatory Overview

THE FCC PLAYS A core role in regulating amateur radio in the United States, maintaining an organized and fair use of the radio spectrum. As an independent U.S. government agency, the FCC oversees all domestic and international communications by radio, television, wire, satellite, and cable. In amateur radio, the FCC's responsibilities include licensing operators, allocating frequency bands, and ensuring that all communications adhere to established rules designed to prevent interference and ensure public safety.

> **T1A02: Which agency regulates and enforces the rules for the Amateur Radio Service in the United States?**
>
> A. FEMA
> B. Homeland Security
> **C. The FCC**
> D. All these choices are correct

Critical rules that you must be aware of as an aspiring or practicing ham include regulations on frequency usage, power limits, and emission types. For example, the FCC dictates which frequency bands are available for amateur use and what power is acceptable for transmission in these bands.

The rationale behind these rules is multifaceted: They prevent interference with other communication services and users, ensure that amateur radio practices do not pose a hazard to public safety, and preserve the integrity and utility of the radio spectrum for all users.

Understanding these rules isn't just about compliance; it's about contributing to a harmonious, interference-free environment where the amateur radio community can thrive. The FCC's regulations are laid out in Part 97 of the Commission's rules, and familiarizing yourself with this document is an excellent start to understanding your obligations and rights as a radio operator.

And why does this all exist?

T1A01: Which of the following is part of the Basis and Purpose of the Amateur Radio Service?

A. Providing personal radio communications for as many citizens as possible
B. Providing communications for international non-profit organizations
C. Advancing skills in the technical and communication phases of the radio art
D. All these choices are correct

The FCC understands the benefits of radio, and a legion of ham operators ensures that the art of radio and the skills involved in its communication continue to advance and be maintained - an indispensable skill during emergencies.

The FCC provides definitions that we will review in this section. Those definitions often appear in questions on the exam, like this one...

T1D10: How does the FCC define broadcasting for the Amateur Radio Service?

A. Two-way transmissions by amateur stations
B. Any transmission made by the licensed station
C. Transmission of messages directed only to amateur operators
D. Transmissions intended for reception by the general public

When operating our radios, we transmit across open radio frequencies. Therefore, anyone may receive our transmissions, implying they are intended for the general public.

Speaking of emergencies:

T1A10: What is the Radio Amateur Civil Emergency Service (RACES)?

A. A radio service using amateur frequencies for emergency management or civil defense communications
B. A radio service using amateur stations for emergency management or civil defense communications
C. An emergency service using amateur operators certified by a civil defense organization as being enrolled in that organization
D. All these choices are correct.

RACES, or the Radio Amateur Civil Emergency Service, is a key component of amateur radio operations in the United States. The FCC established it to provide emergency communication support during civil emergencies. Thus, answer 'A' is correct; it's a radio service using amateur frequencies for emergency communications. Those communications happen on amateur stations/equipment, so answer 'B' is correct.

Managed by local, county, and state emergency agencies, RACES volunteers, who are licensed amateur radio operators, work closely with civil authorities to ensure reliable communication when traditional systems fail. Working closely with civil authorities, we are certified; you have to have a relationship with them ahead of time and enroll with them; you can't just show up and wave your hands around saying, "Pick Me." So, the answer 'C' is correct.

RACES operators are activated only during declared emergencies or drills. They participate in regular training to stay prepared. This service not only exemplifies the public service spirit of ham radio but also enhances community preparedness, provides communication redundancy, and bolsters public trust in amateur radio operators as essential resources during crises.

If answers A, B, and C are all correct by deduction, then 'D' is correct.

Restrictions for U.S. Amateurs in Secondary Segments

U.S. amateurs must be mindful of their operating practices in segments of the radio bands where the Amateur Radio Service is designated as secondary. This designation means primary users, including government or commercial stations, have priority access to those frequencies. As a result, amateur radio operators must ensure they do not interfere with these primary users. If interference occurs, the amateur station must either cease transmission or make necessary adjustments to eliminate the interference.

T1B08: How are U.S. amateurs restricted in segments of bands where the Amateur Radio Service is secondary?

A. U.S. amateurs may find non-amateur stations in those segments and must avoid interfering with them
B. U.S. amateurs must give foreign amateur stations priority in those segments
C. International communications are not permitted in those segments
D. Digital transmissions are not permitted in those segments

Understanding this restriction is essential for responsible amateur radio operations. It emphasizes the need for amateurs to be aware of the band plans and usage designations within the frequency spectrum they are utilizing. By adhering to these guidelines, amateurs help maintain harmonious and efficient use of the radio frequencies, ensuring that all services can coexist without disruption. This knowledge highlights the importance of respecting and cooperating with other spectrum users to preserve the integrity and functionality of the amateur radio service.

Licensing Requirements

To legally operate on amateur radio frequencies in the U.S., you must obtain a license from the FCC. That's why you are here!

T1C01: For which license classes are new licenses currently available from the FCC?

A. Novice, Technician, General, Amateur Extra
B. Technician, Technician Plus, General, Amateur Extra
C. Novice, Technician Plus, General, Advanced
D. Technician, General, Amateur Extra

The important thing to remember here is that other types of licenses were historically issued. But today, we have the Technician, General, and Amateur Extra.

T1A04: How many operator/primary station license grants may be held by any one person?

A. One
B. No more than two
C. One for each band on which the person plans to operate
D. One for each permanent station location from which the person plans to operate

---

Technically, your amateur radio license has two parts: an operator and a station license. The operator license is the personal authorization granted to you as an individual. This license signifies that the holder has demonstrated the knowledge and skills to safely and effectively use radio frequencies allocated for amateur radio use.

The primary station license is tied to the operator license. It authorizes the licensee to set up and operate an amateur radio station. For us hams, the two are combined into one.

T1A05: What proves that the FCC has issued an operator/primary license grant?

A. A printed copy of the certificate of successful completion of examination
B. An email notification from the NCVEC granting the license
C. The license appears in the FCC ULS database
D. All these choices are correct

As simple as it sounds, how do you prove you have a license? You show up in their database.

And showing up in their database is essential. Because...

T1C10: How soon after passing the examination for your first amateur radio license may you transmit on the amateur radio bands?

A. Immediately on receiving your Certificate of Successful Completion of Examination (CSCE)
B. As soon as your operator/station license grant appears on the ARRL website
C. As soon as your operator/station license grant appears in the FCC's license database
D. As soon as you receive your license in the mail from the FCC

That's right. You don't actually have a license – even if you passed the exam - until you show up in their database. Until then, no radio operations!

Being in their database means you must provide an active email address, which is very important.

T1C04: What may happen if the FCC is unable to reach you by email?

A. Fine and suspension of operator license
B. Revocation of the station license or suspension of the operator license
C. Revocation of access to the license record in the FCC system
D. Nothing; there is no such requirement

Yes! If you miss an email from the FCC, they can revoke your license. So, watch your email! Make sure the FCC isn't going to your spam or junk folder. In fact, they are so concerned about you maintaining your email address with them that they ask two questions about it!

T1C07: Which of the following can result in revocation of the station license or suspension of the operator license?

A. Failure to inform the FCC of any changes in the amateur station following performance of an R.F. safety environmental evaluation
B. Failure to provide and maintain a correct email address with the FCC
C. Failure to obtain FCC type acceptance prior to using a home-built transmitter
D. Failure to have a copy of your license available at your station

At this point, you have taken the exam, passed it, and ensured your email is correct in the FCC database and your record in their database is live. You are now officially licensed!

So, how long is your license good for?

T1C08: What is the normal term for an FCC-issued amateur radio license?

A. Five years
B. Life
C. Ten years
D. Eight years

You need to renew your license <u>every 10 years</u>. You will only have to retake the test if your license expires. But...

T1C09: What is the grace period for renewal if an amateur license expires?

A. Two years
B. Three years
C. Five years
D. Ten years

If your license expires, you have <u>two years to renew your license</u> before you have to retake the exam. However, during those two years...

T1C11: If your license has expired and is still within the allowable grace period, may you continue to transmit on the amateur radio bands?

A. Yes, for up to two years
B. Yes, as soon as you apply for renewal
C. Yes, for up to one year
D. No, you must wait until the license has been renewed

You must only continue transmitting on licensed amateur bands with an active license. Please don't do it! Go renew your license.

A final word about licenses: amateur radio clubs can also obtain a license from the FCC.

A club license allows amateur radio operators to collectively operate under a single call sign, facilitating group activities and promoting collaboration among members. <u>To apply for a club license, the club must have at least four members,</u> including a trustee with a current amateur radio license. The trustee is responsible for the club's station and compliance with FCC regulations.

T1F11: Which of the following is a requirement for the issuance of a club station license grant?

A. The trustee must have an Amateur Extra Class operator license grant
B. The club must have at least four members
C. The club must be registered with the American Radio Relay League
D. All these choices are correct

Obtaining a club license involves submitting an application (FCC Form 605) and paying any required fees. Once granted, the club call sign is used by all members when operating the club station, enabling the club to participate in events, contests, and public service activities under a unified identity. Club licenses help foster a sense of community and shared purpose among amateur radio enthusiasts, making organizing and coordinating activities that promote the hobby and its benefits easier.

Transmission Restrictions and Rules

One key aspect of the Federal Communications Commission's (FCC) oversight involves setting restrictions on transmissions to minimize interference and promote orderly communication. In this section, we will explore the various constraints imposed by the FCC on ham radio transmissions, understanding their importance in maintaining the integrity of amateur radio bands and ensuring safe and effective communication for all operators.

Willful Interference

Let's start with one of the most fundamental ones: willful interference with other amateur radio stations is never permitted. The FCC regulations strictly prohibit any actions that intentionally disrupt or interfere with the communications of other amateur radio operators. This rule is fundamental to maintaining the integrity and functionality of the amateur radio bands, ensuring that all operators can communicate effectively and without unnecessary disruption.

T1A11: When is willful interference to other amateur radio stations permitted?

A. To stop another amateur station that is breaking the FCC rules
B. At no time
C. When making short test transmissions
D. At any time, stations in the Amateur Radio Service are not protected from willful interference

You need to understand and abide by this prohibition. Intentional interference violates FCC regulations and undermines the spirit of cooperation and mutual respect central to the amateur radio community. By adhering to this rule, operators help create a respectful and efficient communication environment, fostering positive interactions and reliable transmissions across the amateur radio spectrum. Compliance with this regulation is essential for preserving the quality and reliability of amateur radio operations for everyone involved.

Broadcasting

In amateur radio, one-way transmissions are generally prohibited under the circumstance of broadcasting. Broadcasting refers to transmitting messages intended for reception by the general public. The FCC regulations strictly limit amateur radio operators from broadcasting to prevent using amateur frequencies for purposes other than personal, non-commercial communications. This rule helps maintain the amateur bands for their intended purpose, facilitating individual and emergency communications, technical training, and the advancement of radio art.

T1D02: Under which of the following circumstances are one-way transmissions by an amateur station prohibited?

A. In all circumstances
B. Broadcasting
C. International Morse Code Practice
D. Telecommand or transmissions of telemetry

There are exceptions, however, where amateur stations may transmit information typically associated with broadcasting. According to FCC rules, amateur radio operators can transmit information to support broadcasting, program production, or news gathering if no other means of communication is available and the situation involves the immediate safety of human life or property protection. These exceptions are rare and typically apply in emergency scenarios where alternative communication methods are not viable. Understanding these regulations ensures that amateur radio operations remain compliant with FCC rules and that amateur bands are used appropriately.

T1D09: When may amateur stations transmit information in support of broadcasting, program production, or news gathering, assuming no other means is available?

A. When such communications are directly related to the immediate safety of human life or protection of property
B. When broadcasting communications to or from the space shuttle
C. Where non-commercial programming is gathered and supplied exclusively to the National Public Radio network
D. Never

Indecent or Obscene

The FCC strictly prohibits the transmission of any language that may be considered indecent or obscene on amateur radio frequencies. This rule is in place to ensure that amateur radio remains a respectful and appropriate medium for communication, accessible to operators of all ages and backgrounds. The use of indecent or obscene language is not only against FCC regulations but also against the ethos of amateur radio, which promotes courteous and professional conduct among operators.

T1D06: What, if any, are the restrictions concerning transmission of language that may be considered indecent or obscene?

A. The FCC maintains a list of words that are not permitted to be used on amateur frequencies
B. Any such language is prohibited
C. The ITU maintains a list of words that are not permitted to be used on amateur frequencies
D. There is no such prohibition

Amateur radio is a community-driven activity that relies on mutual respect and adherence to established guidelines to function effectively. Violating these rules by transmitting indecent or obscene language can lead to severe penalties, including fines, suspension, or revocation of the operator's license.

Prohibited Communications

FCC-licensed amateur radio stations are prohibited from exchanging communications with any country that has notified the International Telecommunication Union (ITU) of its objection to such communications. This regulation ensures that amateur radio operators respect international agreements and the sovereignty of other nations. The ITU maintains a list of countries that have objected to amateur radio communications, and operators must stay informed about these restrictions to remain compliant with FCC rules.

T1D01: With which countries are FCC-licensed amateur radio stations prohibited from exchanging communications?

A. Any country whose administration has notified the International Telecommunication Union (ITU) that it objects to such communications
B. Any country whose administration has notified the American Radio Relay League (ARRL) that it objects to such communications
C. Any country banned from such communications by the International Amateur Radio Union (IARU)
D. Any country banned from making such communications by the American Radio Relay League (ARRL)

Understanding this regulation is important as it emphasizes the respect of international protocols and maintaining good relations within the global amateur radio community. By adhering to these restrictions, operators help ensure that amateur radio remains a cooperative and internationally respected hobby, free from political and diplomatic conflicts.

Encoded Transmissions

In amateur radio, messages encoded to obscure their meaning are generally prohibited. This rule ensures transparency and openness in amateur radio communications, fostering an environment where all operators can understand and participate in exchanges. However, this rule has specific exceptions, particularly when transmitting control commands to space stations or radio control craft. In these cases, encoding messages is permissible because it is necessary to maintain the integrity and security of the control functions, preventing unauthorized access or interference.

T1D03: When is it permissible to transmit messages encoded to obscure their meaning?

A. Only during contests
B. Only when transmitting certain approved digital codes
C. Only when transmitting control commands to space stations or radio control craft
D. Never

Operators must be aware that any attempt to encode messages for general communication purposes is prohibited and could lead to penalties. However, recognizing the exceptions for space stations and radio control craft allows operators to engage in these specialized activities without violating the rules. This balance helps maintain the transparency of amateur radio while accommodating the unique needs of certain advanced operations.

Special Conditions and Exceptions in Amateur Radio Operations

In amateur radio, certain transmissions that are typically prohibited can be authorized under specific conditions. For example, transmitting music using a phone emission is generally not allowed. However, there is an exception when the music is incidental to an authorized retransmission of manned spacecraft communications. This means that if music is part of the audio feed from a manned space mission being retransmitted, transmitting that music over amateur radio frequencies is permissible. This exception helps facilitate educational and public outreach efforts related to space missions.

T1D04: Under what conditions is an amateur station authorized to transmit music using a phone emission?

A. When incidental to an authorized retransmission of manned spacecraft communications
B. When the music produces no spurious emissions
C. When transmissions are limited to less than three minutes per hour
D. When the music is transmitted above 1280 MHz

Another exception involves using amateur radio stations to sell or trade equipment. Amateur radio operators can notify other amateurs of equipment availability for sale or trade, provided these activities are not conducted regularly and are limited to amateur radio equipment. This rule ensures that the amateur bands are not used for commercial purposes, maintaining their primary focus on communication, experimentation, and emergency preparedness.

T1D05: When may amateur radio operators use their stations to notify other amateurs of the availability of equipment for sale or trade?

A. Never
B. When the equipment is not the personal property of either the station licensee, or the control operator, or their close relatives
C. When no profit is made on the sale
D. When selling amateur radio equipment and not on a regular basis

Furthermore, amateur radio operators can receive compensation for operating their stations under specific circumstances. One such situation is when the communication is incidental to classroom instruction at an educational institution. Suppose an amateur radio station is part of a class or educational program. In that case, the control operator can be compensated for their involvement. This exception supports the educational use of amateur radio, helping to teach students about radio communications and technology in a hands-on learning environment.

T1D08: In which of the following circumstances may the control operator of an amateur station receive compensation for operating that station?

A. When the communication is related to the sale of amateur equipment by the control operator's employer
B. When the communication is incidental to classroom instruction at an educational institution
C. When the communication is made to obtain emergency information for a local broadcast station
D. All these choices are correct

By understanding these exceptions, amateur radio operators can more effectively navigate the rules and regulations, ensuring compliance while taking advantage of the unique opportunities that amateur radio offers.

International Communications

FCC-licensed amateur radio stations can engage in international communications under specific conditions. These communications must be incidental to the purposes of the Amateur Radio Service, which primarily include technical experimentation, emergency communication, and fostering international goodwill. Additionally, these communications should be personal, meaning they should not be conducted for commercial purposes, broadcasting, or any form of financial interest.

T1C03: What types of international communications are an FCC-licensed amateur radio station permitted to make?

A. Communications incidental to the purposes of the Amateur Radio Service and remarks of a personal character
B. Communications incidental to conducting business or remarks of a personal nature
C. Only communications incidental to contest exchanges; all other communications are prohibited
D. Any communications that would be permitted by an international broadcast station

The emphasis on personal and incidental communications helps ensure that amateur radio remains a hobby focused on experimentation, learning, and public service. For example, an amateur radio operator might converse with a fellow operator in another country about their equipment setups or discuss the technical aspects of radio wave propagation.

Transmission Locations

An FCC-licensed amateur radio station can transmit from any vessel or craft in international waters, provided the vessel is documented or registered in the United States. This is interesting, but it means that amateur radio operators can operate their stations while on ships, boats, or other maritime vessels as long as these vessels are legally recognized as U.S. entities. This allowance supports maritime communication needs, including safety, emergency communication, and continuing amateur radio activities at sea.

> **T1C06: From which of the following locations may an FCC-licensed amateur station transmit?**
>
> A. From within any country that belongs to the International Telecommunication Union
> B. From within any country that is a member of the United Nations
> C. From anywhere within International Telecommunication Union (ITU) Regions 2 and 3
> **D. From any vessel or craft located in international waters and documented or registered in the United States**

It is important to remember this if you, as an amateur radio operator, find yourself traveling or working on vessels in international waters. This provision ensures amateur radio operators can maintain communication capabilities and comply with international and U.S. regulations. It allows for the continuous operation of amateur radio equipment, promoting safety and spreading technical knowledge even when operators are far from the land.

Restrictions on Third-Party Communications with Foreign Stations

Specific restrictions apply when a non-licensed person can speak to a foreign station using a station under the control of a licensed amateur operator. The fundamental limitation is that the foreign station must be in a country with which the United States has a third-party agreement. A third-party agreement is an international understanding that allows individuals who are not licensed amateur radio operators to communicate with foreign stations under the supervision of a licensed operator.

> **T1F07: Which of the following restrictions apply when a non-licensed person is allowed to speak to a foreign station using a station under the control of a licensed amateur operator?**
>
> A. The person must be a U.S. citizen
> **B. The foreign station must be in a country with which the U.S. has a third-party agreement**
> C. The licensed control operator must do the station identification
> D. All these choices are correct

This regulation ensures that communications are conducted legally and within international agreements. Licensed operators must know these agreements to avoid unauthorized communications that could lead to regulatory issues. By adhering to this restriction, amateur radio operators help maintain the integrity of the Amateur Radio Service and foster positive international relations. Understanding these guidelines is essential for operators who wish to allow non-licensed individuals to experience and enjoy amateur radio communications legally and responsibly.

Definition of Third-Party Communications

Third-party communications in amateur radio refer to the transmission of messages by a licensed control operator to another amateur station control operator on behalf of a third person who is not a licensed amateur radio operator. It involves relaying messages between two stations where the content of the message originates from someone other than the licensed operators themselves. This practice is regulated to ensure that all parties involved adhere to legal and operational standards set by the FCC and international agreements.

T1F08: What is the definition of third party communications?

A. A message from a control operator to another amateur station control operator on behalf of another person
B. Amateur radio communications where three stations are in communications with one another
C. Operation when the transmitting equipment is licensed to a person other than the control operator
D. Temporary authorization for an unlicensed person to transmit on the amateur bands for technical experiments

Understanding third-party communications is important, especially involving non-licensed individuals. The control operator must ensure that the transmission complies with all relevant regulations, including verifying that the receiving station is in a country with a third-party agreement with the United States. This ensures that the communication is lawful and respects international protocols, maintaining the integrity and proper functioning of the amateur radio service. Familiarity with the concept and regulations surrounding third-party communications helps operators engage in this practice responsibly and within the legal framework.

Call Signs

Once you pass your FCC exam and obtain your Technician Class license, you will automatically be assigned a call sign based on your geographic location and the sequential issuing system.

Maverick, Goose, and Iceman are classic call signs. Unfortunately, ham radio call signs are a little different.

Understanding the structure and use of call signs in amateur radio is akin to learning how to properly address letters in the postal system. Each part of a call sign holds a specific meaning, and using them correctly ensures clear, efficient, and respectful communication across the airwaves. A call sign is your unique identifier as an amateur radio operator, and it serves multiple purposes:

- Legal identification

- A signal of your geographic location

- A reflection of your license class

Call signs in the United States and globally follow a structure set by international agreements and national regulations. Typically, a call sign consists of one or two letters (prefix), a numeral (indicating the geographic area), and one to three additional letters (suffix) assigned sequentially.

The most common type of Technician class call sign is 2 x 3. U.S. call signs start with a letter (K, N, or W) followed by another. Then, a number indicating your region. They end with three letters, which are assigned sequentially (meaning ABC will be assigned before ABD).

For instance, in the U.S., a call sign like KG9XYZ (just an example call sign) indicates that the operator is licensed in the U.S. and in the region represented by the numeral 9, which includes Wisconsin, Illinois, and Indiana.

Call Sign Number Indicating Region

T1C05: Which of the following is a valid Technician class call sign format?

A. KF1XXX
B. KA1X
C. W1XX
D. All these choices are correct

Many operators opt for vanity call signs—these are custom-selected by the operator and can include combinations that are easier to remember or might spell out initials or words relevant to the operator. Obtaining a vanity call sign involves applying through the FCC, and a fee is involved. Still, many find that the personalization is worth the effort. Vanity call signs are available to anyone who has already obtained their ham radio license.

Special event call signs are temporary and used to mark significant events or anniversaries in the amateur radio community. They are often sought after for their unique or commemorative value and help promote the event or celebration within and beyond the amateur radio community. For example, a special event station might use a call sign like W100NASA to mark NASA's 100th anniversary.

T1C02: Who may select a desired call sign under the vanity call sign rules?

A. Only a licensed amateur with a General or Amateur Extra Class license
B. Only a licensed amateur with an Amateur Extra Class license
C. Only a licensed amateur who has been licensed continuously for more than 10 years
D. Any licensed amateur

Using your call sign correctly during communications is not just a legal requirement—it fosters clear and effective exchanges. Whenever you initiate a contact or QSO, your call sign should be clearly stated at the beginning of the communication. This helps identify you with other operators. Additionally, regulations require that you broadcast your call sign at least every ten minutes during and at the end of your communications. This protocol ensures listeners can easily identify who is transmitting, enhancing transparency and accountability in the airwaves.

However, legally, you don't need to state your call sign at the beginning of a conversation. That's just part of being courteous and introducing yourself.

T1F03: When are you required to transmit your assigned call sign?

A. At the beginning of each contact and every 10 minutes thereafter
B. At least once during each transmission
C. At least every 15 minutes during and at the end of a communication
D. At least every 10 minutes during and at the end of a communication

Now, the FCC throws another almost identical question but phrases it using a specific scenario. Just remember, the answer doesn't change!

T1F02: How often must you identify with your FCC-assigned call sign when using tactical call signs such as "ace Headquarters."

A. Never, the tactical call is sufficient
B. Once during every hour
C. At the end of each communication and every ten minutes during a communication
D. At the end of every transmission

Your call sign is more than just a series of letters and numbers—it is your signature across the airwaves, representing your identity and ethics as an operator. Your reputation will precede you!

FCC and Amateur Self-Management

In the amateur radio community, voluntary management plays a central role in maintaining efficient and orderly use of the radio spectrum. This voluntary management cooperates with the Federal Communications Commission (FCC), the official regulatory body overseeing amateur radio operations in the United States. While the FCC establishes the legal framework and regulations for amateur radio, including frequency allocations, licensing requirements, and technical standards, volunteer organizations and individuals within the amateur radio community often manage and coordinate frequency use.

One key aspect of this voluntary management is the role of Frequency Coordinators. Local or regional amateur radio operators typically recognize these coordinators. They are responsible for recommending specific frequency allocations and operational parameters for repeaters, auxiliary stations, and other uses within the amateur bands. Although Frequency Coordinators are not formally appointed by the FCC, their recommendations are generally respected and followed by the amateur radio community to minimize interference and ensure effective spectrum use.

The cooperation between voluntary management and the FCC is based on mutual respect and the goal of maintaining an organized and functional radio environment. The FCC relies on the expertise and local knowledge of Frequency Coordinators and other volunteer organizations to manage the complexities of frequency use and to address issues such as interference and congestion. In turn, the amateur radio community adheres to the guidelines and regulations set forth by the FCC, ensuring that their operations are legal and compliant.

This collaborative approach allows the amateur radio community to self-manage many aspects of its operations while still adhering to the overarching regulatory framework established by the FCC. It leverages amateur radio operators' collective knowledge and experience to maintain efficient and effective spectrum use, ensuring the hobby is enjoyable and accessible for all participants.

Frequency Coordinator

A Frequency Coordinator is an individual or organization responsible for managing and assigning frequencies within amateur radio bands to ensure efficient and orderly spectrum use. This role is vital for coordinating repeater frequencies to prevent interference and ensure repeaters operate effectively within a given area. Frequency Coordinators work closely with local amateur radio clubs and operators to assign frequencies for repeaters, simplex channels, and other communication needs.

The primary goal of a Frequency Coordinator is to minimize conflicts and interference between different users of the amateur radio spectrum. They maintain databases of assigned frequencies and work to resolve any disputes or issues that arise. By coordinating frequencies, these individuals help maintain a harmonious and functional radio environment, allowing operators to enjoy clear and reliable communications. Understanding the role of a Frequency Coordinator is essential for amateur radio operators, especially those involved in setting up or operating repeaters, as it ensures that their equipment operates within the guidelines established to protect all spectrum users.

Local amateur radio operators recognize Volunteer Frequency Coordinators to recommend transmit/receive channels and other parameters for auxiliary and repeater stations. These coordinators analyze the needs of the local amateur community and suggest appropriate frequency allocations and operational parameters for repeaters and auxiliary stations to minimize conflicts and maximize the effective use of available frequencies. By coordinating these recommendations, Volunteer Frequency Coordinators help maintain orderly and reliable communication networks within the amateur radio bands. Their work is essential for preventing frequency conflicts that could disrupt communication and ensuring that repeaters and auxiliary stations operate smoothly.

T1A08: Which of the following entities recommends transmit/receive channels and other parameters for auxiliary and repeater stations?

A. Frequency Spectrum Manager appointed by the FCC
B. Volunteer Frequency Coordinator recognized by local amateurs
C. FCC Regional Field Office
D. International Telecommunication Union

Amateur operators select Frequency Coordinators in a local or regional area whose stations are eligible to be a repeater or auxiliary stations. These operators choose a coordinator based on the individual or organization's ability to manage and assign frequencies within the amateur radio bands. The selection process is often based on the coordinator's experience, knowledge of the local radio environment, and ability to work collaboratively with the amateur radio community. This collaborative selection process ensures that the coordinator has the support and trust of the local amateur radio operators, leading to more effective and harmonious frequency management.

T1A09: Who selects a Frequency Coordinator?

A. The FCC Office of Spectrum Management and Coordination Policy
B. The local chapter of the Office of National Council of Independent Frequency Coordinators
C. Amateur operators in a local or regional area whose stations are eligible to be repeater or auxiliary stations
D. FCC Regional Field Office

Understanding the selection and role of Frequency Coordinators highlights the importance of community involvement in maintaining an organized and functional amateur radio environment. Their work ensures efficient spectrum use, minimizes interference, and promotes reliable communication across the amateur radio community.

Chapter 28

What's Legal for a Technician?

IT'S IMPORTANT TO UNDERSTAND that the Technician license has certain limitations regarding the radio spectrum and power output. Let's review those restrictions and what you will have access to.

Bands

This section will provide an overview of the privileges and opportunities available as a newly licensed Technician, helping you make the most of your amateur radio experience.

Understanding Band Plans

A band plan is a <u>voluntary guideline the amateur radio community uses to organize different modes and activities within an amateur band</u>. While the FCC establishes the legal frequency privileges for various license classes, band plans provide additional structure to ensure that the spectrum is used efficiently and harmoniously. Amateur radio organizations create these plans and reflect the collective agreement of operators on how to allocate the best frequencies for various modes of operation, such as voice, digital, CW (Morse code), and satellite communications.

> **T2A10: What is a band plan, beyond the privileges established by the FCC?**
>
> **A. A voluntary guideline for using different modes or activities within an amateur band**
> B. A list of operating schedules
> C. A list of available net frequencies
> D. A plan devised by a club to indicate frequency band usage

Band plans help minimize interference and promote a more orderly use of the radio spectrum by designating specific segments for different activities. For example, one part of a band might be recommended for SSB phone operations, another for digital modes, and another for CW. By following these guidelines, amateur radio operators can enjoy better communication experiences and contribute to a more organized and cooperative use of amateur bands.

Band Plan Adherence

Adherence to designated band plans and frequency allocations is not merely a legal requirement but a best practice that all amateur operators are expected to follow. Band plans are developed by the amateur radio community and coordinated through the ARRL (American Radio Relay League). These plans outline which segments of the amateur bands are to be used for different types of communications, such as voice, Morse code, or digital modes.

Following these plans helps prevent interference between users operating different modes of communication within the same band. For instance, if digital modes are relegated to specific frequencies within a band, sticking to these guidelines ensures that your digital signals do not interfere with ongoing voice communications elsewhere in the band. Such structure facilitates more efficient spectrum use and enhances the overall experience by reducing conflicts and maximizing the clarity and reach of communications.

Band Segments

Technicians generally have access to all amateur radio bands above 30 MHz, which are ideal for local communications and some limited long-distance communications under certain atmospheric conditions.

This includes the popular 2-meter (VHF) and 70-centimeter bands (UHF), ideal for local and regional communication. Technicians also have limited privileges on specific HF bands (10-meter).

Here is a cheat sheet or quick reference guide to the band segments you can access with a technician's license: **www.MorseCodePublishing.com/TechExam**

VHF/UHF Band Segments Limited to CW Only

Technician class operators can access various VHF and UHF band segments, some designated exclusively for Continuous Wave (CW) operation.

The specific segments limited to CW only are 50.0 MHz to 50.1 MHz on the 6-meter band and 144.0 MHz to 144.1 MHz on the 2-meter band. These segments are reserved for Morse code communications.

T1B07: Which of the following VHF/UHF band segments are limited to CW only?

A. 50.0 MHz to 50.1 MHz and 144.0 MHz to 144.1 MHz
B. 219 MHz to 220 MHz and 420.0 MHz to 420.1 MHz
C. 902.0 MHz to 902.1 MHz
D. All these choices are correct

Memorization Trick for CW-Only Segments

To help you remember the specific segments limited to CW (Continuous Wave) only, consider these as small ranges at the start of their respective bands.

Here's a mnemonic to assist: "Start Small with CW" on both the 6-meter and 2-meter bands:

- 6-meter band: think of "50 to 50.1" as a tiny segment at the beginning.

- 2-meter band: "144 to 144.1" is the small starting segment.

Just remember, CW starts right at the beginning of these bands!

The allocation of these CW-only segments helps ensure that Morse code enthusiasts have dedicated frequencies where they can practice and communicate without interference from other modes. This setup promotes the preservation and continuation of CW as a skill and mode of communication.

Phone (Voice)

What is meant by a phone sub-band in amateur radio? No, you don't need a phone like you think. It refers to specific portions of the radio frequency spectrum <u>designated for voice communications</u>, also known as "phone" operations. These sub-bands are allocated by regulatory bodies such as the Federal Communications Commission (FCC). They are part of the broader amateur radio bands. Within these phone sub-bands, amateur radio operators can use various voice modulation methods, such as amplitude modulation (AM), frequency modulation (FM), and single sideband (SSB) modulation, to communicate.

The allocation of phone sub-bands ensures that voice communications do not interfere with other transmissions, such as digital modes or Morse code (CW). Each amateur radio band typically has specific sub-bands for different operations, allowing for organized and efficient spectrum use.

Technician class operators have phone (voice) privileges on only one HF band: the <u>10-meter band.</u> Specifically, Technician licensees can operate phone modes from <u>28.300 MHz to 28.500 MHz</u> within this band. This allocation provides an excellent opportunity for new operators to experience HF voice communication and make contacts over long distances, particularly during favorable propagation conditions.

Operating on the 10-meter band allows Technician class operators to enjoy the benefits of HF communication, including the potential for international contacts and participation in various amateur radio activities and contests.

T1B06: On which HF bands does a Technician class operator have phone privileges?

A. None
B. 10 meter band only
C. 80 meter, 40 meter, 15 meter, and 10 meter bands
D. 30 meter band only

And within the 10-meter band...

T1B01: Which of the following frequency ranges are available for phone operation by Technician licensees?

A. 28.050 MHz to 28.150 MHz
B. 28.100 MHz to 28.300 MHz
C. 28.300 MHz to 28.500 MHz
D. 28.500 MHz to 28.600 MHz

This one is tricky. If you glance, all the answers are very close and almost identical. You must memorize this one; remember, it's the 300-500 number you want. Good luck!

Here is what I do. I see this question, and each answer is 28 MHz, so I know we are talking about the '28 club.' Within the '28 club,' only 3 to 5 members are allowed in at once. So, the answer is 28.3 to 28.5! That's what I do.

Identifying Your Station on Phone Sub-Bands

When operating in a phone sub-band, it's essential to correctly identify your station to ensure clear and legal communication. The language used for identification must be <u>English</u>. This requirement helps maintain consistency and clarity across international communications, making it easier for operators worldwide to understand and identify each other accurately.

T1F04: What language may you use for identification when operating in a phone sub-band?

A. Any language recognized by the United Nations
B. Any language recognized by the ITU
C. English
D. English, French, or Spanish

The method of call sign identification required for a station transmitting phone signals is either <u>sending the call sign using a CW (Morse code) or a phone emission (voice).</u> This dual option allows flexibility while ensuring the station identification is clear and meets regulatory standards. Proper identification complies with FCC regulations and promotes good operating practices by ensuring that all operators can easily recognize each other on the airwaves.

T1F05: What method of call sign identification is required for a station transmitting phone signals?

A. Send the call sign followed by the indicator RPT
B. Send the call sign using a CW or phone emission
C. Send the call sign followed by the indicator R
D. Send the call sign using only a phone emission

Additionally, operators may include self-assigned indicators to provide additional information about their location or operating conditions when using phone transmissions. Acceptable self-assigned indicators include formats like "KL7CC <u>stroke</u> W3," "KL7CC <u>slant</u> W3," or "KL7CC <u>slash</u> W3." The words stroke, slant, or slash are just different regional ways to pronounce the symbol shown here: / as in KL7CC/W3

T1F06: Which of the following self-assigned indicators are acceptable when using a phone transmission?

A. KL7CC stroke W3
B. KL7CC slant W3
C. KL7CC slash W3
D. All these choices are correct

SSB Phone (Voice)

Single-sideband (SSB) phone operation is a widely used voice communication mode in amateur radio. It is valued for its efficient use of bandwidth and power. For technician-class operators, SSB phones can be used <u>in at least some segment of all amateur bands above 50 MHz.</u> This includes popular VHF and UHF bands such as the 6-meter band (50-54 MHz), the 2-meter band (144-148 MHz), and the 70-centimeter band (420-450 MHz).

T1B10: Where may SSB phone be used in amateur bands above 50 MHz?

A. Only in sub-bands allocated to General class or higher licensees
B. Only on repeaters
C. In at least some segment of all these bands
D. On any band, if the power is limited to 25 watts

The availability of SSB phone segments in these higher-frequency bands allows for versatile communication options, enabling long-distance contacts under favorable conditions.

Selecting the correct receiver filter bandwidth for Single-Sideband (SSB) reception is essential to achieving the best signal-to-noise ratio. A bandwidth of 2400 Hz (2.4 kHz) is ideal for SSB. This bandwidth is wide enough to pass the entire SSB signal, which typically ranges from about 300 Hz to 3000 Hz, while also narrow enough to exclude most of the noise and interference from adjacent channels.

T4B10: Which of the following receiver filter bandwidths provides the best signal-to-noise ratio for SSB reception?

A. 500 Hz
B. 1000 Hz
C. 2400 Hz
D. 5000 Hz

Using a 2400 Hz filter helps enhance the received signal's clarity and intelligibility. It ensures that the voice signals are not distorted or clipped, providing a clear and crisp audio output. This balance between signal fidelity and noise reduction is pivotal for effective communication, especially in crowded band conditions or weak signals.

Digital

The 219 to 220 MHz segment of the 1.25-meter band is explicitly allocated for fixed digital message forwarding systems only. This means amateur radio operators can use this frequency range exclusively for digital communications involving automated message forwarding between fixed stations. This allocation supports activities such as packet radio networks and other digital communication systems that rely on efficiently transferring data over long distances.

T1B05: How may amateurs use the 219 to 220 MHz segment of 1.25 meter band?

A. Spread spectrum only
B. Fast-scan television only
C. Emergency traffic only
D. Fixed digital message forwarding systems only

By restricting the 219 to 220 MHz segment to fixed digital message forwarding, the FCC ensures that this portion of the spectrum is used effectively for high-speed, reliable digital communications. This helps reduce congestion in other parts of the amateur bands and promotes the development and use of advanced digital communication technologies.

Power Output

As a Technician class licensee, you must know the specific power output restrictions that apply to your operating privileges. While Technician license holders enjoy access to various frequency bands and modes, the FCC has set limits on the maximum power you can use. These restrictions are in place to ensure safe and efficient radio spectrum use and minimize interference with other users.

Power Output for Frequencies Above 30 MHz

Technician class operators are allowed a maximum peak envelope power (PEP) output of 1500 watts on frequencies above 30 MHz. This high power limit allows for robust communications over longer distances, particularly on popular VHF and UHF bands like the 2-meter and 70-centimeter bands. However, it's essential to remember that while 1500 watts is the upper limit, effective communication often requires much less power. Using the minimum power necessary to maintain a reliable connection is a good practice to reduce interference and conserve energy.

T1B12: Except for some specific restrictions, what is the maximum peak envelope power output for Technician class operators using frequencies above 30 MHz?

A. 50 watts
B. 100 watts
C. 500 watts
D. 1500 watts

Power Output for HF Band Segments

For the HF band segments that Technician licensees are permitted to use, the maximum PEP output is <u>limited to 200 watts</u>. The 200-watt limit is designed to provide sufficient power for making contacts over longer distances typical of HF propagation while reducing the risk of interference with other HF users. As with VHF and UHF operations, using the minimum power necessary to make contact effectively is essential.

T1B11: What is the maximum peak envelope power output for Technician class operators in their HF band segments?

A. 200 watts
B. 100 watts
C. 50 watts
D. 10 watts

Understanding the Difference in Power Limits for Technician Licensees

The significant difference in power limits between HF and frequencies above 30 MHz for Technician licensees is primarily due to the different propagation characteristics and potential for interference associated with these frequency bands.

Power Limits for Frequencies Above 30 MHz

Frequencies above 30 MHz, including the VHF and UHF bands, have more predictable and generally shorter-range propagation characteristics. These frequencies are primarily used for local and regional communications, where higher power can help overcome obstacles, terrain, and other local interference to ensure reliable contacts. The 1500-watt power limit allows Technician operators to effectively communicate over greater distances within these bands, especially in challenging environments or during adverse conditions.

Power Limits for HF Band Segments

In contrast, HF bands (below 30 MHz) have different propagation characteristics, often allowing for long-distance (DX) communication due to ionospheric reflection. Signals in the HF bands can travel thousands of miles, bouncing off the ionosphere, especially during favorable propagation conditions. Because HF signals can cover much larger areas, there is a higher potential for interference with other users. The 200-watt power limit for Technician licensees in their HF segments helps minimize this risk. Lower power levels are typically sufficient for making long-distance contacts in the HF bands, and the 200-watt limit strikes a balance between effective communication and reducing the likelihood of causing interference.

Remember to grab the quick reference guide. Again, it's one of those things you print off and keep at your radio. Over time, it will become memorized. For now, refer to the guide!

Chapter 29

Public Service in Ham Radio

PUBLIC SERVICE IS A cornerstone of amateur radio, offering operators a unique opportunity to support their communities during emergencies, public events, and disasters. Ham radio operators provide reliable communication when traditional systems fail or are overloaded. Whether it's coordinating relief efforts during a natural disaster, supporting communication at a marathon, or participating in community events, amateur radio operators are there to assist.

Understanding the rules and regulations that govern public service activities in ham radio is essential. These rules ensure that operators use their skills and equipment responsibly and effectively. In this section, we will explore the various aspects of public service in amateur radio, including the types of events where ham operators can contribute, the specific regulations that apply, and best practices for ensuring efficient and effective communication.

RACES and ARES

RACES (Radio Amateur Civil Emergency Service) and ARES (Amateur Radio Emergency Service) are vital organizations within the amateur radio community that provide vital communication services during emergencies.

RACES (Radio Amateur Civil Emergency Service)

RACES is a service regulated by the Federal Communications Commission (FCC) - a unique amateur radio service regulated under Part 97 of the FCC rules - and operates under the auspices of local, county, and state emergency management agencies. It is designed to provide emergency communication services during civil emergencies, such as natural disasters, terrorist attacks, or other significant incidents. RACES activation is usually coordinated by government emergency management agencies, and its members are trained and prepared to operate under the direction of these agencies during emergencies.

T2C04: What is RACES?

A. An emergency organization combining amateur radio and citizens band operators and frequencies
B. An international radio experimentation society
C. A radio contest held in a short period, sometimes called a "sprint."
D. An FCC part 97 amateur radio service for civil defense communications during national emergencies

---

ARES (Amateur Radio Emergency Service)

ARES is a volunteer-based organization organized by the American Radio Relay League (ARRL). Unlike RACES, ARES is more flexible and can be activated for a broader range of emergency situations, including non-governmental and community events. ARES members provide communication support during disasters, public service events, and other community activities. Membership in ARES is voluntary and open to any licensed amateur radio operator, and training focuses on developing the skills needed to provide effective emergency communications.

T2C06: What is the Amateur Radio Emergency Service (ARES)?

A. A group of licensed amateurs who have voluntarily registered their qualifications and equipment for communications duty in the public service
B. A group of licensed amateurs who are members of the military and who voluntarily agreed to provide message handling services in the case of an emergency
C. A training program that provides licensing courses for those interested in obtaining an amateur license to use during emergencies
D. A training program that certifies amateur operators for membership in the Radio Amateur Civil Emergency Service

Key Differences and Collaboration

- **Regulation and Activation**: RACES operates under government regulation and is activated by governmental agencies. ARES is more community-oriented and can be activated to meet various public service needs.

- **Flexibility**: ARES can be used in a broader range of situations than RACES, which is specifically for civil emergencies.

- **Membership and Training**: Both organizations require training, but RACES is typically more formal and structured due to its government affiliation.

Despite these differences, RACES and ARES often collaborate to provide comprehensive emergency communication services. Understanding the roles and functions of both organizations is key for amateur radio operators who wish to contribute effectively to public service and emergency response efforts.

Here's a simplified way to remember the difference between the two groups: When you see 'ARES,' think of the first 'A' for "Amateur," which suggests a less formal, volunteer-based organization. For 'RACES,' the 'C' stands for "Civil," which reminds you of "Civil service" and indicates that it's a government-run organization. This isn't a perfect rule, but it can be a helpful way to distinguish between the two.

American Radio Relay League (ARRL)

The ARRL (American Radio Relay League) is the national association for amateur radio in the United States, founded in 1914. It advocates for hams' interests, provides educational resources, supports emergency communication through ARES, coordinates licensing and testing, fosters community through events, and advances technical standards. The ARRL plays a role in promoting and supporting amateur radio, ensuring the hobby's growth and vitality.

Their website has many great, and often very technical, radio readings and resources.

Nets in Ham Radio

A "net" in ham radio refers to a scheduled on-air meeting of amateur radio operators, organized for various purposes such as sharing information, coordinating activities, providing emergency communications, or simply socializing. Nets are typically run by a net control station (NCS), which facilitates the orderly flow of communication, ensures that all participants have a chance to speak, and maintains the structure and purpose of the net.

Key Features and Types of Nets

1. **Regularly Scheduled**: Nets usually occur at specific times and frequencies, allowing operators to plan their participation. Schedules for nets can often be found on club websites, newsletters, or through on-air announcements.

2. **Net Control Station (NCS):** The NCS plays a role in managing the net, <u>calling the net to order, directing and coordinating the order of speakers,</u> and ensuring the net runs smoothly and efficiently. The NCS helps to prevent chaos and overlapping transmissions by controlling who speaks and when.

T2C02: Which of the following are typical duties of a Net Control Station?

A. Choose the regular net meeting time and frequency
B. Ensure that all stations checking into the net are properly licensed for operation on the net frequency
C. Call the net to order and direct communications between stations checking in
D. All these choices are correct

Types of Nets:

- **Traffic Nets**: These nets handle formal message traffic, ensuring that important messages are relayed accurately and efficiently across distances.

- **Emergency Nets**: Activated during emergencies or disasters, these nets provide communication links for coordinating relief efforts, reporting conditions, and supporting emergency services.

- **Social Nets**: These are informal gatherings where operators check in, share news, discuss topics of interest, and enjoy fellowship.

- **Special Interest Nets**: Focused on specific topics, such as technical discussions, DXing (long-distance communications), contesting, or modes like digital or CW (Morse code).

Participating in a Net

When participating in a net, <u>it is standard practice to transmit only when directed by the net control station (NCS) unless you report an emergency.</u> The NCS manages the flow of communication, ensuring that all participants can speak in an orderly manner without causing interference or confusion. By waiting for the NCS to call on you, you help maintain the net's structure and efficiency, allowing for clear and effective communication.

T2C07: Which of the following is standard practice when you participate in a net?

A. When first responding to the net control station, transmit your call sign, name, and address as in the FCC database
B. Record the time of each of your transmissions
C. Unless you are reporting an emergency, transmit only when directed by the net control station
D. All these choices are correct

This practice enables the smooth operation of the net, as it prevents overlapping transmissions and ensures that important messages are conveyed accurately. You should immediately report the situation in an emergency, as emergency traffic always takes priority. Understanding and following this protocol is essential for all amateur radio operators, as it demonstrates respect for the net's organization and enhances the overall communication experience.

Net Operation

In the context of net operation, <u>"traffic" refers to the messages exchanged by net stations.</u> These messages can be routine communications, formal messages, or emergency information that needs to be relayed to other stations. Managing traffic efficiently is essential for maintaining clear and organized communication, especially during emergency operations or coordinated events.

Traffic in net operations is typically categorized and prioritized to ensure that urgent and important messages are handled promptly. Formal traffic handling follows a structured format to ensure accuracy and clarity, making it easier for operators to pass messages accurately without misunderstandings. Understanding the concept of traffic and how it is managed in net operations is essential for all amateur radio operators, as it ensures effective communication and coordination within the network. This knowledge is also part of exam preparation, highlighting the organized nature of amateur radio communications.

T2C05: What does the term "traffic" refer to in net operation?

A. Messages exchanged by net stations
B. The number of stations checking in and out of a net
C. Operation by mobile or portable stations
D. Requests to activate the net by a served agency

Good Traffic Handling

Good traffic handling in amateur radio involves passing messages precisely as received, without alteration or interpretation. This precision is beneficial because even minor changes in the message content can lead to misunderstandings, incorrect actions, or failed communications, especially during emergencies. The integrity of the message must be maintained to ensure that the recipient receives the information as the sender intended.

T2C08: Which of the following is a characteristic of good traffic handling?

A. Passing messages exactly as received
B. Making decisions as to whether messages are worthy of relay or delivery
C. Ensuring that any newsworthy messages are relayed to the news media
D. All these choices are correct

Traffic handling refers to relaying messages between stations in a network, often within organized nets. This can include routine communications, formal messages, and emergency information. Operators must follow standardized procedures and use specific formats to ensure clarity and accuracy. This involves using the standard phonetic alphabet for clarity (spelling out the words), confirming the receipt of each message, and maintaining detailed logs of all traffic handled. By adhering to these practices, amateur radio operators ensure reliable and effective communication, which is key in coordinated operations, especially during emergencies.

T2C03: What technique is used to ensure that voice messages containing unusual words are received correctly?

A. Send the words by voice and Morse code
B. Speak very loudly into the microphone
C. Spell the words using a standard phonetic alphabet
D. All these choices are correct

The Parts of the Message

Understanding the Preamble in Formal Traffic Messages

The preamble of a formal traffic message contains essential information needed to track the message as it moves through various stations. This message section typically includes details such as the message number, the originating station's call sign, the destination, the date and time of origination, and the message's priority level. This information ensures the message can be accurately tracked, identified, and managed as it is relayed from one operator to another.

Including a detailed preamble is vital for effective traffic handling. It allows operators to verify the authenticity and urgency of the message, ensure it reaches the correct destination, and maintain an accurate log of all communications. This structured approach helps prevent errors, provides accountability, and enhances the reliability of the communication process.

T2C10: What information is contained in the preamble of a formal traffic message?

A. The email address of the originating station
B. The address of the intended recipient
C. The telephone number of the addressee
D. Information needed to track the message

Radiogram

A radiogram is a standardized format for sending formal messages in amateur radio communications, particularly within traffic nets. Developed by the National Traffic System (NTS), radiograms facilitate clear and precise message handling. Each radiogram includes a preamble (containing the check, the message number, origin, destination, and priority), the recipient's address, the text of the message, and the sender's signature. This format ensures that messages are transmitted consistently, making them easier to relay accurately across multiple stations. Understanding the components of a radiogram, including the "check," is essential for effective participation in traffic handling and for preparing for the amateur radio exam.

In a radiogram header, "check" <u>refers to the number of words or word equivalents</u> in the message's text portion. This count helps ensure that the message has been received accurately and completely. When the receiving operator verifies the check, they count the words in the message text and compare them to the number in the header. If the numbers match, it confirms that the entire message has been transmitted without omissions or errors.

T2C11: What is meant by "check" in a radiogram header?

A. The number of words or word equivalents in the text portion of the message
B. The call sign of the originating station
C. A list of stations that have relayed the message
D. A box on the message form that indicates that the message was received and/or relayed

Rules in Emergencies and Public Service

Effective communication is vital during emergencies and in group settings, and amateur radio operators play a vital role in these scenarios. Whether coordinating disaster relief efforts, supporting public events, or participating in organized nets, following established rules and protocols ensures that communication remains clear, efficient, and effective.

This section will delve into the specific rules that apply during emergencies and when operating within groups. By adhering to these guidelines, amateur radio operators can provide invaluable support during critical times, enhancing safety and operational success.

FCC Rules and Emergency Operations in Amateur Radio

<u>FCC rules always apply to the operation of an amateur station, even during emergencies</u>. This ensures that all communication remains orderly, efficient, and within legal guidelines. Adherence to FCC rules becomes even more important during emergencies as it helps manage the limited communication resources and prevents interference with key operations.

T2C01: When do FCC rules NOT apply to the operation of an amateur station?

A. When operating a RACES station
B. When operating under special FEMA rules
C. When operating under special ARES rules
D. FCC rules always apply

While the primary focus in emergencies is facilitating effective communication, operators must still follow established protocols such as identifying their stations, using appropriate frequencies, and maintaining proper power levels. These regulations ensure that all stations can operate harmoniously and that emergency communications are prioritized without interference.

Operating Outside Frequency Privileges in Emergencies

Under normal circumstances, amateur station control operators must adhere strictly to the frequency privileges of their license class. However, there is an exception to this rule in situations involving the immediate safety of human life or property protection. In such emergencies, operators can operate outside their assigned frequency privileges to facilitate urgent communications necessary to address the crisis.

This exception ensures amateur radio operators can provide communication support when most needed, regardless of their license class restrictions. Despite this allowance, operators must still follow all other FCC rules and regulations, such as identifying their stations and using appropriate communication protocols. Understanding this exception is crucial for both practical emergency response and exam preparation. It highlights the flexibility within the regulatory framework to prioritize human safety and property protection in emergency situations, even though FCC rules always apply.

T2C09: Are amateur station control operators ever permitted to operate outside the frequency privileges of their license class?

A. No
B. Yes, but only when part of a FEMA emergency plan
C. Yes, but only when part of a RACES emergency plan
D. Yes, but only in situations involving the immediate safety of human life or the protection of property

Not confusing at all... is it!

Public service is a cornerstone of amateur radio, allowing operators to support their communities during emergencies, public events, and disasters. Understanding the rules and regulations governing public service activities is essential for responsible and effective communication.

Chapter 30

The Amateur Station and Control

IN THIS CHAPTER, WE will delve into the essentials of station control and the operational aspects of your ham radio. Understanding these fundamentals is necessary for the effective and compliant operation within the amateur radio service. From learning the responsibilities of the control operator to mastering the procedures for safe and efficient station management, this section will provide you with the knowledge needed to control and operate your ham radio station confidently.

Control Operator

A control operator is an individual responsible for properly operating an amateur radio station. This person holds a valid amateur radio license and ensures all transmissions comply with FCC rules and regulations. The control operator must be present and control the station whenever it is transmitting. Their duties include managing the station's frequency usage, adhering to power limits, and ensuring all communications are conducted legally and ethically.

The control operator's role is central to maintaining the integrity of the amateur radio service. By overseeing the station's operation, the control operator helps prevent interference with other communications, ensures the safety of radio operations, and upholds the standards the FCC sets. This responsibility highlights the importance of knowledge and adherence to regulations in the amateur radio community, making the control operator a key figure in any station's operation.

Presumed Control Operator of an Amateur Station

The FCC presumes the station licensee to be the control operator of an amateur station unless there is documentation in the station records indicating otherwise. This means that, by default, the person or entity that holds the license for the amateur radio station is responsible for its operation and ensuring compliance with all FCC regulations. The station licensee is assumed to be in control unless it is clearly documented that another qualified operator has been designated as the control operator for specific periods or operations.

T1E11: Who does the FCC presume to be the control operator of an amateur station unless documentation to the contrary is in the station records?

A. The station custodian
B. The third party participant
C. The person operating the station equipment
D. The station licensee

Designation of the Station Control Operator

The station licensee must designate the station control operator. The station licensee is the individual or entity that holds the license for the amateur radio station and is ultimately responsible for its operations. By designating a control operator, the licensee ensures that a qualified individual can manage the station's transmissions and adhere to FCC regulations.

T1E03: Who must designate the station control operator?

A. The station licensee
B. The FCC
C. The frequency coordinator
D. Any licensed operator

This designation process helps ensure that all operations are conducted legally and ethically, with a responsible person overseeing the use of the radio equipment. It emphasizes the importance of accountability and proper management within the amateur radio community, reinforcing the need for all stations to operate under the supervision of a knowledgeable and licensed control operator.

Control Operator Privileges

Under normal circumstances, a Technician class licensee may never be the control operator of a station operating in an Amateur Extra Class band segment. The FCC regulations strictly limit the operating privileges of amateur radio licensees based on their license class, and each class grants access to specific frequency bands. Technician class licensees are restricted to certain VHF and UHF bands and do not have the authority to operate in the frequency segments reserved for Amateur Extra Class licensees.

T1E06: When, under normal circumstances, may a Technician class licensee be the control operator of a station operating in an Amateur Extra Class band segment?

A. At no time
B. When designated as the control operator by an Amateur Extra Class licensee
C. As part of a multi-operator contest team
D. When using a club station whose trustee holds an Amateur Extra Class license

---

This restriction ensures that only those who have passed the more advanced licensing exams and demonstrate a deeper understanding of radio theory, regulations, and operating practices can access the broader and more powerful segments of the amateur bands.

Responsibility for Proper Operation

When the control operator is not the station licensee, both the control operator AND the station licensee share the responsibility for the proper station operation. This means that while the control operator is actively managing the station's transmissions, ensuring compliance with FCC regulations and operational standards, the station licensee retains overall responsibility for the station's activities and must ensure that any designated control operators are qualified and compliant with all relevant rules.

T1E07: When the control operator is not the station licensee, who is responsible for the proper operation of the station?

A. All licensed amateurs who are present at the operation
B. Only the station licensee
C. Only the control operator
D. The control operator and the station licensee

This dual responsibility ensures that checks and balances are in place, promoting accountability and adherence to regulations. The control operator must operate within the privileges of their license class and follow all operational guidelines. At the same time, the station licensee must ensure that their station is used appropriately and legally.

Repeaters

When a repeater inadvertently retransmits communications that violate FCC rules, the control operator of the originating station is held accountable. This means the individual who controls the station from which the violating communication originated is responsible for ensuring compliance with FCC regulations. Even though the repeater may automatically retransmit the communication, it is the responsibility of the originating station's control operator to ensure that their transmissions adhere to the rules.

T1F10: Who is accountable if a repeater inadvertently retransmits communications that violate the FCC rules?

A. The control operator of the originating station
B. The control operator of the repeater
C. The owner of the repeater
D. Both the originating station and the repeater owner

This accountability emphasizes the importance of operators being vigilant and always responsible for their transmissions. Operators must monitor their content and avoid prohibited communications, such as obscene language, deliberate interference, or unlicensed operations.

Identifying Your Station During On-The-Air Test Transmissions

When making on-the-air test transmissions, it is essential to identify the transmitting station. This requirement is part of the FCC regulations to ensure that all transmissions can be traced back to a licensed operator, maintaining accountability and order on the amateur radio bands. Proper identification involves stating your call sign at regular intervals during the test transmission, typically every ten minutes and at the end of the transmission.

T2A06: Which of the following is required when making on-the-air test transmissions?

A. Identify the transmitting station
B. Conduct tests only between 10 p.m. and 6 a.m. local time
C. Notify the FCC of the transmissions
D. All these choices are correct

Identifying your station during test transmissions complies with regulatory requirements and helps other operators know who is conducting the tests. This transparency prevents confusion and interference, allowing the amateur radio community to function smoothly.

When Identification is Not Required for Transmissions

Under FCC regulations, an amateur station may transmit without identifying on the air only in specific circumstances, such as when transmitting signals to <u>control model craft</u>. This exemption is designed to facilitate the operation of remote-controlled devices, like model airplanes or boats, which often require rapid and frequent transmission of control signals. In these cases, continuously identifying the station could interfere with the effective control of the model craft.

T1D11: When may an amateur station transmit without identifying on the air?

A. When the transmissions are of a brief nature to make station adjustments
B. When the transmissions are unmodulated
C. When the transmitted power level is below 1 watt
D. When transmitting signals to control model craft

This narrow and specific exception emphasizes the importance of proper station identification in most amateur radio operations, allowing for accountability and ensuring that transmissions comply with FCC rules.

Amateur Station

Control Operator Requirement for Amateur Stations

An amateur station is <u>NOT permitted</u> to transmit without a control operator. According to FCC regulations, a control operator must be present and in charge of the station's operations whenever it is transmitting. The control operator ensures that all transmissions comply with FCC rules and regulations, including frequency use, power limits, and communication content.

T1E01: When may an amateur station transmit without a control operator?

A. When using automatic control, such as in the case of a repeater
B. When the station licensee is away and another licensed amateur is using the station
C. When the transmitting station is an auxiliary station
D. Never

Understanding this requirement is needed for all operators, as it emphasizes the responsibility of operating a station. Transmissions could easily violate regulations without a control operator, leading to potential interference, legal issues, and disruption of the amateur radio community.

Frequency Privileges

The transmitting frequency privileges of an amateur station <u>are determined by the operator license class</u> held by the control operator. The FCC issues different classes of amateur radio licenses, each granting varying levels of access to the radio frequency spectrum.

T1E04: What determines the transmitting frequency privileges of an amateur station?

A. The frequency authorized by the frequency coordinator
B. The frequencies printed on the license grant
C. The highest class of operator license held by anyone on the premises
D. The class of operator license held by the control operator

The control operator's license class dictates which frequencies can be used, ensuring that operators transmit only on frequencies they are authorized to use.

Station and Records for FCC Inspection

The FCC requires that an amateur radio station and its associated records be <u>available for inspection at any time</u> upon request by an FCC representative. This rule ensures that amateur radio operators comply with FCC regulations and promptly demonstrate their adherence to proper operational standards. The records typically include the station log, licenses, and documentation of control operators, which collectively provide evidence of lawful operation and proper station management.

T1F01: When must the station and its records be available for FCC inspection?

A. At any time ten days after notification by the FCC of such an inspection
B. At any time upon request by an FCC representative
C. At any time after written notification by the FCC of such inspection
D. Only when presented with a valid warrant by an FCC official or government agent

Preparing for an FCC inspection means keeping all records accurate, up-to-date, and easily accessible. This readiness demonstrates a commitment to compliance and helps prevent any potential legal issues arising from improper station management.

Amateur Station's Control Point

An amateur station's control point is <u>where the control operator performs their function</u>. This is where the operator can manage and control the station's transmissions, ensuring compliance with FCC regulations. The control point is critical because it is where the operator can monitor and adjust the station's operations in real-time, maintaining proper frequency use, power levels, and adherence to communication protocols.

T1E05: What is an amateur station's control point?

A. The location of the station's transmitting antenna
B. The location of the station's transmitting apparatus
C. The location at which the control operator function is performed
D. The mailing address of the station licensee

Knowing the concept of a control point is essential for amateur radio operators because it defines the operational center of their station. Whether the control point is a physical location, like a designated radio room, or a remote setup managed via computer software, it is the hub where the operator exercises authority and responsibility. This setup ensures that every transmission is supervised and that the station operates within the legal and technical parameters established by the FCC.

Automatic Retransmission of Signals

Certain amateur stations, specifically <u>repeater, auxiliary, and space stations</u>, are permitted to retransmit the signals of other amateur stations <u>automatically</u>. Repeaters are commonly used to extend the range of communications, receiving a signal on one frequency and retransmitting it on another, typically with higher power and from a better location. This allows operators to communicate over greater distances than possible with direct point-to-point communication.

T1D07: What types of amateur stations can automatically retransmit the signals of other amateur stations?

A. Auxiliary, beacon, or Earth stations
B. Earth, repeater, or space stations
C. Beacon, repeater, or space stations
D. Repeater, auxiliary, or space stations

The key word in this question is automatically.

Auxiliary stations are similar but are used to support the primary operations of a station, often facilitating control or linking between repeaters. Space stations like those on satellites can also automatically retransmit signals, allowing for global communication coverage. Understanding these capabilities is key as it helps utilize the full potential of the amateur radio infrastructure, enhancing communication possibilities and operational flexibility. These systems play a vital role in expanding the reach and effectiveness of amateur radio networks, making it possible to maintain reliable communication in various scenarios.

Automatic Control

Automatic control in amateur radio refers to the operation of a station without the need for continuous real-time human intervention. A prime example of this is <u>repeater operation</u>. Repeaters are designed to receive signals on one frequency and <u>automatically</u> retransmit them on another, allowing for extended communication ranges. This process is entirely automated, meaning the repeater can operate independently, continually receiving and retransmitting signals without a control operator always being present.

T1E08: Which of the following is an example of automatic control?

A. Repeater operation
B. Controlling a station over the internet
C. Using a computer or other device to send CW automatically
D. Using a computer or other device to identify automatically

---

Remote Control Operation

Remote control operation in amateur radio involves managing a station from a location other than where the radio equipment is physically situated. Specific requirements must be met for this type of operation to ensure compliance with FCC regulations. First, <u>a control operator must be at the control point</u> where the station is remotely operated. This ensures that a qualified individual constantly oversees the station's transmissions and adheres to all relevant rules and guidelines.

Additionally, a <u>control operator is always required during remote control operations</u>. This constant oversight is there to maintain the integrity and proper functioning of the amateur radio station. The <u>control operator must indirectly manipulate the station's controls</u>, typically software or other remote-control technologies, to manage frequency changes, power levels, and other operational parameters. Understanding these requirements helps amateur radio operators ensure that their remote control operations are legal, safe, and effective, maintaining the high standards of the amateur radio community.

T1E09: Which of the following are required for remote control operation?

A. The control operator must be at the control point
B. A control operator is required at all times
C. The control operator must indirectly manipulate the controls
D. All these choices are correct

Example of Remote Control in Amateur Radio

As defined in Part 97 of the FCC regulations, remote control in amateur radio involves operating a station from a distance without being physically present at the station's location. A typical example of this is operating the station over the internet. This setup allows a licensed amateur radio operator to control their equipment from virtually anywhere, using computer software and internet connectivity to adjust frequencies, power levels, and other operational settings.

T1E10: Which of the following is an example of remote control as defined in Part 97?

A. Repeater operation
B. Operating the station over the internet
C. Controlling a model aircraft, boat, or car by amateur radio
D. All these choices are correct

This is beneficial for operators who need to manage their stations while away from home or for those who want to remotely take advantage of better propagation conditions or more favorable locations. Remote control helps operators utilize modern technology to enhance their radio operations, ensuring they remain compliant with FCC rules while enjoying the flexibility and convenience that remote control offers. It also underscores the importance of maintaining proper control and supervision, as the control operator must still ensure all transmissions adhere to regulatory standards.

Beacons

According to FCC Part 97, a beacon is defined as an amateur station transmitting communications for the purpose of observing propagation or conducting related experimental activities. Beacons are tools in the amateur radio community, as they provide valuable information about the conditions of the ionosphere and other propagation mediums. By continuously transmitting a signal, beacons allow operators to monitor the strength and stability of signals over various frequencies and distances, helping to predict the best times and frequencies for effective communication.

T1A06: What is the FCC Part 97 definition of a beacon?

A. A government transmitter marking the amateur radio band edges
B. A bulletin sent by the FCC to announce a national emergency
C. A continuous transmission of weather information authorized in the amateur bands by the National Weather Service
D. An amateur station transmitting communications for the purposes of observing propagation or related experimental activities

Beacons serve an essential function in propagation studies and experimentation. By analyzing beacon signals, operators can gain insights into the current state of the radio bands and make informed decisions about when and how to conduct their transmissions.

Expanding Your Ham Experience

EMBARKING ON THE PATH of amateur radio is akin to setting out on a vast sea with endless horizons to explore. Each new skill you acquire and every piece of knowledge you gain is like catching a favorable wind, pushing you further along this exciting voyage, looking for more adventures.

After you get licensed, many opportunities open up to you. Let's examine a few of them.

Chapter 31

Hams Having Fun

Contests

Ham radio contests, often known as "radiosport," provide an exhilarating opportunity for operators of all skill levels to test their abilities in a structured competitive environment. For you as a newly licensed Technician, participating in these contests can significantly enhance your operating skills, broaden your understanding of radio propagation, and deepen your engagement with the regional amateur radio community.

Contests vary widely, ranging from local VHF competitions to worldwide DX contests. Each contest has its own set of rules, objectives, and modes of operation, which can include making as many contacts as possible within a certain period or contacting as many geographic areas as possible.

T8C03: What operating activity involves contacting as many stations as possible during a specified period?

A. Simulated emergency exercises
B. Net operations
C. Public service events
D. Contesting

To begin your adventure in radiosport, the first step is finding contests that align with your license privileges and interests. Many contests are designed to include newcomers and may have categories or power restrictions ensuring a level playing field.

The American Radio Relay League (ARRL) website is a tremendous resource, listing various upcoming contests with detailed descriptions of their rules and eligibility criteria. Platforms like ContestCalendar.com aggregate information about ham radio contests worldwide, providing a comprehensive schedule to help you plan your participation months in advance.

When choosing a contest, consider the required bands, modes, and duration to ensure it matches your available equipment and personal schedule. Some contests, like those dedicated to digital modes, also need specific software for logging contacts or participation.

Understanding and adhering to contest etiquette ensures fair play and fosters participant camaraderie. One fundamental aspect of contest etiquette is precise and efficient communication. Unlike regular QSOs, contest exchanges are typically brief, focusing on the essential information required by the contest rules, such as signal report, call sign, and location. Maintaining a brisk but polite pace helps keep the contest moving and allows more participants to make contacts.

T8C04: Which of the following is good procedure when contacting another station in a contest?

A. Sign only the last two letters of your call if there are many other stations calling
B. Contact the station twice to be sure that you are in his log
C. Send only the minimum information needed for proper identification and the contest exchange
D. All these choices are correct

Respecting the frequency rights of others is also essential; if you find a frequency in use, it's courteous to move to another one rather than causing interference. Additionally, self-spotting, or announcing your frequency on spotting networks to attract contacts, is generally frowned upon unless explicitly allowed by the contest rules.

Logging during contests is more than just a formality—it's a core part of the strategy and integrity of radiosport. Each contact made during the contest must be meticulously logged, with details including the time of contact, the call sign of the other station, and the exchange information. Accuracy is paramount, as errors can lead to penalties or disqualification from the contest results. Many operators use specialized logging software that helps record contacts and check for duplicate contacts, which are usually not allowed. These programs can also provide real-time scores and projections to help you adjust your strategy.

Grid Locators

A grid locator is a letter-number designator assigned to a specific geographic location, used primarily in amateur radio to identify the exact position of a station. This system, known as the Maidenhead Locator System, divides the world into a grid of squares, each represented by a unique combination of letters and numbers. For example, a grid locator might look like "FN31pr," where "FN" identifies a larger geographic area, "31" pinpoints a more specific region within that area, and "pr" provides an even more precise location.

Grid locators are essential for several reasons. They allow amateur radio operators to accurately log their contacts while participating in contests.

Understanding that a grid locator is a geographic designator consisting of letters and numbers helps operators easily communicate their location, making it a crucial tool in the ham radio community.

T8C05: What is a grid locator?

A. A letter-number designator assigned to a geographic location
B. A letter-number designator assigned to an azimuth and elevation
C. An instrument for neutralizing a final amplifier
D. An instrument for radio direction finding

After the contest, submitting your log is the final step in your participation. Each contest has specific rules about how and when logs should be submitted, often through a web upload interface or email. Timely submission is essential, as most contests have strict deadlines for log entries, typically within a few days to a week after the event concludes. Once submitted, your log will be checked against the logs of other participants, a process that helps ensure the accuracy and fairness of the scoring. After all logs are evaluated, results are published, detailing scores and standings. These results can provide valuable insights into your performance and areas for improvement.

Partaking in contests and striving for awards brings excitement and recognition and significantly contributes to your growth as an amateur radio operator. Each contest challenges you to apply your skills, adapt to changing conditions, and interact with a diverse array of operators, each of which enriches your experience and builds your proficiency in the hobby. As you continue to participate, you'll likely find that the thrill of competition, the joy of achievement, and the camaraderie of the community become enduring motivators in your ongoing journey in amateur radio.

Hidden Transmitter Hunts: Fox Hunts

A fox hunt, also known as a hidden transmitter hunt, is a popular activity in the amateur radio community. Participants use radio direction-finding techniques to locate a hidden transmitter called the "fox." Equipped with directional antennas and radio equipment, hunters search for the fox by following the strongest signal directions. The goal is to find the exact location of the hidden transmitter as quickly as possible. Fox hunts are fun and competitive, help improve radio direction-finding skills, and promote fellowship among radio enthusiasts. This engaging activity demonstrates the practical applications of radio technology and provides valuable experience in signal tracking and problem-solving.

A directional antenna is an indispensable tool for fox hunting. This type of antenna focuses on the reception of signals in a specific direction, making it easier to determine the direction from which a signal is coming. By rotating the directional antenna and observing where the signal strength is strongest, hunters can pinpoint the location of the hidden transmitter.

T8C02: Which of these items would be useful for a hidden transmitter hunt?

A. Calibrated SWR meter
B. A directional antenna
C. A calibrated noise bridge
D. All these choices are correct

Using a directional antenna simplifies the process of locating the hidden transmitter by providing a clear indication of direction, which is much more efficient than using a non-directional antenna that receives signals equally from all directions.

This technique is essential for hidden transmitter hunts, allowing participants to quickly and accurately find the transmitter. In addition, because a directional antenna helps identify the direction of signals, it can help us locate sources of interference or jamming.

Radio direction finding is a method for locating noise interference or jamming sources by determining the direction from which a radio signal originates. This technique uses directional antennas that can focus on signals from specific directions. By rotating the antenna and noting the direction where the signal is strongest, operators can triangulate and pinpoint the source of the interference.

T8C01: Which of the following methods is used to locate sources of noise interference or jamming?

A. Echolocation
B. Doppler radar
C. Radio direction finding
D. Phase locking

Welcome to the excitement known as ham contests and fox hunts, where you can test your skills, challenge yourself, and enjoy friendly competition. Whether you're chasing signals or hunting hidden transmitters, these activities offer a fun and engaging way to hone your radio expertise and connect with fellow enthusiasts.

Chapter 32

Upgrading Your License: From Technician to General

AS YOU BEGIN TO feel more comfortable with your Technician License, you may look towards broader seas, yearning to delve deeper and reach further. This is where upgrading your license from Technician to General comes into play, opening up a world of enhanced frequencies and international communication opportunities.

Benefits of Upgrading

Upgrading to a General class license is not just a step up—it's a gateway to a new realm of possibilities in the amateur radio community. This upgrade allows you to access additional frequency bands below 30 MHz, primarily for high-frequency (HF) communications. These bands are prized for their ability to communicate internationally, harnessing the ionosphere to bounce radio waves across oceans and continents. This capability expands your operational reach and immerses you in a global network of amateur radio operators. Engaging with this community can enrich your experience with diverse cultural exchanges and deepen your understanding of international communication dynamics from the comfort of your radio station.

Moreover, the General class license opens up more bandwidth in the HF bands, allowing you to experiment with a broader range of modes and activities, including contesting and emergency communications on a global scale. These activities enhance your technical skills and contribute to your personal growth within the hobby, offering new challenges and the satisfaction of overcoming them.

Keeping the Hobby Alive

NOW THAT YOU HAVE everything you need to pass your Technician Class License exam and dive into the exciting world of ham radio, it's time to share your newfound knowledge and help others on their journey.

Would you help someone you've never met, even if you never got credit for it?

That person might be a lot like you were when you first picked up this book—curious about ham radio, eager to learn, and looking for guidance. Your honest review can be the light that guides them to success.

At Morse Code Publishing, we aim to make ham radio accessible to everyone. But to reach more people and make a bigger impact, we need your help.

Most people judge a book by its cover—and its reviews. You can make a difference by taking just 60 seconds to leave a review on Amazon. Your review could help:

- one more beginner discover amateur radio

- one more student pass their Technician exam

Your review won't cost you anything but could change someone's life.

Simply scan the QR code or click the link below to leave your review:

Leave a Review

https://mybook.to/HamTechReview

Thank you for your support. Ham radio thrives when we pass on our knowledge—and with your help, we can keep the passion alive and growing.

Welcome to the club! Your biggest fan,

Morse Code Publishing

PS – When you help someone else, you become part of their success story. If you believe this book will help others, consider sharing it with them. Let's keep the goodwill going!

Conclusion

As we turn the final page of this journey together, take a moment to reflect on the incredible path you've navigated—from a curious beginner to a proud holder of the Technician Class license (or soon-to-be license holder) poised at the threshold of the vast and vibrant hobby of ham radio. Throughout this book, we have traversed the essentials of ham radio operations, tackled the intricacies of FCC regulations, and mastered the knowledge necessary to pass the Technician Class exam. But more importantly, you've taken your first steps into a global community rich with continuous learning, friendship, and service opportunities.

Remember, the license you've worked so hard to acquire is much more than a license - it's your ticket to endless exploration and innovation in radio communications. The real adventure begins now, with each frequency you tune into and every connection you make expanding your horizons.

Connect with local clubs, participate in online forums, and attend hamfests. These platforms are not just avenues for deepening your technical knowledge—they are gateways to forging lasting friendships and contributing to a hobby that thrives on active participation and mutual support.

Ham radio offers unparalleled opportunities for personal growth and public service. Whether it's experimenting with digital modes, communicating through satellites, or providing emergency comms, you have the power to make a significant impact.

Now, I call on you to share your journey. Inspire others by recounting your experience obtaining your Technician Class license. Whether through social media, a blog, or casual conversations within your community, share your story of successfully obtaining your license.

Looking ahead, consider the next challenge. The General and Extra Class licenses await, opening new frequencies and possibilities.

Thank you for allowing us to participate in your entry into the ham radio world. It's been a privilege to guide and accompany you on this initial leg of what I hope will be a long and fulfilling adventure. Continue to push the boundaries of what you can achieve, and remember that each frequency tuned and each call made is a note in the ongoing symphony of global communication.

Finally, view your Technician license as the beginning of a continuous learning path in amateur radio. Continuous learning will expand your operational capabilities and deepen your enjoyment and engagement with the hobby. Participate in forums, join clubs, attend ham fests, and perhaps most importantly, stay curious. Amateur radio is vast and varied, and there is always something new to discover.

Welcome to the community—we can't wait to hear your call sign on the air.

- 73

Jared Johnson, KF0RTU @ Morse Code Publishing

Exam Question Index

T0 - Safety
Group T0A
T0A01 150
T0A02 147
T0A03 149
T0A04 148
T0A05 148
T0A06 150
T0A07 152
T0A08 149
T0A09 150
T0A10 150
T0A11 150
T0A12 102

Group T0B
T0B01 162
T0B02 160
T0B03 160
T0B04 157
T0B05 159
T0B06 157
T0B07 159
T0B08 161
T0B09 157
T0B10 162
T0B11 161

Group T0C
T0C01 142
T0C02 144
T0C03 143
T0C04 142
T0C05 144
T0C06 146
T0C07 145
T0C08 145
T0C09 152
T0C10 143
T0C11 143
T0C12 142
T0C13 137

T1 - Commission's Rules
Group T1A
T1A01 212
T1A02 211
T1A03 165
T1A04 213
T1A05 214
T1A06 243
T1A07 180
T1A08 224
T1A09 224
T1A10 212
T1A11 216

Group T1B
T1B01 227
T1B02 180
T1B03 72
T1B04 73
T1B05 229
T1B06 227
T1B07 226
T1B08 213
T1B09 172
T1B10 228
T1B11 230
T1B12 230

Group T1C
T1C01 213
T1C02 222
T1C03 219
T1C04 214
T1C05 222
T1C06 220
T1C07 214
T1C08 215
T1C09 215
T1C10 214
T1C11 215

Group T1D
T1D01 217
T1D02 216
T1D03 218
T1D04 218
T1D05 219
T1D06 217
T1D07 242
T1D08 219
T1D09 217
T1D10 212
T1D11 240

Group T1E
T1E01 240
T1E02 179
T1E03 238
T1E04 241
T1E05 241
T1E06 238
T1E07 239
T1E08 242
T1E09 243
T1E10 243
T1E11 237

Group T1F
T1F01 241
T1F02 223
T1F03 223
T1F04 228
T1F05 228
T1F06 228
T1F07 220
T1F08 221
T1F09 174
T1F10 239
T1F11 215

T2 - Operating Procedures
Group T2A
T2A01 175
T2A02 170
T2A03 176
T2A04 177
T2A05 173
T2A06 239
T2A07 175
T2A08 171
T2A09 176
T2A10 225
T2A11 167
T2A12 171

Group T2B
T2B01 108
T2B02 169
T2B03 177
T2B04 206
T2B05 204
T2B06 198
T2B07 192
T2B08 209
T2B09 178
T2B10 166
T2B11 166
T2B12 190
T2B13 168

Group T2C
T2C01 236
T2C02 233
T2C03 234
T2C04 231
T2C05 234
T2C06 232
T2C07 233
T2C08 234
T2C09 236
T2C10 235
T2C11 235

T3 - Radio Wave Propagation
Group T3A
T3A01 55
T3A02 49
T3A03 123
T3A04 124
T3A05 207
T3A06 55
T3A07 50
T3A08 55
T3A09 124
T3A10 56
T3A11 61
T3A12 49

Group T3B
T3B01 43
T3B02 43
T3B03 42
T3B04 41
T3B05 65
T3B06 66
T3B07 71
T3B08 71
T3B09 71
T3B10 71
T3B11 42

Group T3C
T3C01 64
T3C02 64
T3C03 62
T3C04 61
T3C05 53
T3C06 57
T3C07 63
T3C08 58
T3C09 61
T3C10 62
T3C11 58

T4 - Amateur Radio Practices
Group T4A
T4A01 141
T4A02 127
T4A03 141
T4A04 188
T4A05 155
T4A06 186
T4A07 186
T4A08 146
T4A09 139
T4A10 186
T4A11 140
T4A12 112

Group T4B
T4B01 206
T4B02 111
T4B03 168
T4B04 109
T4B05 109
T4B06 206
T4B07 189
T4B08 109
T4B09 192
T4B10 229
T4B11 193
T4B12 172

T5 - Electrical Principles
Group T5A
T5A01 22
T5A02 24
T5A03 22
T5A04 24
T5A05 23
T5A06 28
T5A07 29
T5A08 29
T5A09 24
T5A10 25
T5A11 29
T5A12 28

Group T5B
T5B01 17
T5B02 18
T5B03 19
T5B04 19
T5B05 19
T5B06 20
T5B07 20
T5B08 20
T5B09 25
T5B10 26
T5B11 27
T5B12 20
T5B13 21

Group T5C
T5C01 38
T5C02 38
T5C03 39
T5C04 39
T5C05 40
T5C06 28
T5C07 16
T5C08 36
T5C09 37
T5C10 37
T5C11 37
T5C12 40
T5C13 16

Group T5D
T5D01 32
T5D02 32
T5D03 33
T5D04 33
T5D05 34
T5D06 34
T5D07 34
T5D08 34
T5D09 34
T5D10 35
T5D11 35
T5D12 35
T5D13 30
T5D14 31

T6 - Electrical Components
Group T6A
T6A01 84
T6A02 90
T6A03 90
T6A04 85
T6A05 85
T6A06 96
T6A07 96
T6A08 87
T6A09 86
T6A10 138
T6A11 139
T6A12 86

Group T6B
T6B01 88
T6B02 87
T6B03 92
T6B04 93
T6B05 93
T6B06 88
T6B07 89
T6B08 93
T6B09 88
T6B10 94
T6B11 94
T6B12 93

Group T6C
T6C01 83
T6C02 92
T6C03 92
T6C04 94
T6C05 95
T6C06 85
T6C07 89
T6C08 89
T6C09 90
T6C10 96
T6C11 97
T6C12 83

Group T6D

T6D01 98
T6D02 87
T6D03 130
T6D04 98
T6D05 98
T6D06 91
T6D07 89
T6D08 98
T6D09 98
T6D10 92
T6D11 98

T7 - Practical Circuits
Group T7A

T7A01 111
T7A02 107
T7A03 110
T7A04 112
T7A05 110
T7A06 111
T7A07 110
T7A08 74
T7A09 113
T7A10 112
T7A11 113

Group T7B

T7B01 205
T7B02 201
T7B03 200
T7B04 205
T7B05 202
T7B06 203
T7B07 201
T7B08 203
T7B09 202
T7B10 204
T7B11 203

Group T7C

T7C01 154
T7C02 154
T7C03 155
T7C04 126
T7C05 129
T7C06 126
T7C07 127
T7C08 126
T7C09 132
T7C10 132
T7C11 133

Group T7D

T7D01 101
T7D02 102
T7D03 103
T7D04 102
T7D05 ..... removed from pool
T7D06 105
T7D07 104
T7D08 106
T7D09 106
T7D10 104
T7D11 103

T8 - Signals And Emissions
Group T8A

T8A01 75
T8A02 76
T8A03 75
T8A04 77
T8A05 80
T8A06 76
T8A07 77
T8A08 78
T8A09 79
T8A10 80
T8A11 80
T8A12 78

Group T8B

T8B01 182
T8B02 185
T8B03 184
T8B04 182
T8B05 182
T8B06 184
T8B07 183
T8B08 185
T8B09 183
T8B10 181
T8B11 181
T8B12 185

Group T8C

T8C01 247
T8C02 247
T8C03 245
T8C04 246
T8C05 246
T8C06 198
T8C07 197
T8C08 198
T8C09 199
T8C10 199
T8C11 197

Group T8D

T8D01 187
T8D02 191
T8D03 196
T8D04 199
T8D05 195
T8D06 196
T8D07 190
T8D08 194
T8D09 80
T8D10 189
T8D11 195
T8D12 197
T8D13 188

T9 - Antennas / Feedlines
Group T9A

T9A01 120
T9A02 122
T9A03 117
T9A04 121
T9A05 117
T9A06 120
T9A07 121
T9A08 119
T9A09 118
T9A10 117
T9A11 121
T9A12 122

Group T9B

T9B01 127
T9B02 130
T9B03 130
T9B04 153
T9B05 131
T9B06 136
T9B07 135
T9B08 131
T9B09 128
T9B10 134
T9B11 134
T9B12 126

Glossary

- **Absorbed:** When a radio wave loses energy as it passes through a medium, such as a building or the atmosphere, reducing signal strength.

- **ALARA:** An acronym for "As Low As Reasonably Achievable," a safety principle in ham radio to minimize exposure to radio frequency energy, especially in antenna placement and power levels.

- **Alternating Current (AC):** Electrical current that flows first in one direction in a wire and then in the other. The applied voltage is also changing polarity. This direction reversal continues at a rate that depends on the frequency of the AC.

- **Amateur Operator:** A person holding a written authorization to be the control operator of an amateur station.

- **Amateur Service:** A radiocommunication service for the purpose of self-training, intercommunication, and technical investigations carried out by amateurs, that is, duly authorized persons interested in radio technique solely with a personal aim and without pecuniary interest.

- **Amateur Station:** A station licensed in the amateur service, including necessary equipment, used for amateur communication.

- **Ammeter:** A test instrument that measures current.

- **Ampere (A):** The basic unit of electrical current. Current is a measure of the electron flow through a circuit.

- **Amplitude Modulation (AM):** A modulation technique that encodes information by varying the amplitude of the radio carrier signal. Used in AM broadcast radio, it is more susceptible to noise than FM.

- **Analog:** Representation of signals as continuous waveforms rather than discrete digital data. Analog voice transmission is common in handheld radios.

- **Antenna:** A device that picks up or sends out radio frequency energy.

- **Antenna Gain:** The measure of how well an antenna directs or concentrates radio frequency energy in a specific direction compared to an isotropic radiator. Higher gain indicates a more focused signal, often measured in dBi (decibels relative to an isotropic antenna).

- **Antenna Switch:** A switch used to connect one transmitter, receiver, or transceiver to several different antennas.

- **Antenna Tuner:** A device used to match the impedance of an antenna to the transmitter or receiver, ensuring efficient power transfer and reducing signal reflection. It allows the use of antennas that might not be naturally resonant at the operating frequency.

- **APRS (Automatic Packet Reporting System):** A digital communication protocol used in amateur radio to transmit real-time data such as location, weather information, and messages.

- **Attenuation:** The decrease in signal strength as a radio wave travels through space or materials. It can be caused by distance, physical obstructions, and atmospheric conditions.

- **Autopatch:** A device that allows repeater users to make telephone calls through a repeater.

- **Automatic Gain Control (AGC):** A feature in receivers that automatically adjusts the gain to maintain a constant output level, even when the received signal strength varies.

- **Balun:** Contraction for balanced to unbalanced. A device to couple a balanced load to an unbalanced source, or vice versa.

- **Band Plans:** Agreed-upon allocations of frequency ranges within the amateur radio bands, designating specific uses like voice, CW, or digital modes to minimize interference.

- **Band Spread:** A receiver quality used to describe how far apart stations on different nearby frequencies will seem to be. Band spread determines how easily signals can be tuned.

- **Bandwidth:** The range of frequencies a radio can receive or transmit on. Wider bandwidth allows receiving multiple signals simultaneously.

- **Base Station:** A fixed radio installation, typically at a home or command center, used for effective long-range communication. It often includes a more powerful radio unit and larger antenna systems than portable units.

- **Battery:** A device that converts chemical energy into electrical energy.

- **Beacon:** A continuous or periodic signal transmitted by a station to indicate its presence and location, often used in propagation studies to assess the conditions of a particular band.

- **Beam Antenna:** A directional antenna. A beam antenna must be rotated to provide coverage in different directions.

- **Bluetooth:** A wireless technology standard for exchanging data over short distances, used in radios for audio accessories, data transfer, and programming.

- **Break:** A term used during voice communication to indicate a pause or request to interrupt ongoing communication, often to pass an urgent message.

- **Call Sign:** A unique identifier assigned to a radio operator by their country's telecommunications authority. It's used to legally identify the operator or station during transmissions.

- **Carrier Squelch:** A radio receiver function that mutes audio unless a signal is detected, preventing static noise. It activates with an incoming transmission's carrier wave, filtering out background noise.

- **Channel:** A labeled radio memory location containing preset receive and transmit frequencies for convenient recall, allowing quick switching between saved frequencies.

- **Chirp:** A slight shift in transmitter frequency each time you key the transmitter.

- **Closed Repeater:** A repeater that restricts access to those who know a special code.

- **Coaxial Cable:** A type of feed line with one conductor inside the other.

- **CQ:** A general call to all stations, indicating that the operator is available for communication. For example, "CQ CQ CQ, this is K1ABC calling CQ."

- **CTCSS (Continuous Tone-Coded Squelch System):** A subaudible tone transmitted along with voice signals to prevent interference from other users on the same frequency.

- **CW (Continuous Wave):** Morse code telegraphy.

- **DCS (Digital Code Squelch):** Digitally encoded subaudible codes transmitted with your audio to block unwanted receptions unless the code matches.

- **Decibel (dB):** A logarithmic unit used to measure the relative difference in power, often used in describing gains, losses, and signal strength in radio systems.

- **Delta Loop Antenna:** A variation of the cubical quad with triangular elements.

- **Digital:** Representation of signals as discrete binary data rather than continuous waveforms. Digital modes convert voice and data to binary for transmission.

- **Digipeater:** A packet-radio station used to retransmit signals that are specifically addressed to be retransmitted by that station.

- **Dipole Antenna:** A simple and widely used antenna consisting of two equal-length conductive elements that radiate radio waves.

- **Directional Antenna:** An antenna that concentrates the signal in one direction.

- **Duplex:** Using two distinct frequencies for transmitting and receiving, allowing simultaneous sending and receiving.

- **Duplexer:** A device that allows simultaneous transmission and reception on different frequencies using the same antenna. It's commonly used in repeaters.

- **Dummy Load:** A station accessory that allows you to test or adjust transmitting equipment without sending a signal out over the air. Also called dummy antenna.

- **Dual-Band Radio:** A radio that can operate on two distinct frequency bands, like VHF and UHF, allowing increased versatility.

- **Dual Watch:** Monitoring two different frequencies or channels simultaneously by rapidly switching between them.

- **DXing:** The hobby of receiving or sending long-distance communications. "DX" is shorthand for "distance" or "distant."

- **Earth Ground:** A circuit connection to a ground rod driven into the Earth or to a cold-water pipe made of copper that goes into the ground.

- **Earth-Moon-Earth (EME):** A mode of communication that involves bouncing radio signals off the moon's surface to reach distant stations. Also known as "moonbounce."

- **Electromagnetic Interference (EMI):** Unwanted noise or signals that interfere with the operation of electronic devices, often caused by other electrical equipment or power lines.

- **Elmer:** An informal term in the ham radio community for an experienced ham who mentors or guides newcomers.

- **Emergency:** A situation where there is a danger to lives or property.

- **Emergency Traffic:** Messages with life and death urgency or requests for medical help and supplies that leave an area shortly after an emergency.

- **Emission:** The transmitted signal from an amateur station.

- **Feedline:** The cable or transmission line that connects the radio to the antenna, crucial for efficiently transferring power. Types include coaxial cable and ladder line.

- **Ferrite Beads:** Small components made of ferrite material, used to suppress high-frequency noise in electronic circuits by absorbing unwanted signals.

- **Final:** The last transmission in a contact before signing off.

- **FM Repeater:** A device that receives an FM signal on one frequency, amplifies it, and retransmits it on another frequency, typically with an offset. Repeaters extend the communication range of handheld and mobile radios.

- **Fox Hunt:** An amateur radio activity where participants use radio direction-finding techniques to locate a transmitter at an unknown location.

- **Frequency:** The number of cycles a radio wave completes per second, measured in Hertz (Hz).

- **Frequency Modulation (FM):** A modulation technique that encodes information by varying the frequency of the radio carrier signal. Used in two-way handheld radios for voice communication.

- **Gain:** The increase in signal strength or amplification provided by an antenna or amplifier. Gain is usually measured in decibels (dB) and can enhance the range and clarity of communication.

- **Ground Loop:** An unwanted electrical current that flows in a looped grounding system, often causing noise and interference in radio equipment.

- **Ground Wave:** A type of radio wave that travels along the Earth's surface, typically used for short to medium-range communication, especially at lower frequencies.

- **Grounding:** The practice of connecting equipment to the Earth or a common ground point to reduce electrical noise, enhance safety, and improve signal quality.

- **Ham Radio (Amateur Radio):** A hobby involving radio frequencies for non-commercial communication, experimentation, and emergency services. It requires licensing.

- **High Gain Antenna:** An antenna that amplifies signal strength in a specific direction, enhancing long-distance communication.

- **Hertz (Hz):** The unit of frequency, equal to one cycle per second.

- **HT (Handheld Transceiver):** A portable, handheld radio used for two-way communication. HTs are popular among new ham radio operators for their portability and ease of use.

- **Impedance:** The resistance to the flow of alternating current (AC) in a circuit, combining resistance and reactance.

- **Intermediate Frequency (IF):** A lower frequency to which a received signal is shifted to simplify processing and amplification in a receiver.

- **IP Rating (Ingress Protection):** A standard that defines the levels of protection against intrusion from foreign bodies and moisture in electrical enclosures.

- **IP67 Rating:** Indicates that a device is entirely dust-tight and can be submerged in water up to 1 meter deep for 30 minutes without damage.

- **Ionosphere:** A region of electrically charged (ionized) gases high in the atmosphere that bends radio waves as they travel through it, returning them to Earth.

- **Isotropic Radiator:** A theoretical antenna that radiates equally in all directions, used as a reference point for measuring antenna gain.

- **ITU (International Telecommunication Union):** A specialized agency of the United Nations that coordinates global telecommunications standards, including frequency allocations for amateur radio.

- **J-Pole Antenna:** An omnidirectional antenna, typically for VHF/UHF bands, characterized by a distinctive 'J' shape. It's popular for its simplicity and low SWR.

- **Li-ion (Lithium-ion):** A battery chemistry commonly used in modern handheld radios. Offers good energy density and requires protection circuitry for safe charging.

- **Linking (Repeater Linking):** Connecting multiple repeaters via the internet or RF to create a larger coverage area.

- **Mobile Radio:** A radio designed for vehicle use, providing better performance than handhelds but less than base stations.

- **Mode:** The type of signal modulation used in radio communication, such as AM, FM, SSB (Single Sideband), CW (Continuous Wave), or digital modes like PSK31 or RTTY.

- **MR (Memory Recall):** A mode that allows users to access and operate on frequencies previously programmed and stored in the radio's memory channels.

- **Net Control:** The designated station in an amateur radio net that manages communications and directs net operations.

- **NiMH (Nickel-Metal Hydride):** A battery chemistry often used in older handheld radios, more susceptible to performance degradation over time than Li-ion.

- **NVIS (Near Vertical Incidence Skywave):** A propagation method where radio signals are directed nearly vertically to reflect off the ionosphere and return to Earth over short to medium distances.

- **Offset:** The difference between the receive and transmit frequencies required for repeaters. It allows simultaneous reception and transmission.

- **Oscillator:** An electronic circuit that produces a continuous, oscillating electrical signal, often used as a frequency reference in transmitters and receivers.

- **Packet Radio:** A digital mode of communication that transmits data in packets using amateur radio frequencies.

- **Parity:** A method of adding a simple checksum to transmitted data bits to detect errors in received data packets, used in digital transmission schemes.

- **PL Tone (Private Line):** A pilot tone squelch system using subaudible tones similar to CTCSS for selectively receiving transmissions encoded with a matching tone.

- **PL-259 Connector:** A type of coaxial connector commonly used in ham radio for connecting coaxial cable to radios, antennas, and other equipment.

- **Power Supply:** A device that provides electrical power to a radio, typically converting AC from a wall outlet to the DC required by the radio.

- **Propagation:** The way radio waves travel through the atmosphere and environment between transmitting and receiving antennas, influenced by factors like frequency, distance, terrain, and atmospheric conditions.

- **PSK31 (Phase Shift Keying, 31 Baud):** A popular digital mode used in ham radio for low-power communications, known for its narrow bandwidth and efficiency in poor conditions.

- **PTT (Push To Talk):** A button that initiates voice transmissions in half-duplex radio systems. The transceiver switches to transmit mode when the operator presses PTT.

- **Q Codes:** A standardized collection of three-letter message encodings, used in Morse code and voice communication to convey common phrases efficiently.

- **QRM:** A Q code used to describe interference from other stations. For example, "I am receiving QRM" means there is interference affecting your reception.

- **QRN:** A Q code used to describe natural interference, such as static from thunderstorms.

- **QRP Operation:** Transmitting with low power, often less than 5 watts, in ham radio. It's a challenge to make distant contacts with minimal power output.

- **QSL Card:** A written confirmation of two-way radio communication between two amateur radio stations or a one-way reception of a signal.

- **QSO:** A radio communication or conversation between two ham radio operators.

- **Rag Chew:** An informal, often lengthy conversation via radio on non-technical subjects.

- **Radiosonde:** A balloon-borne device that measures various atmospheric parameters and transmits the data back to a ground receiver via radio.

- **RDIS (Radio Data Information Service):** Digital data streams encoded alongside analog FM voice transmissions to convey identifying and messaging information.

- **Receiver:** A device that picks up radio signals from an antenna, processes them to extract the desired information, and converts them to a form that can be heard or read.

- **Reflected:** Describes a radio wave that bounces off a surface, such as the ground or an object, affecting signal strength and quality.

- **Refracted:** Describes a radio wave that bends as it passes through different layers of the atmosphere or materials, affecting the signal path.

- **Repeater:** A device that receives radio signals on one frequency and retransmits them at higher power on another frequency to extend range.

- **Repeater Directory:** A listing or database of repeater frequencies and information, often used by ham radio operators to find local repeaters.

- **Repeater Offset:** The difference between the repeater's receive frequency (input) and transmit frequency (output). Allows simultaneous reception and retransmission without interference between the frequencies.

- **RF (Radio Frequency):** The range of electromagnetic waves used in wireless communication, oscillating between 20 kHz and 300 GHz, enabling wireless communication.

- **RF Gain:** Adjusts the radio's receiver sensitivity to incoming signals, allowing for better signal reception.

- **RFA (Radio Frequency Adapter):** A device that converts between different radio bands or frequency ranges, allowing interoperability between diverse radio types.

- **RF Interference (RFI):** Unwanted reception of RF signals that disrupt normal radio operations, a common issue in densely populated areas.

- **RSSI (Received Signal Strength Indicator):** A measurement of the strength or power level of received radio signals, displayed by the radio as a signal meter.

- **S-Meter:** A meter on a receiver that measures the strength of the received signal, usually calibrated in S-units.

- **Silent Key (SK):** A term used to refer to a deceased ham radio operator.

- **Simplex:** Communication where signals are transmitted and received on the same frequency channel but not simultaneously.

- **Skip:** A phenomenon where radio waves reflect off the ionosphere, allowing long-distance communication beyond the normal line-of-sight range.

- **Sky Wave:** A radio wave that is refracted or reflected back to Earth by the ionosphere, allowing long-distance communication beyond the horizon.

- **SMA (SubMiniature version A):** A type of RF coaxial connector used in various applications, including antennas, radios, and telecommunications equipment.

- **Squelch:** Mutes the radio speaker when no transmission is received to reduce background noise. Adjusting the squelch threshold filters out weak or irrelevant signals.

- **Spurious Emissions:** Unwanted signals generated by a transmitter that are outside the intended transmission band.

- **Standing Wave:** A stationary wave pattern formed on a transmission line when there is a mismatch between the load and the transmission line, often indicated by a high SWR.

- **Stealth Antenna:** A type of antenna designed to be unobtrusive or hidden, often used by amateur radio operators in areas with restrictions on visible antennas.

- **SSB (Single Sideband):** A mode of amplitude modulation that eliminates the carrier and one of the sidebands, making it more efficient for voice communication, especially on HF bands.

- **SWR (Standing Wave Ratio):** A measure of the radio antenna system's efficiency in transmitting power. A lower SWR indicates better efficiency.

- **SWR Meter:** A device used to measure the Standing Wave Ratio (SWR) of an antenna system. It helps ensure the antenna is properly tuned and the radio is operating efficiently.

- **Tactical Call Signs:** Temporary call signs used for simplicity and clarity during emergency operations or events.

- **Time-Out Timer (TOT):** A safety feature that limits the maximum duration of radio transmissions to prevent overheating or hogging the channel.

- **TPU (Thermoplastic Polyurethane) Case:** A case that blends rubber's flexibility with plastic's strength, offering protection against impacts and scratches for electronic devices.

- **Traffic:** Messages passed via radio, especially within nets, for relaying information such as health and welfare updates during emergencies.

- **Transceiver:** A single device that functions as both a transmitter and a receiver, commonly used in ham radios for two-way communication.

- **Transmitter:** A device that generates and sends radio frequency signals through an antenna to communicate with other radios.

- **Tropospheric Ducting:** A type of VHF propagation that can occur when warm air overruns cold air, creating a duct in which radio signals can travel over longer distances.

- **UHF (Ultra High Frequency):** Radio frequency ranges from 300 MHz to 3 GHz, used for two-way radio, Wi-Fi, Bluetooth, and other applications.

- **VE (Volunteer Examiner):** A licensed amateur radio operator who is certified to administer licensing exams to other amateur radio candidates.

- **VFO (Variable Frequency Oscillator):** Allows a radio receiver or transmitter to be tuned to different frequencies manually.

- **VHF (Very High Frequency):** Radio frequency ranges from 30–300 MHz, commonly used for two-way radio, FM, and television broadcasting.

- **VOX (Voice-Operated Transmission):** A feature that allows hands-free automatic transmission based on detecting your speech input via a microphone.

- **Wavelength:** The physical length of one cycle of a radio wave, inversely related to frequency.

- **Yagi Antenna:** A directional antenna with multiple elements, including a driven element, reflector, and directors, used for focusing radio signals in a specific direction.

- **Zero Beat:** The point at which two frequencies match exactly, often used when tuning in a signal in CW or SSB modes to ensure accurate frequency alignment.

References

- Aberle, S. (2017, June 21). HAM radio in emergency operations. Domestic Preparedness. https://domesticprepar edness.com/articles/ham-radio-in-emergency-operations

- American Radio Relay League (ARRL). (n.d.). Amateur radio communication: Amateur radio emergency service. https://www.arrl.org/amateur-radio-emergency-communication

- American Radio Relay League (ARRL). (n.d.). Building simple antennas. https://www.arrl.org/building-simple -antennas

- American Radio Relay League (ARRL). (n.d.). NTS standard net procedures. https://www.arrl.org/chapter-five -nts-standard-net-procedures

- American Radio Relay League (ARRL). (n.d.). What is ham radio? https://www.arrl.org/what-is-ham-radio

- Britannica. (n.d.). Amateur radio. https://www.britannica.com/technology/amateur-radio

- Federal Communications Commission (FCC). (n.d.). Amateur radio service. https://www.fcc.gov/wireless/burea u-divisions/mobility-division/amateur-radio-service

- Federal Communications Commission (FCC). (n.d.). 47 CFR Part 97 -- Amateur radio service. https://www.ecfr .gov/current/title-47/chapter-I/subchapter-D/part-97

- Ham Radio for Nontechies. (2024). A beginner's guide to HAM radio. https://hamradiofornontechies.com/the -definitive-guide-to-ham-radio/

- Ham Radio Prep. (2024). Ham radio emergency communications guide. https://hamradioprep.com/ham-radio-i n-emergencies/

- Institute For Building Technology and Safety. (2024). Tips for HAM radio operators: Natural disaster communica- tions best practices. https://ibtsonhand.org/resource/tips-for-ham-radio-operators-natural-disaster-communicati ons-best-practices/

- Racoma, A. J. (2020, October 6). The prepper's guide to emergency communications. https://n2rac.com/the-pre ppers-guide-to-emergency-communications-37f438db250

- Radio Design Group, Inc. (2023, October 9). The vital role of HAM radio in disaster preparedness. https://www .radiodesigngroup.com/blog/the-vital-role-of-ham-radio-in-disaster-preparedness

- Stathis, J. (2020, September 16). There's no better time to be an amateur radio geek. Wired. https://www.wired.c om/story/amateur-radio-disaster-preparedness/

- Stryker Radios. (2023, June 22). Ham radio emergency frequencies and common uses. https://strykerradios.com /ham-radios/ham-radio-emergency-frequencies-common-uses/

Made in United States
Troutdale, OR
12/08/2024

26163748R00151